C-4526   CAREER EXAMINATION SERIES

This is your
PASSBOOK for...

Supervising Carpenter

Test Preparation Study Guide
Questions & Answers

COPYRIGHT NOTICE

This book is SOLELY intended for, is sold ONLY to, and its use is RESTRICTED to individual, bona fide applicants or candidates who qualify by virtue of having seriously filed applications for appropriate license, certificate, professional and/or promotional advancement, higher school matriculation, scholarship, or other legitimate requirements of education and/or governmental authorities.

This book is NOT intended for use, class instruction, tutoring, training, duplication, copying, reprinting, excerption, or adaptation, etc., by:

1) Other publishers
2) Proprietors and/or Instructors of "Coaching" and/or Preparatory Courses
3) Personnel and/or Training Divisions of commercial, industrial, and governmental organizations
4) Schools, colleges, or universities and/or their departments and staffs, including teachers and other personnel
5) Testing Agencies or Bureaus
6) Study groups which seek by the purchase of a single volume to copy and/or duplicate and/or adapt this material for use by the group as a whole without having purchased individual volumes for each of the members of the group
7) Et al.

Such persons would be in violation of appropriate Federal and State statutes.

PROVISION OF LICENSING AGREEMENTS – Recognized educational, commercial, industrial, and governmental institutions and organizations, and others legitimately engaged in educational pursuits, including training, testing, and measurement activities, may address request for a licensing agreement to the copyright owners, who will determine whether, and under what conditions, including fees and charges, the materials in this book may be used them. In other words, a licensing facility exists for the legitimate use of the material in this book on other than an individual basis. However, it is asseverated and affirmed here that the material in this book CANNOT be used without the receipt of the express permission of such a licensing agreement from the Publishers. Inquiries re licensing should be addressed to the company, attention rights and permissions department.

All rights reserved, including the right of reproduction in whole or in part, in any form or by any means, electronic or mechanical, including photocopying, recording, or by any information storage and retrieval system, without permission in writing from the Publisher.

Copyright © 2024 by
National Learning Corporation

212 Michael Drive, Syosset, NY 11791
(516) 921-8888 • www.passbooks.com
E-mail: info@passbooks.com

PUBLISHED IN THE UNITED STATES OF AMERICA

PASSBOOK® SERIES

THE *PASSBOOK® SERIES* has been created to prepare applicants and candidates for the ultimate academic battlefield – the examination room.

At some time in our lives, each and every one of us may be required to take an examination – for validation, matriculation, admission, qualification, registration, certification, or licensure.

Based on the assumption that every applicant or candidate has met the basic formal educational standards, has taken the required number of courses, and read the necessary texts, the *PASSBOOK® SERIES* furnishes the one special preparation which may assure passing with confidence, instead of failing with insecurity. Examination questions – together with answers – are furnished as the basic vehicle for study so that the mysteries of the examination and its compounding difficulties may be eliminated or diminished by a sure method.

This book is meant to help you pass your examination provided that you qualify and are serious in your objective.

The entire field is reviewed through the huge store of content information which is succinctly presented through a provocative and challenging approach – the question-and-answer method.

A climate of success is established by furnishing the correct answers at the end of each test.

You soon learn to recognize types of questions, forms of questions, and patterns of questioning. You may even begin to anticipate expected outcomes.

You perceive that many questions are repeated or adapted so that you can gain acute insights, which may enable you to score many sure points.

You learn how to confront new questions, or types of questions, and to attack them confidently and work out the correct answers.

You note objectives and emphases, and recognize pitfalls and dangers, so that you may make positive educational adjustments.

Moreover, you are kept fully informed in relation to new concepts, methods, practices, and directions in the field.

You discover that you are actually taking the examination all the time: you are preparing for the examination by "taking" an examination, not by reading extraneous and/or supererogatory textbooks.

In short, this PASSBOOK®, used directedly, should be an important factor in helping you to pass your test.

SUPERVISING CARPENTER

DUTIES
Supervisor Carpenters, under general direction, supervise, direct and are responsible for the work of Carpenters and other assigned employees. They assign and lay out jobs for Carpenters and closely allied workers; supervise, direct and inspect the work of Carpenters relating to the installation and/or replacement of flooring, doors, building hardware, trim, window frames, sashes, partition, etc.; estimate job requirements from plans and specifications and/or field surveys; requisition materials and equipment; supervise, direct and are responsible for the proper operation of the departmental carpentry shop(s); when required, lay out and supervise the heavy and rough carpentry work in construction, maintenance, and repair of shoring, bulkheads, scaffolds, dock facilities, construction sheds, promenades, etc.; keep records and prepare reports; and may operate a motor vehicle. All Supervisor Carpenters perform related work.

SCOPE OF THE EXAMINATION
The multiple-choice test is designed to assess the extent to which candidates have certain knowledge and abilities determined to be important to the performance of the tasks of a Supervisor Carpenter. Task areas are as follows:

Conducting meetings with subordinates to review work progress; generating work orders using computer software system; visiting workplace to collect the data to prepare estimates for potential work; drawing/sketching/listing details for specifications; reviewing work order for required repairs; assigning work to carpenters; checking progress of work; inspecting shops to make sure they are safe and clean; erecting scaffolds, ramps, platforms and structures; contacting and resolving problems with vendors/tenants/employees; preparing documents and/or ordering materials needed for jobs; writing and generating weekly/quarterly reports; reviewing and approving time, vacation and leaves; attending meetings and providing input on job assessment; using laser and other tools to layout work; making proposals for alternative work solutions; coordinating work with other trade personnel; building ramps, staircases, and partitions using hand and power tools; installing building hardware; fixing and installing doors, windows, walls, ceilings, cabinetry, floors, etc.

The test will include questions which may require the technical knowledge on safety practices and procedures applicable to the carpentry trade; techniques and materials used in the carpentry trade; project management; tools and equipment used in the carpentry trade; budgeting, estimation and job-related calculations; reading/interpreting blueprints and/or sketches; applicable building codes; departmental policies and procedures; standards of proper employee ethical conduct; and other related areas.

The test may also include questions requiring the use of any of the following abilities:

Analytical Thinking: Analyzing information and using logic to address specific work-related issues and problems; involves the identification of problems, not implementation of solutions. Example: A Supervisor Carpenter inspects a job completed and pinpoints errors in the work.

Judgment and Decision-Making: Reviewing information to develop and evaluate the relative costs and benefits of potential solutions to problems and choosing the most appropriate one; implementing a course of action determined by thinking analytically. While similar to Planning & Organizing, Judgment and Decision-Making are typically applied over a shorter time frame. Example: A Supervisor Carpenter addresses problems with contractors.

Planning and Organizing: Establishing a method of execution to accomplish a specific goal over an extended period of time; determining appropriate assignments and allocation of resources. Example: A Supervisor Carpenter plans and then assigns work to subordinates/personnel.

Management of Material Resources: Obtaining and seeing to the appropriate use of equipment, facilities and materials needed to do certain work; managing the things needed for work to be accomplished. Example: A Supervisor Carpenter assesses how much material is needed to install partitions.

Management of Personnel Resources: Motivating, developing and directing people as they work, identifying the best people for the job; managing employees needed to accomplish tasks. Example: A Supervisor Carpenter assigns appropriate number of Carpenters to complete a construction project on time.

Written Comprehension: Understanding the information and ideas presented in written sentences and paragraphs in work-related documents. Example: A Supervisor Carpenter reads and understands work orders.

Written Expression: Appropriately communicating information and ideas in written words and sentences so intended audience will understand. Example: A Supervisor Carpenter writes reports free of grammatical errors.

Updating and Using Relevant Knowledge: Keeping up-to-date technically and applying new knowledge to the job. Example: A Supervisor Carpenter keeps up-to-date with new construction techniques, tools and equipment.

Certain questions may need to be answered on the basis of documents or other information supplied to the candidates on the date of the multiple-choice exam.

HOW TO TAKE A TEST

I. YOU MUST PASS AN EXAMINATION

A. *WHAT EVERY CANDIDATE SHOULD KNOW*

Examination applicants often ask us for help in preparing for the written test. What can I study in advance? What kinds of questions will be asked? How will the test be given? How will the papers be graded?

As an applicant for a civil service examination, you may be wondering about some of these things. Our purpose here is to suggest effective methods of advance study and to describe civil service examinations.

Your chances for success on this examination can be increased if you know how to prepare. Those "pre-examination jitters" can be reduced if you know what to expect. You can even experience an adventure in good citizenship if you know why civil service exams are given.

B. *WHY ARE CIVIL SERVICE EXAMINATIONS GIVEN?*

Civil service examinations are important to you in two ways. As a citizen, you want public jobs filled by employees who know how to do their work. As a job seeker, you want a fair chance to compete for that job on an equal footing with other candidates. The best-known means of accomplishing this two-fold goal is the competitive examination.

Exams are widely publicized throughout the nation. They may be administered for jobs in federal, state, city, municipal, town or village governments or agencies.

Any citizen may apply, with some limitations, such as the age or residence of applicants. Your experience and education may be reviewed to see whether you meet the requirements for the particular examination. When these requirements exist, they are reasonable and applied consistently to all applicants. Thus, a competitive examination may cause you some uneasiness now, but it is your privilege and safeguard.

C. *HOW ARE CIVIL SERVICE EXAMS DEVELOPED?*

Examinations are carefully written by trained technicians who are specialists in the field known as "psychological measurement," in consultation with recognized authorities in the field of work that the test will cover. These experts recommend the subject matter areas or skills to be tested; only those knowledges or skills important to your success on the job are included. The most reliable books and source materials available are used as references. Together, the experts and technicians judge the difficulty level of the questions.

Test technicians know how to phrase questions so that the problem is clearly stated. Their ethics do not permit "trick" or "catch" questions. Questions may have been tried out on sample groups, or subjected to statistical analysis, to determine their usefulness.

Written tests are often used in combination with performance tests, ratings of training and experience, and oral interviews. All of these measures combine to form the best-known means of finding the right person for the right job.

II. HOW TO PASS THE WRITTEN TEST

A. NATURE OF THE EXAMINATION

To prepare intelligently for civil service examinations, you should know how they differ from school examinations you have taken. In school you were assigned certain definite pages to read or subjects to cover. The examination questions were quite detailed and usually emphasized memory. Civil service exams, on the other hand, try to discover your present ability to perform the duties of a position, plus your potentiality to learn these duties. In other words, a civil service exam attempts to predict how successful you will be. Questions cover such a broad area that they cannot be as minute and detailed as school exam questions.

In the public service similar kinds of work, or positions, are grouped together in one "class." This process is known as *position-classification*. All the positions in a class are paid according to the salary range for that class. One class title covers all of these positions, and they are all tested by the same examination.

B. FOUR BASIC STEPS

1) Study the announcement

How, then, can you know what subjects to study? Our best answer is: "Learn as much as possible about the class of positions for which you've applied." The exam will test the knowledge, skills and abilities needed to do the work.

Your most valuable source of information about the position you want is the official exam announcement. This announcement lists the training and experience qualifications. Check these standards and apply only if you come reasonably close to meeting them.

The brief description of the position in the examination announcement offers some clues to the subjects which will be tested. Think about the job itself. Review the duties in your mind. Can you perform them, or are there some in which you are rusty? Fill in the blank spots in your preparation.

Many jurisdictions preview the written test in the exam announcement by including a section called "Knowledge and Abilities Required," "Scope of the Examination," or some similar heading. Here you will find out specifically what fields will be tested.

2) Review your own background

Once you learn in general what the position is all about, and what you need to know to do the work, ask yourself which subjects you already know fairly well and which need improvement. You may wonder whether to concentrate on improving your strong areas or on building some background in your fields of weakness. When the announcement has specified "some knowledge" or "considerable knowledge," or has used adjectives like "beginning principles of..." or "advanced ... methods," you can get a clue as to the number and difficulty of questions to be asked in any given field. More questions, and hence broader coverage, would be included for those subjects which are more important in the work. Now weigh your strengths and weaknesses against the job requirements and prepare accordingly.

3) Determine the level of the position

Another way to tell how intensively you should prepare is to understand the level of the job for which you are applying. Is it the entering level? In other words, is this the position in which beginners in a field of work are hired? Or is it an intermediate or advanced level? Sometimes this is indicated by such words as "Junior" or "Senior" in the class title. Other jurisdictions use Roman numerals to designate the level – Clerk I, Clerk II, for example. The word "Supervisor" sometimes appears in the title. If the level is not indicated by the title, check the description of duties. Will you be working under very close supervision, or will you have responsibility for independent decisions in this work?

4) Choose appropriate study materials

Now that you know the subjects to be examined and the relative amount of each subject to be covered, you can choose suitable study materials. For beginning level jobs, or even advanced ones, if you have a pronounced weakness in some aspect of your training, read a modern, standard textbook in that field. Be sure it is up to date and has general coverage. Such books are normally available at your library, and the librarian will be glad to help you locate one. For entry-level positions, questions of appropriate difficulty are chosen – neither highly advanced questions, nor those too simple. Such questions require careful thought but not advanced training.

If the position for which you are applying is technical or advanced, you will read more advanced, specialized material. If you are already familiar with the basic principles of your field, elementary textbooks would waste your time. Concentrate on advanced textbooks and technical periodicals. Think through the concepts and review difficult problems in your field.

These are all general sources. You can get more ideas on your own initiative, following these leads. For example, training manuals and publications of the government agency which employs workers in your field can be useful, particularly for technical and professional positions. A letter or visit to the government department involved may result in more specific study suggestions, and certainly will provide you with a more definite idea of the exact nature of the position you are seeking.

III. KINDS OF TESTS

Tests are used for purposes other than measuring knowledge and ability to perform specified duties. For some positions, it is equally important to test ability to make adjustments to new situations or to profit from training. In others, basic mental abilities not dependent on information are essential. Questions which test these things may not appear as pertinent to the duties of the position as those which test for knowledge and information. Yet they are often highly important parts of a fair examination. For very general questions, it is almost impossible to help you direct your study efforts. What we can do is to point out some of the more common of these general abilities needed in public service positions and describe some typical questions.

1) General information

Broad, general information has been found useful for predicting job success in some kinds of work. This is tested in a variety of ways, from vocabulary lists to questions about current events. Basic background in some field of work, such as sociology or economics, may be sampled in a group of questions. Often these are principles which have become familiar to most persons through exposure rather than through formal training. It is difficult to advise you how to study for these questions; being alert to the world around you is our best suggestion.

2) Verbal ability

An example of an ability needed in many positions is verbal or language ability. Verbal ability is, in brief, the ability to use and understand words. Vocabulary and grammar tests are typical measures of this ability. Reading comprehension or paragraph interpretation questions are common in many kinds of civil service tests. You are given a paragraph of written material and asked to find its central meaning.

3) Numerical ability

Number skills can be tested by the familiar arithmetic problem, by checking paired lists of numbers to see which are alike and which are different, or by interpreting charts and graphs. In the latter test, a graph may be printed in the test booklet which you are asked to use as the basis for answering questions.

4) Observation

A popular test for law-enforcement positions is the observation test. A picture is shown to you for several minutes, then taken away. Questions about the picture test your ability to observe both details and larger elements.

5) Following directions

In many positions in the public service, the employee must be able to carry out written instructions dependably and accurately. You may be given a chart with several columns, each column listing a variety of information. The questions require you to carry out directions involving the information given in the chart.

6) Skills and aptitudes

Performance tests effectively measure some manual skills and aptitudes. When the skill is one in which you are trained, such as typing or shorthand, you can practice. These tests are often very much like those given in business school or high school courses. For many of the other skills and aptitudes, however, no short-time preparation can be made. Skills and abilities natural to you or that you have developed throughout your lifetime are being tested.

Many of the general questions just described provide all the data needed to answer the questions and ask you to use your reasoning ability to find the answers. Your best preparation for these tests, as well as for tests of facts and ideas, is to be at your physical and mental best. You, no doubt, have your own methods of getting into an exam-taking mood and keeping "in shape." The next section lists some ideas on this subject.

IV. KINDS OF QUESTIONS

Only rarely is the "essay" question, which you answer in narrative form, used in civil service tests. Civil service tests are usually of the short-answer type. Full instructions for answering these questions will be given to you at the examination. But in case this is your first experience with short-answer questions and separate answer sheets, here is what you need to know:

1) Multiple-choice Questions

Most popular of the short-answer questions is the "multiple choice" or "best answer" question. It can be used, for example, to test for factual knowledge, ability to solve problems or judgment in meeting situations found at work.

A multiple-choice question is normally one of three types—
- It can begin with an incomplete statement followed by several possible endings. You are to find the one ending which *best* completes the statement, although some of the others may not be entirely wrong.
- It can also be a complete statement in the form of a question which is answered by choosing one of the statements listed.

- It can be in the form of a problem – again you select the best answer.

Here is an example of a multiple-choice question with a discussion which should give you some clues as to the method for choosing the right answer:

When an employee has a complaint about his assignment, the action which will *best* help him overcome his difficulty is to
   A. discuss his difficulty with his coworkers
   B. take the problem to the head of the organization
   C. take the problem to the person who gave him the assignment
   D. say nothing to anyone about his complaint

In answering this question, you should study each of the choices to find which is best. Consider choice "A" – Certainly an employee may discuss his complaint with fellow employees, but no change or improvement can result, and the complaint remains unresolved. Choice "B" is a poor choice since the head of the organization probably does not know what assignment you have been given, and taking your problem to him is known as "going over the head" of the supervisor. The supervisor, or person who made the assignment, is the person who can clarify it or correct any injustice. Choice "C" is, therefore, correct. To say nothing, as in choice "D," is unwise. Supervisors have and interest in knowing the problems employees are facing, and the employee is seeking a solution to his problem.

2) True/False Questions

The "true/false" or "right/wrong" form of question is sometimes used. Here a complete statement is given. Your job is to decide whether the statement is right or wrong.

SAMPLE: A roaming cell-phone call to a nearby city costs less than a non-roaming call to a distant city.

This statement is wrong, or false, since roaming calls are more expensive.

This is not a complete list of all possible question forms, although most of the others are variations of these common types. You will always get complete directions for answering questions. Be sure you understand *how* to mark your answers – ask questions until you do.

V. RECORDING YOUR ANSWERS

Computer terminals are used more and more today for many different kinds of exams.
For an examination with very few applicants, you may be told to record your answers in the test booklet itself. Separate answer sheets are much more common. If this separate answer sheet is to be scored by machine – and this is often the case – it is highly important that you mark your answers correctly in order to get credit.
An electronic scoring machine is often used in civil service offices because of the speed with which papers can be scored. Machine-scored answer sheets must be marked with a pencil, which will be given to you. This pencil has a high graphite content which responds to the electronic scoring machine. As a matter of fact, stray dots may register as answers, so do not let your pencil rest on the answer sheet while you are pondering the correct answer. Also, if your pencil lead breaks or is otherwise defective, ask for another.

Since the answer sheet will be dropped in a slot in the scoring machine, be careful not to bend the corners or get the paper crumpled.

The answer sheet normally has five vertical columns of numbers, with 30 numbers to a column. These numbers correspond to the question numbers in your test booklet. After each number, going across the page are four or five pairs of dotted lines. These short dotted lines have small letters or numbers above them. The first two pairs may also have a "T" or "F" above the letters. This indicates that the first two pairs only are to be used if the questions are of the true-false type. If the questions are multiple choice, disregard the "T" and "F" and pay attention only to the small letters or numbers.

Answer your questions in the manner of the sample that follows:

32. The largest city in the United States is
    A. Washington, D.C.
    B. New York City
    C. Chicago
    D. Detroit
    E. San Francisco

1) Choose the answer you think is best. (New York City is the largest, so "B" is correct.)
2) Find the row of dotted lines numbered the same as the question you are answering. (Find row number 32)
3) Find the pair of dotted lines corresponding to the answer. (Find the pair of lines under the mark "B.")
4) Make a solid black mark between the dotted lines.

VI. BEFORE THE TEST

Common sense will help you find procedures to follow to get ready for an examination. Too many of us, however, overlook these sensible measures. Indeed, nervousness and fatigue have been found to be the most serious reasons why applicants fail to do their best on civil service tests. Here is a list of reminders:

- Begin your preparation early – Don't wait until the last minute to go scurrying around for books and materials or to find out what the position is all about.
- Prepare continuously – An hour a night for a week is better than an all-night cram session. This has been definitely established. What is more, a night a week for a month will return better dividends than crowding your study into a shorter period of time.
- Locate the place of the exam – You have been sent a notice telling you when and where to report for the examination. If the location is in a different town or otherwise unfamiliar to you, it would be well to inquire the best route and learn something about the building.
- Relax the night before the test – Allow your mind to rest. Do not study at all that night. Plan some mild recreation or diversion; then go to bed early and get a good night's sleep.
- Get up early enough to make a leisurely trip to the place for the test – This way unforeseen events, traffic snarls, unfamiliar buildings, etc. will not upset you.
- Dress comfortably – A written test is not a fashion show. You will be known by number and not by name, so wear something comfortable.

- Leave excess paraphernalia at home – Shopping bags and odd bundles will get in your way. You need bring only the items mentioned in the official notice you received; usually everything you need is provided. Do not bring reference books to the exam. They will only confuse those last minutes and be taken away from you when in the test room.
- Arrive somewhat ahead of time – If because of transportation schedules you must get there very early, bring a newspaper or magazine to take your mind off yourself while waiting.
- Locate the examination room – When you have found the proper room, you will be directed to the seat or part of the room where you will sit. Sometimes you are given a sheet of instructions to read while you are waiting. Do not fill out any forms until you are told to do so; just read them and be prepared.
- Relax and prepare to listen to the instructions
- If you have any physical problem that may keep you from doing your best, be sure to tell the test administrator. If you are sick or in poor health, you really cannot do your best on the exam. You can come back and take the test some other time.

VII. AT THE TEST

The day of the test is here and you have the test booklet in your hand. The temptation to get going is very strong. Caution! There is more to success than knowing the right answers. You must know how to identify your papers and understand variations in the type of short-answer question used in this particular examination. Follow these suggestions for maximum results from your efforts:

1) Cooperate with the monitor

The test administrator has a duty to create a situation in which you can be as much at ease as possible. He will give instructions, tell you when to begin, check to see that you are marking your answer sheet correctly, and so on. He is not there to guard you, although he will see that your competitors do not take unfair advantage. He wants to help you do your best.

2) Listen to all instructions

Don't jump the gun! Wait until you understand all directions. In most civil service tests you get more time than you need to answer the questions. So don't be in a hurry. Read each word of instructions until you clearly understand the meaning. Study the examples, listen to all announcements and follow directions. Ask questions if you do not understand what to do.

3) Identify your papers

Civil service exams are usually identified by number only. You will be assigned a number; you must not put your name on your test papers. Be sure to copy your number correctly. Since more than one exam may be given, copy your exact examination title.

4) Plan your time

Unless you are told that a test is a "speed" or "rate of work" test, speed itself is usually not important. Time enough to answer all the questions will be provided, but this does not mean that you have all day. An overall time limit has been set. Divide the total time (in minutes) by the number of questions to determine the approximate time you have for each question.

5) Do not linger over difficult questions

If you come across a difficult question, mark it with a paper clip (useful to have along) and come back to it when you have been through the booklet. One caution if you do this – be sure to skip a number on your answer sheet as well. Check often to be sure that you have not lost your place and that you are marking in the row numbered the same as the question you are answering.

6) Read the questions

Be sure you know what the question asks! Many capable people are unsuccessful because they failed to *read* the questions correctly.

7) Answer all questions

Unless you have been instructed that a penalty will be deducted for incorrect answers, it is better to guess than to omit a question.

8) Speed tests

It is often better NOT to guess on speed tests. It has been found that on timed tests people are tempted to spend the last few seconds before time is called in marking answers at random – without even reading them – in the hope of picking up a few extra points. To discourage this practice, the instructions may warn you that your score will be "corrected" for guessing. That is, a penalty will be applied. The incorrect answers will be deducted from the correct ones, or some other penalty formula will be used.

9) Review your answers

If you finish before time is called, go back to the questions you guessed or omitted to give them further thought. Review other answers if you have time.

10) Return your test materials

If you are ready to leave before others have finished or time is called, take ALL your materials to the monitor and leave quietly. Never take any test material with you. The monitor can discover whose papers are not complete, and taking a test booklet may be grounds for disqualification.

VIII. EXAMINATION TECHNIQUES

1) Read the general instructions carefully. These are usually printed on the first page of the exam booklet. As a rule, these instructions refer to the timing of the examination; the fact that you should not start work until the signal and must stop work at a signal, etc. If there are any *special* instructions, such as a choice of questions to be answered, make sure that you note this instruction carefully.

2) When you are ready to start work on the examination, that is as soon as the signal has been given, read the instructions to each question booklet, underline any key words or phrases, such as *least, best, outline, describe* and the like. In this way you will tend to answer as requested rather than discover on reviewing your paper that you *listed without describing*, that you selected the *worst* choice rather than the *best* choice, etc.

3) If the examination is of the objective or multiple-choice type – that is, each question will also give a series of possible answers: A, B, C or D, and you are called upon to select the best answer and write the letter next to that answer on your answer paper – it is advisable to start answering each question in turn. There may be anywhere from 50 to 100 such questions in the three or four hours allotted and you can see how much time would be taken if you read through all the questions before beginning to answer any. Furthermore, if you come across a question or group of questions which you know would be difficult to answer, it would undoubtedly affect your handling of all the other questions.

4) If the examination is of the essay type and contains but a few questions, it is a moot point as to whether you should read all the questions before starting to answer any one. Of course, if you are given a choice – say five out of seven and the like – then it is essential to read all the questions so you can eliminate the two that are most difficult. If, however, you are asked to answer all the questions, there may be danger in trying to answer the easiest one first because you may find that you will spend too much time on it. The best technique is to answer the first question, then proceed to the second, etc.

5) Time your answers. Before the exam begins, write down the time it started, then add the time allowed for the examination and write down the time it must be completed, then divide the time available somewhat as follows:
    - If 3-1/2 hours are allowed, that would be 210 minutes. If you have 80 objective-type questions, that would be an average of 2-1/2 minutes per question. Allow yourself no more than 2 minutes per question, or a total of 160 minutes, which will permit about 50 minutes to review.
    - If for the time allotment of 210 minutes there are 7 essay questions to answer, that would average about 30 minutes a question. Give yourself only 25 minutes per question so that you have about 35 minutes to review.

6) The most important instruction is to *read each question* and make sure you know what is wanted. The second most important instruction is to *time yourself properly* so that you answer every question. The third most important instruction is to *answer every question*. Guess if you have to but include something for each question. Remember that you will receive no credit for a blank and will probably receive some credit if you write something in answer to an essay question. If you guess a letter – say "B" for a multiple-choice question – you may have guessed right. If you leave a blank as an answer to a multiple-choice question, the examiners may respect your feelings but it will not add a point to your score. Some exams may penalize you for wrong answers, so in such cases *only*, you may not want to guess unless you have some basis for your answer.

7) Suggestions
    a. Objective-type questions
        1. Examine the question booklet for proper sequence of pages and questions
        2. Read all instructions carefully
        3. Skip any question which seems too difficult; return to it after all other questions have been answered
        4. Apportion your time properly; do not spend too much time on any single question or group of questions

5. Note and underline key words – *all, most, fewest, least, best, worst, same, opposite*, etc.
6. Pay particular attention to negatives
7. Note unusual option, e.g., unduly long, short, complex, different or similar in content to the body of the question
8. Observe the use of "hedging" words – *probably, may, most likely*, etc.
9. Make sure that your answer is put next to the same number as the question
10. Do not second-guess unless you have good reason to believe the second answer is definitely more correct
11. Cross out original answer if you decide another answer is more accurate; do not erase until you are ready to hand your paper in
12. Answer all questions; guess unless instructed otherwise
13. Leave time for review

b. Essay questions
1. Read each question carefully
2. Determine exactly what is wanted. Underline key words or phrases.
3. Decide on outline or paragraph answer
4. Include many different points and elements unless asked to develop any one or two points or elements
5. Show impartiality by giving pros and cons unless directed to select one side only
6. Make and write down any assumptions you find necessary to answer the questions
7. Watch your English, grammar, punctuation and choice of words
8. Time your answers; don't crowd material

8) Answering the essay question

Most essay questions can be answered by framing the specific response around several key words or ideas. Here are a few such key words or ideas:

M's: manpower, materials, methods, money, management
P's: purpose, program, policy, plan, procedure, practice, problems, pitfalls, personnel, public relations

  a. Six basic steps in handling problems:
    1. Preliminary plan and background development
    2. Collect information, data and facts
    3. Analyze and interpret information, data and facts
    4. Analyze and develop solutions as well as make recommendations
    5. Prepare report and sell recommendations
    6. Install recommendations and follow up effectiveness

  b. Pitfalls to avoid
    1. *Taking things for granted* – A statement of the situation does not necessarily imply that each of the elements is necessarily true; for example, a complaint may be invalid and biased so that all that can be taken for granted is that a complaint has been registered

2. *Considering only one side of a situation* – Wherever possible, indicate several alternatives and then point out the reasons you selected the best one
3. *Failing to indicate follow up* – Whenever your answer indicates action on your part, make certain that you will take proper follow-up action to see how successful your recommendations, procedures or actions turn out to be
4. *Taking too long in answering any single question* – Remember to time your answers properly

IX. AFTER THE TEST

Scoring procedures differ in detail among civil service jurisdictions although the general principles are the same. Whether the papers are hand-scored or graded by machine we have described, they are nearly always graded by number. That is, the person who marks the paper knows only the number – never the name – of the applicant. Not until all the papers have been graded will they be matched with names. If other tests, such as training and experience or oral interview ratings have been given, scores will be combined. Different parts of the examination usually have different weights. For example, the written test might count 60 percent of the final grade, and a rating of training and experience 40 percent. In many jurisdictions, veterans will have a certain number of points added to their grades.

After the final grade has been determined, the names are placed in grade order and an eligible list is established. There are various methods for resolving ties between those who get the same final grade – probably the most common is to place first the name of the person whose application was received first. Job offers are made from the eligible list in the order the names appear on it. You will be notified of your grade and your rank as soon as all these computations have been made. This will be done as rapidly as possible.

People who are found to meet the requirements in the announcement are called "eligibles." Their names are put on a list of eligible candidates. An eligible's chances of getting a job depend on how high he stands on this list and how fast agencies are filling jobs from the list.

When a job is to be filled from a list of eligibles, the agency asks for the names of people on the list of eligibles for that job. When the civil service commission receives this request, it sends to the agency the names of the three people highest on this list. Or, if the job to be filled has specialized requirements, the office sends the agency the names of the top three persons who meet these requirements from the general list.

The appointing officer makes a choice from among the three people whose names were sent to him. If the selected person accepts the appointment, the names of the others are put back on the list to be considered for future openings.

That is the rule in hiring from all kinds of eligible lists, whether they are for typist, carpenter, chemist, or something else. For every vacancy, the appointing officer has his choice of any one of the top three eligibles on the list. This explains why the person whose name is on top of the list sometimes does not get an appointment when some of the persons lower on the list do. If the appointing officer chooses the second or third eligible, the No. 1 eligible does not get a job at once, but stays on the list until he is appointed or the list is terminated.

X. HOW TO PASS THE INTERVIEW TEST

The examination for which you applied requires an oral interview test. You have already taken the written test and you are now being called for the interview test – the final part of the formal examination.

You may think that it is not possible to prepare for an interview test and that there are no procedures to follow during an interview. Our purpose is to point out some things you can do in advance that will help you and some good rules to follow and pitfalls to avoid while you are being interviewed.

What is an interview supposed to test?

The written examination is designed to test the technical knowledge and competence of the candidate; the oral is designed to evaluate intangible qualities, not readily measured otherwise, and to establish a list showing the relative fitness of each candidate – as measured against his competitors – for the position sought. Scoring is not on the basis of "right" and "wrong," but on a sliding scale of values ranging from "not passable" to "outstanding." As a matter of fact, it is possible to achieve a relatively low score without a single "incorrect" answer because of evident weakness in the qualities being measured.

Occasionally, an examination may consist entirely of an oral test – either an individual or a group oral. In such cases, information is sought concerning the technical knowledges and abilities of the candidate, since there has been no written examination for this purpose. More commonly, however, an oral test is used to supplement a written examination.

Who conducts interviews?

The composition of oral boards varies among different jurisdictions. In nearly all, a representative of the personnel department serves as chairman. One of the members of the board may be a representative of the department in which the candidate would work. In some cases, "outside experts" are used, and, frequently, a businessman or some other representative of the general public is asked to serve. Labor and management or other special groups may be represented. The aim is to secure the services of experts in the appropriate field.

However the board is composed, it is a good idea (and not at all improper or unethical) to ascertain in advance of the interview who the members are and what groups they represent. When you are introduced to them, you will have some idea of their backgrounds and interests, and at least you will not stutter and stammer over their names.

What should be done before the interview?

While knowledge about the board members is useful and takes some of the surprise element out of the interview, there is other preparation which is more substantive. It *is* possible to prepare for an oral interview – in several ways:

1) Keep a copy of your application and review it carefully before the interview

This may be the only document before the oral board, and the starting point of the interview. Know what education and experience you have listed there, and the sequence and dates of all of it. Sometimes the board will ask you to review the highlights of your experience for them; you should not have to hem and haw doing it.

2) Study the class specification and the examination announcement

Usually, the oral board has one or both of these to guide them. The qualities, characteristics or knowledges required by the position sought are stated in these documents. They offer valuable clues as to the nature of the oral interview. For example, if the job involves supervisory responsibilities, the announcement will usually indicate that knowledge of modern supervisory methods and the qualifications of the candidate as a supervisor will be tested. If so, you can expect such questions, frequently in the form of a hypothetical situation which you are expected to solve. NEVER go into an oral without knowledge of the duties and responsibilities of the job you seek.

3) Think through each qualification required

Try to visualize the kind of questions you would ask if you were a board member. How well could you answer them? Try especially to appraise your own knowledge and background in each area, *measured against the job sought*, and identify any areas in which you are weak. Be critical and realistic – do not flatter yourself.

4) Do some general reading in areas in which you feel you may be weak

For example, if the job involves supervision and your past experience has NOT, some general reading in supervisory methods and practices, particularly in the field of human relations, might be useful. Do NOT study agency procedures or detailed manuals. The oral board will be testing your understanding and capacity, not your memory.

5) Get a good night's sleep and watch your general health and mental attitude

You will want a clear head at the interview. Take care of a cold or any other minor ailment, and of course, no hangovers.

What should be done on the day of the interview?

Now comes the day of the interview itself. Give yourself plenty of time to get there. Plan to arrive somewhat ahead of the scheduled time, particularly if your appointment is in the fore part of the day. If a previous candidate fails to appear, the board might be ready for you a bit early. By early afternoon an oral board is almost invariably behind schedule if there are many candidates, and you may have to wait. Take along a book or magazine to read, or your application to review, but leave any extraneous material in the waiting room when you go in for your interview. In any event, relax and compose yourself.

The matter of dress is important. The board is forming impressions about you – from your experience, your manners, your attitude, and your appearance. Give your personal appearance careful attention. Dress your best, but not your flashiest. Choose conservative, appropriate clothing, and be sure it is immaculate. This is a business interview, and your appearance should indicate that you regard it as such. Besides, being well groomed and properly dressed will help boost your confidence.

Sooner or later, someone will call your name and escort you into the interview room. *This is it.* From here on you are on your own. It is too late for any more preparation. But remember, you asked for this opportunity to prove your fitness, and you are here because your request was granted.

What happens when you go in?

The usual sequence of events will be as follows: The clerk (who is often the board stenographer) will introduce you to the chairman of the oral board, who will introduce you to the other members of the board. Acknowledge the introductions before you sit down. Do not be surprised if you find a microphone facing you or a stenotypist sitting by. Oral interviews are usually recorded in the event of an appeal or other review.

Usually the chairman of the board will open the interview by reviewing the highlights of your education and work experience from your application – primarily for the benefit of the other members of the board, as well as to get the material into the record. Do not interrupt or comment unless there is an error or significant misinterpretation; if that is the case, do not hesitate. But do not quibble about insignificant matters. Also, he will usually ask you some question about your education, experience or your present job – partly to get you to start talking and to establish the interviewing "rapport." He may start the actual questioning, or turn it over to one of the other members. Frequently, each member undertakes the questioning on a particular area, one in which he is perhaps most competent, so you can expect each member to participate in the examination. Because time is limited, you may also expect some rather abrupt switches in the direction the questioning takes, so do not be upset by it. Normally, a board member will not pursue a single line of questioning unless he discovers a particular strength or weakness.

After each member has participated, the chairman will usually ask whether any member has any further questions, then will ask you if you have anything you wish to add. Unless you are expecting this question, it may floor you. Worse, it may start you off on an extended, extemporaneous speech. The board is not usually seeking more information. The question is principally to offer you a last opportunity to present further qualifications or to indicate that you have nothing to add. So, if you feel that a significant qualification or characteristic has been overlooked, it is proper to point it out in a sentence or so. Do not compliment the board on the thoroughness of their examination – they have been sketchy, and you know it. If you wish, merely say, "No thank you, I have nothing further to add." This is a point where you can "talk yourself out" of a good impression or fail to present an important bit of information. Remember, *you close the interview yourself*.

The chairman will then say, "That is all, Mr. _____, thank you." Do not be startled; the interview is over, and quicker than you think. Thank him, gather your belongings and take your leave. Save your sigh of relief for the other side of the door.

How to put your best foot forward

Throughout this entire process, you may feel that the board individually and collectively is trying to pierce your defenses, seek out your hidden weaknesses and embarrass and confuse you. Actually, this is not true. They are obliged to make an appraisal of your qualifications for the job you are seeking, and they want to see you in your best light. Remember, they must interview all candidates and a non-cooperative candidate may become a failure in spite of their best efforts to bring out his qualifications. Here are 15 suggestions that will help you:

1) Be natural – Keep your attitude confident, not cocky

If you are not confident that you can do the job, do not expect the board to be. Do not apologize for your weaknesses, try to bring out your strong points. The board is interested in a positive, not negative, presentation. Cockiness will antagonize any board member and make him wonder if you are covering up a weakness by a false show of strength.

2) Get comfortable, but don't lounge or sprawl

Sit erectly but not stiffly. A careless posture may lead the board to conclude that you are careless in other things, or at least that you are not impressed by the importance of the occasion. Either conclusion is natural, even if incorrect. Do not fuss with your clothing, a pencil or an ashtray. Your hands may occasionally be useful to emphasize a point; do not let them become a point of distraction.

3) Do not wisecrack or make small talk

This is a serious situation, and your attitude should show that you consider it as such. Further, the time of the board is limited – they do not want to waste it, and neither should you.

4) Do not exaggerate your experience or abilities

In the first place, from information in the application or other interviews and sources, the board may know more about you than you think. Secondly, you probably will not get away with it. An experienced board is rather adept at spotting such a situation, so do not take the chance.

5) If you know a board member, do not make a point of it, yet do not hide it

Certainly you are not fooling him, and probably not the other members of the board. Do not try to take advantage of your acquaintanceship – it will probably do you little good.

6) Do not dominate the interview

Let the board do that. They will give you the clues – do not assume that you have to do all the talking. Realize that the board has a number of questions to ask you, and do not try to take up all the interview time by showing off your extensive knowledge of the answer to the first one.

7) Be attentive

You only have 20 minutes or so, and you should keep your attention at its sharpest throughout. When a member is addressing a problem or question to you, give him your undivided attention. Address your reply principally to him, but do not exclude the other board members.

8) Do not interrupt

A board member may be stating a problem for you to analyze. He will ask you a question when the time comes. Let him state the problem, and wait for the question.

9) Make sure you understand the question

Do not try to answer until you are sure what the question is. If it is not clear, restate it in your own words or ask the board member to clarify it for you. However, do not haggle about minor elements.

10) Reply promptly but not hastily

A common entry on oral board rating sheets is "candidate responded readily," or "candidate hesitated in replies." Respond as promptly and quickly as you can, but do not jump to a hasty, ill-considered answer.

11) Do not be peremptory in your answers

A brief answer is proper – but do not fire your answer back. That is a losing game from your point of view. The board member can probably ask questions much faster than you can answer them.

12) Do not try to create the answer you think the board member wants

He is interested in what kind of mind you have and how it works – not in playing games. Furthermore, he can usually spot this practice and will actually grade you down on it.

13) Do not switch sides in your reply merely to agree with a board member

Frequently, a member will take a contrary position merely to draw you out and to see if you are willing and able to defend your point of view. Do not start a debate, yet do not surrender a good position. If a position is worth taking, it is worth defending.

14) Do not be afraid to admit an error in judgment if you are shown to be wrong

The board knows that you are forced to reply without any opportunity for careful consideration. Your answer may be demonstrably wrong. If so, admit it and get on with the interview.

15) Do not dwell at length on your present job

The opening question may relate to your present assignment. Answer the question but do not go into an extended discussion. You are being examined for a *new* job, not your present one. As a matter of fact, try to phrase ALL your answers in terms of the job for which you are being examined.

Basis of Rating

Probably you will forget most of these "do's" and "don'ts" when you walk into the oral interview room. Even remembering them all will not ensure you a passing grade. Perhaps you did not have the qualifications in the first place. But remembering them will help you to put your best foot forward, without treading on the toes of the board members.

Rumor and popular opinion to the contrary notwithstanding, an oral board wants you to make the best appearance possible. They know you are under pressure – but they also want to see how you respond to it as a guide to what your reaction would be under the pressures of the job you seek. They will be influenced by the degree of poise you display, the personal traits you show and the manner in which you respond.

ABOUT THIS BOOK

This book contains tests divided into Examination Sections. Go through each test, answering every question in the margin. We have also attached a sample answer sheet at the back of the book that can be removed and used. At the end of each test look at the answer key and check your answers. On the ones you got wrong, look at the right answer choice and learn. Do not fill in the answers first. Do not memorize the questions and answers, but understand the answer and principles involved. On your test, the questions will likely be different from the samples. Questions are changed and new ones added. If you understand these past questions you should have success with any changes that arise. Tests may consist of several types of questions. We have additional books on each subject should more study be advisable or necessary for you. Finally, the more you study, the better prepared you will be. This book is intended to be the last thing you study before you walk into the examination room. Prior study of relevant texts is also recommended. NLC publishes some of these in our Fundamental Series. Knowledge and good sense are important factors in passing your exam. Good luck also helps. So now study this Passbook, absorb the material contained within and take that knowledge into the examination. Then do your best to pass that exam.

EXAMINATION SECTION

EXAMINATION SECTION
TEST 1

DIRECTIONS: Each question or incomplete statement is followed by several suggested answers or completions. Select the one that BEST answers the question or completes the statement. *PRINT THE LETTER OF THE CORRECT ANSWER IN THE SPACE AT THE RIGHT.*

1. A percentage of the payment for a contract is held back until the job is completed for one year.
   The MAIN reason for this practice is to insure that the

   A. city doesn't overpay the contractor for the job
   B. contractor will return to correct defective work after the job is completed
   C. contractor will not make unwarranted claims against the city
   D. contractor will pay all his subcontractors

   1.____

2. There are four separate major contracts on a certain building construction project.
   The MAJOR disadvantage of this practice, as compared to the practice of having a single contract, is

   A. the difficulty in coordinating the work
   B. the low level of productivity of the tradesman
   C. cost of the material going into the building is greater
   D. the difficulty in finding competent bidders on the contracts

   2.____

3. Of the following, the PREFERRED way to authorize a contractor to perform work other than required by the contract is by a

   A. T & M order
   B. unit price order
   C. lump sum modification
   D. change order

   3.____

4. A contract requires that the prime contractor do a certain minimum percentage of the work with his own forces.
   Of the following, the BEST reason for this requirement is to

   A. insure good work
   B. discourage bidders who may not have the ability to do the job
   C. encourage more people to bid the job, thus lowering the bid price
   D. freeze out incompetent subcontractors

   4.____

5. In computing an extra based on the actual cost of work done, the THREE MAJOR items that go into the cost are

   A. taxes, labor, and material
   B. time, taxes, and material
   C. labor, material, and equipment
   D. taxes, labor, and equipment

   5.____

6. A contractor is to be penalized if he exceeds a certain completion date. There is a major strike lasting a month that shuts down all construction.
   Under these conditions, the completion date should be

   6.____

A. held unchanged
B. made two weeks later than the original date
C. made one month later than the original date
D. made six weeks later than the original completion date

7. The one of the following that refers to a Federal safety program in construction is 7.___

   A. OSHA   B. AISC   C. AIEE   D. UL

8. With regard to the placing of concrete, the contractor is GENERALLY 8.___

   A. limited to a specific method by the contract
   B. not permitted to rent equipment to place the concrete
   C. not permitted to pump the concrete into place
   D. permitted to choose his own method of placing the concrete

9. The MOST practical control the inspector or resident engineer has over the contractor when the inspector is not satisfied with the quality of the work is to 9.___

   A. discuss withholding payment on that part of the work that is unsatisfactory
   B. threaten to have the contractor thrown off the job
   C. request that the contractor fire the men responsible for the unsatisfactory work
   D. call the owner of the company and explain the situation to him

10. The MOST practical method of being sure that the architect will be satisfied with the appearance of the exterior brick work for a building is to 10.___

    A. build a sample wall section, for the architect's approval, with the brick that is delivered to the job site
    B. send the architect to the plant supplying the brick to insure that the color and tone of the brick is satisfactory
    C. have the architect's representative on the job while the brick work is being erected to be sure the finished product is satisfactory
    D. put a damage clause in the contract penalizing the contractor if the brick work is not satisfactory to the architect

11. Of the following, the MOST frequent problem that will arise during the construction of a building is 11.___

    A. inability to fit all the reinforcing steel in the space allotted to it
    B. interference in piping and ductwork
    C. inability to keep walls level
    D. settling of the foundation as the load comes on the building

12. To find the number of reinforcing bars that should be in a slab, the inspector SHOULD refer to the 12.___

    A. architect's plan
    B. reinforcing steel design drawings
    C. standard detail drawings
    D. reinforcing steel detail drawings

13. The specifications for a building state that a certain brick type shall be *Stark Brick type* 13.____
    XX or equal.
    The BEST reason for inserting the *or equal* clause is to

    A. permit other companies to compete in supplying the brick
    B. allow other companies to submit their product to determine which is best
    C. limit the suppliers only to those companies whose product is superior to that produced by Stark
    D. allow Stark Brick Company to set the standard for the industry

14. In the absence of a formal training program for inspectors, the BEST of the following 14.____
    ways to train a new man who is to do inspection work is to

    A. give him the literature on the subject so that he can learn what he has to know
    B. have him accompany an inspector as the inspector does his work so that he can learn by observing
    C. assign him the job and let him learn on his own
    D. tell him to go to a school at night that specializes in this field so that he will gain the necessary background

15. Of the following, the safety practice that is REQUIRED on the construction job site is 15.____

    A. safety shoes must be worn by all workers
    B. safety goggles must be worn by all workers
    C. safety helmets must be worn by all workers
    D. all workers must have a safety kit in their possession

16. Safety on the job is the concern of 16.____

    A. the individual workman only
    B. the contractor only
    C. all parties on the job
    D. the insuring company only

17. Frequently, payments due the contractor are delayed many months because of a backlog 17.____
    of work in the agency.
    This practice is considered

    A. *good* because the city saves money by delaying payment
    B. *poor* because the contractors will raise their bids in the future to compensate for the added cost
    C. *poor* because it becomes difficult to compute payments
    D. *good* because it forces the contractor to do good work in order to be sure that he will receive payment

18. Provisions are made in a contract for payment for certain items when delivered to the job 18.____
    before installation.
    The MAIN reason for this practice is to

    A. enable better inspection of the items
    B. prevent bottlenecks during construction
    C. give the contractor a quick profit on the items
    D. allow the contractor more time to shop for the items

19. The agency that approves payments to building contractors is the 19.____

   A. Corporation Counsel B. Comptroller's Office
   C. Board of Estimate D. City Planning Commission

20. The bond that the contractor puts up to insure that he will start work is the 20.____

   A. Bid Bond B. Payment Bond
   C. Performance Bond D. Liability Insurance

21. Of the following, the BEST practice to follow in order to minimize claims of damage to 21.____
    adjacent buildings during the construction of a building is to

   A. take out special insurance against such claims
   B. make a detailed survey of the condition of the nearby buildings before construction begins
   C. make a payment to adjacent property owners in advance so that they waive claims of damage to their property
   D. have the buildings underpinned

22. The four MAJOR contracts on a building project are: 22.____

   A. General Construction, Electrical, Plumbing and Drainage, Heating, Ventilating and Air Conditioning
   B. Plumbing, Heating and Ventilating, Air Conditioning, and General Construction
   C. Foundations, Superstructure, Mechanical, and Electrical
   D. Air Conditioning, Electrical, Mechanical, and Structural

23. Oil tanks, when set in place inside a building, are frequently filled with water. 23.____
    The BEST reason for this practice is

   A. to prevent them from floating off their foundation if water fills the room
   B. to enable them to be lifted up more easily
   C. to prevent them from becoming rusted
   D. for emergency use in case of fire

24. The filing system used in the field for correspondence is required to be uniform for all 24.____
    jobs.
    The BEST reason for this requirement is that

   A. there is only one good way of setting up the filing system
   B. the standardized system is compact, thereby saving space
   C. other interested parties such as engineers from the main office will be able to use the files
   D. the contractor's forces will understand the filing system and will be able to extract necessary correspondence

25. Upon excavation to the subgrade of a footing to be placed on piles, the inspector finds 25.____
    that the soil is very poor.
    Of the following, the PROPER action for the inspector to take is to

   A. do nothing
   B. add 20% to the number of piles
   C. notify the engineer's office of this condition
   D. order the contractor to keep excavating until he hits better soil

26. The general contractor is required to submit a progress schedule before starting work. Of the following, the BEST reason for this requirement is to

    A. determine if the contractor intends to complete the job
    B. enable the inspector to determine whether the contractor is on schedule
    C. enable the inspector to estimate monthly payments
    D. check minority hiring

27. If a contractor is falling behind schedule, the FIRST thing to check if the inspector is looking for the cause of this condition is the

    A. number of men he has on the job
    B. efficiency of his crew
    C. availability of equipment needed to do the job
    D. availability of the latest drawings needed by the contractor

28. The critical path method is a method for

    A. finding the best material needed for a specific use
    B. determining the best arrangement of equipment
    C. determining the best time to replace a piece of machinery
    D. scheduling work

29. The contractor states to the inspector that a given structural detail is undersized and unsafe.
    Of the following, the BEST action for the inspector to take in this situation is to

    A. ignore the complaint since the contractor is not an engineer
    B. change the detail by issuing a change order
    C. notify your superiors of the contractor's statements
    D. allow the contractor to modify the detail since it is his responsibility

30. The contractor proposes to use an additive to the concrete to accelerate its set. He asks you, the inspector, for permission to use it.
    Of the following, the FIRST action to take in response to his request is to

    A. check if the use of the additive is permitted by the specifications
    B. tell him to put the request in writing
    C. ask your superior if the use of the additive is acceptable
    D. deny him permission since additives to concrete are not permitted

KEY (CORRECT ANSWERS)

1.	B	16.	C
2.	A	17.	B
3.	D	18.	B
4.	B	19.	B
5.	C	20.	A
6.	C	21.	B
7.	A	22.	A
8.	D	23.	A
9.	A	24.	C
10.	A	25.	A
11.	B	26.	B
12.	D	27.	A
13.	A	28.	D
14.	B	29.	C
15.	C	30.	A

EXAMINATION SECTION
TEST 1

DIRECTIONS: Each question or incomplete statement is followed by several suggested answers or completions. Select the one that BEST answers the question or completes the statement. *PRINT THE LETTER OF THE CORRECT ANSWER IN THE SPACE AT THE RIGHT.*

Questions 1-3.

DIRECTIONS: Questions 1 through 3, inclusive, are to be answered on the basis of the following specification.

Cellar entrance doors shall be paneled type of Northern White Pine or Idaho White Pine for painted finish. These doors shall be built up of solid stiles and rails, with mortised, tenoned, and pinned joints. Panels shall be not less than 1/8 inch thick (after sanding) and of same materials as stiles and rails. Upper panels shall be divided with muntins with removable molds on inside for glazing. The lower panels shall be installed so as to allow for movement and shall be primed before being set in place.

1. The specification requires that the joints between adjacent members in the frame of the door should be as in

   A.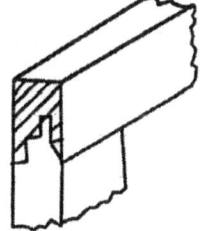
   B.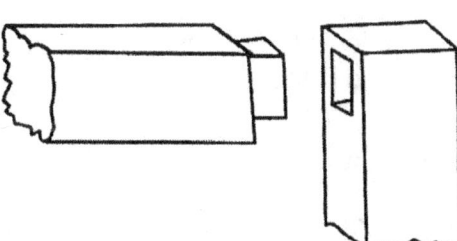
   C.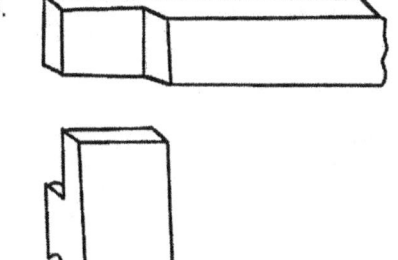
   D.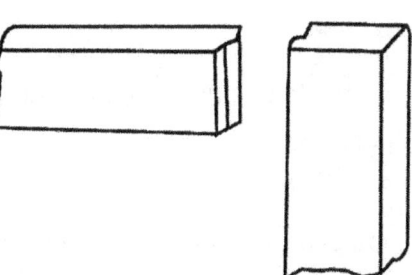

1._____

2. Of the following, the one that is MOST likely to be used for the face veneer of the panels is

   A. birch
   B. oak
   C. northern white pine
   D. hickory

2._____

3. If the three-ply panel is 1/2 inch thick, the core must be _____ inch thick.

   A. 3/8
   B. 1/8
   C. not more than ¼
   D. not less than ¼

4. The term *matched lumber* refers to which of the following types of sections?

   A. Splined plank
   B. Tongue and groove
   C. Shiplap
   D. Beveled siding

5. Rigidity of the hammer handle enables the operator to control and direct the force of the blow.
   As used above, *rigidity* means MOST NEARLY

   A. straightness
   B. strength
   C. shape
   D. stiffness

6. Open-end wrenches are usually made with the sides of the jaws at about a 15° angle to the centerline of the handle. The purpose of this type of design is that it

   A. increases the leverage of the wrench
   B. enables the wrench to lock on to the bolt head
   C. is useful when using the wrench in close quarters
   D. prevents extending the handle with a piece of pipe

7. The type of tool which is used with a portable electric drill to cut 2-inch diameter circular holes in wood is the

   A. reamer
   B. twist drill
   C. hole saw
   D. circular saw

8. The symbol shown at the right on a building plan indicates a
   A. chute
   B. storm window
   C. fireplace
   D. door

9. The size of moulds would be shown on the

   A. plot plan
   B. front elevation
   C. detail sheet
   D. floor plan

10. The location of a partition would be shown on the

    A. front elevation
    B. plot plan
    C. floor plan
    D. detail sheet

11. A finished piece of lumber whose nominal dimensions are 2" x 4" is MOST NEARLY

    A. 1 7/8" x 3 7/8"
    B. 1 3/4" x 3 3/4"
    C. 1 5/8" x 3 5/8"
    D. 1 1/2" x 4 1/2"

12. To measure the width of a piece of finish flooring, include

    A. the groove but not the tongue
    B. the tongue but not the groove
    C. neither the tongue nor the groove
    D. both the tongue and the groove

13. The BEST size of nail to use when nailing two 2" x 2" (S4S) pieces of lumber together is _____ d.

    A. 3   B. 6   C. 10   D. 20

14. The BEST of the following sources of information to use to obtain information concerning the product of a particular manufacturer of flooring is

    A. Sweet's Catalogue
    B. Architectural Standards
    C. The Flooring Institute
    D. The ASTM

15. A requisition for lag screws does NOT require stating the

    A. diameter
    B. quantity
    C. threads per inch
    D. length

16. In an accident report, the information which may be MOST useful in decreasing the recurrence of similar type accidents is the

    A. extent of injuries sustained
    B. time the accident happened
    C. number of people involved
    D. cause of the accident

17. A nail set is a tool used for

    A. straightening bent nails
    B. measuring nail sizes
    C. cutting nails to specified size
    D. driving a nail head into wood

18. To cut a number of 2" x 4" lengths of wood accurately at an angle of 45°, it is BEST to use a

    A. protractor
    B. mitre-box
    C. triangle
    D. square

19. When applied to lumber, the designation *S4S* means

    A. all sides are rough
    B. all four sides are of the same size
    C. fourth grade lumber
    D. all sides are dressed

20. To guard against accidents in connection with wood scaffolding,

    A. inspect the nailing before the scaffold is loaded
    B. never put a heavy load on a scaffold
    C. use only heavy timber for scaffold construction
    D. do not build high scaffolds

21. Lumber in quantity is ordered by 21.___

    A. cubic feet   B. foot board measure
    C. lineal feet   D. weight and length

22. For finishing of wood, BEST results are obtained by sanding 22.___

    A. with a circular motion
    B. against the grain
    C. with the grain
    D. with a circular motion on edges and against the grain on the flat parts

23. Of the following items, the item which is LEAST related to the others is 23.___

    A. putty   B. sash weight
    C. glazier's points   D. lights

24. Assume that a wood-frame house has studs of 2 x 4's. Placing the studs so that the 24.___
    wider dimension is parallel to the wall is

    A. *good* because it provides a wider nailing surface for sheathing and lathing
    B. *bad* because it reduces the open space available for windows
    C. *good* because it stiffens the frame
    D. *bad* because it reduces the load-carrying capacity of the studs

25. Where a 2" solid laminated gypsum wallboard partition, consisting of two 1" wallboards, 25.___
    assembled back to back on the job, abuts a joint, the specifications require that the panel
    be secured to the continuous metal fins or anchors.
    Of the following, the hardware MOST LIKELY to be specified for fastening the gypsum
    panel to the joint is

    A. speed clinch fasteners
    B. 1/2-inch hardened stud nails
    C. U shaped metal joint clips
    D. 2 1/2 inch number 10 sheet metal screws

KEY (CORRECT ANSWERS)

1. B
2. C
3. C
4. B
5. D

6. C
7. C
8. D
9. C
10. C

11. C
12. A
13. C
14. A
15. C

16. D
17. D
18. B
19. D
20. A

21. B
22. C
23. B
24. D
25. C

TEST 2

DIRECTIONS: Each question or incomplete statement is followed by several suggested answers or completions. Select the one that BEST answers the question or completes the statement. *PRINT THE LETTER OF THE CORRECT ANSWER IN THE SPACE AT THE RIGHT.*

1. A board 10'6" long is to have 5 holes drilled along its length. The distances between centers of adjacent holes are to be equal and the distance from each end of the board to the center of the nearest hole is to be twice the distance between centers of adjacent holes. The distance between centers of adjacent holes will be

   A. 14" B. 15 3/4" C. 18" D. 21"

2. Lumber used in certain types of outdoor construction work is treated with creosote before being used.
   The creosote serves to

   A. decrease the rusting of the nails used for fastening
   B. prevent the lumber from checking or peeling
   C. act as a good undercoat for paint
   D. prevent the lumber from rotting

3. On a drawing, the symbol shown at the right represents

   A. stone B. steel C. glass D. wood

4. In building construction, an apron would MOST likely be installed by a

   A. carpenter   B. sheet metal worker
   C. bricklayer   D. glazier

5. In a building with masonry walls, furring

   A. is of no advantage
   B. is of no help in preventing wetting of plaster
   C. is used only because it provides a nailing surface
   D. adds to the insulating quality of the wall

6. In the picture shown at the right, which of the numbered arrows points to the door *jamb*?
   A. 1
   B. 2
   C. 3
   D. 4

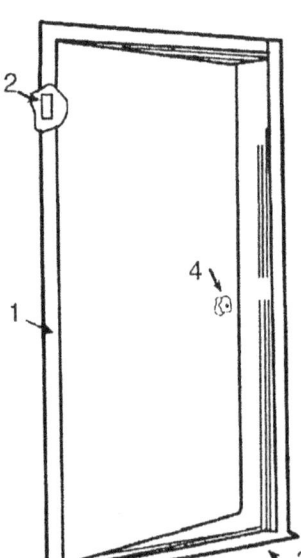

7. Board measure is a measure of

   A. length   B. area   C. volume   D. weight

8. ———— 3'-0" ————

   The above appears on a floor plan. The 3'0" MOST likely represents a

   A. double acting door 3'0" wide
   B. fire door
   C. door, 3'0" wide
   D. masonry opening, 3'0" wide

9. In the city, *drywall* is installed by

   A. plasterers   B. carpenters
   C. bricklayers   D. cement masons

10. The end of a wood joist resting directly on a concrete wall has to be brought up to level. The BEST material to use as a shim for this purpose is

    A. slate   B. wood shingles
    C. dressed wood   D. grout

11. In setting diagonal cross-bridging on wood joists, the BEST method is to

    A. nail at top and bottom before subflooring is in place
    B. nail at bottom, place subflooring, then nail at top
    C. nail at top, place subflooring, then nail at bottom
    D. place subflooring, then nail at top and bottom

12. The dressed size of lumber is

    A. smaller than the nominal size
    B. depends upon the grade of the lumber
    C. its size as finally used on the job
    D. not related to its nominal size

13. Of the following types of joints, the one which is LEAST related to the others is

    A. raked   B. weather
    C. construction   D. struck

14. Of the following, the problem that occurs MOST frequently during the construction of a school building is

    A. cracking of the concrete
    B. cracking of the brickwork
    C. interference between ductwork and piping
    D. settlement of the foundation

13

15. Wainscoting is USUALLY found on

   A. floors　　B. walls　　C. ceilings　　D. roofs

16. Joists spaced 16" o.c. on a 12'0" span support a floor which is to carry a live load of 80 pounds per square foot.
   The TOTAL live load carried by a single joist is, in pounds,

   A. 590　　B. 920　　C. 1195　　D. 1280

17. Pointing up around the end of a joist resting on a brick wall is

   A. *good* because it improves appearance
   B. *bad* because it may cause rotting of joist
   C. *good* because it results in a more solid wall
   D. *bad* because it interferes with firestopping

18. The type of construction MOST commonly used in new wood frame dwellings is the _____ frame.

   A. platform　　B. braced　　C. balloon　　D. butt

19. Plank clips that are .062 inches thick are MOST NEARLY _____ " thick.

   A. 1/32　　B. 2/32　　C. 3/32　　D. 4/32

20. The specification for a wood door states: Stiles and rails of doors M & T together and assembled with hardwood wedges.
   M & T stands for

   A. mitred and tongued
   B. matches and tacked
   C. milled and tacked
   D. mortise and tenon

21. The specifications state that the ends of a wood beam shall be firecut. The end of the beam would appear in place as shown in

22. The CHIEF objection to the use of green lumber in wood construction relates to its

   A. color
   B. strength
   C. lack of dimensional stability
   D. nailing

23. The joints in 2" face wood flooring are MOST likely to be

   A. mortise and tenon
   B. tongue and groove
   C. butt
   D. dove-tail

24. Of the following species of wood, the one that is MOST likely to be specified for finish flooring in a school or housing project is

    A. douglas fir
    B. sitka spruce
    C. northern hard maple
    D. hickory

25. Good practice dictates that an adjustable open-end wrench should be used PRIMARILY when the

    A. nut to be turned is soft and must not be scored
    B. extra leverage is needed
    C. proper size of fixed wrench is not available
    D. location is cramped permitting only a small turning angle

KEY (CORRECT ANSWERS)

1.	B	11.	C
2.	D	12.	A
3.	D	13.	C
4.	A	14.	C
5.	D	15.	B
6.	A	16.	D
7.	C	17.	B
8.	C	18.	A
9.	B	19.	B
10.	A	20.	D

21. C
22. C
23. B
24. C
25. C

TEST 3

DIRECTIONS: Each question or incomplete statement is followed by several suggested answers or completions. Select the one that BEST answers the question or completes the statement. *PRINT THE LETTER OF THE CORRECT ANSWER IN THE SPACE AT THE RIGHT.*

1. The multiple dwelling law states that for stairs each tread shall be not less than nine and one-half inches wide; each riser shall not exceed seven and three-quarters inches in height; and the product of the number of inches in the width of the tread and the number of inches in the height of the riser shall be at least seventy and at most seventy-five. The one of the following sets of dimensions that is ACCEPTABLE for the stairs of a multiple dwelling is tread _____; riser _____".

    A. 9 3/4; 7 1/8
    B. 9 1/4; 8
    C. 10 1/4; 7 1/8
    D. 10 1/2; 7 1/2

2. A bearing wall is a wall which

    A. carries its own weight *only*
    B. carries load other than its own weight
    C. bears on structural supports at each story
    D. is more than 12 feet high

3. A column is an _____ member.

    A. upright compression
    B. inclined compression
    C. upright tension
    D. inclined tension

4. The advantage of using screws instead of nails is:

    A. They have greater holding power
    B. They are available in a greater variety than are nails
    C. A hammer is not required for joining wood members
    D. They are less expensive

5. If a keg of nails had on it the words *Net Weight 10 pounds*, it would mean that the

    A. keg weighed 10 pounds without the nails
    B. nails and the keg together weighed 10 pounds
    C. nails weighed 10 pounds without the keg
    D. weight of 10 pounds is approximate

6. If green lumber is used for joists, shrinkage will have its MOST serious effect in _____ of joists.

    A. length   B. width   C. depth   D. weight

7. To make driving of a screw into hard wood easier, it is BEST to lubricate the threads of the screw with

    A. varnoline
    B. penetrating oil
    C. beeswax
    D. cutting oil

8. To hold a piece of lumber in place, the length of nail should be _____ the thickness of the lumber.

   A. three times
   B. equal to
   C. one and one-half times
   D. half

9. The cap screw which is specifically designed for a counterboard hole is No.

   A. 1
   B. 2
   C. 3
   D. 4

10. The carpenter's hand screw is numbered

    A. 1
    B. 2
    C. 3
    D. 4

11. The tool that is BEST suited for use with a wood chisel is numbered,

    A. 1
    B. 2
    C. 3
    D. 4

12. The FINEST sandpaper from among the following is No.

    A. 3
    B. 1
    C. 2/0
    D. 6/0

13. A screw whose head is buried below the surface of the wood that it is screwed into is said to be

    A. countersunk
    B. scalloped
    C. expanded
    D. flushed

14. The one of the following devices which is used to measure angles is the

    A. caliper
    B. protractor
    C. marking gauge
    D. divider

15. A woodworking tool used to bore odd-size holes for which there is no standard auger bit is a(n)

    A. single twist auger
    B. double twist auger
    C. expansive bit
    D. straight fluted drill

16. Soap is sometimes applied to wood screws in order to

    A. prevent rust
    B. make a tight fit
    C. make insertion easier
    D. prevent wood splitting

17. The following is taken from a specification for kitchen cabinets: Rails and stiles of full front frames on all cabinets shall be of hardwood 4/4 stock, maple or birch or southern poplar.
    Of the following, the 4/4 stock means

    A. 4 x 4 lumber nominal size stock
    B. 1 inch thick rough stock
    C. 2 x 4 lumber nominal size stock
    D. finished four sides

18. After a file has been used on soft material, the BEST way to clean the file is to use a

    A. file card
    B. fine emery cloth
    C. bench brush
    D. cleaning solution

19. The type of wrench that should be used to tighten a nut or bolt to a specified number of foot-pounds is a _____ wrench.

    A. torque   B. spanner   C. box   D. lug

20. The rounded, projecting edge of a stair tread is the

    A. coping   B. nosing   C. rising   D. stringing

21. A fire tower differs from fire stairs PRINCIPALLY in

    A. capacity
    B. location
    C. height
    D. tread and riser requirements

22. The type of chain used with sash weights is _____ link.

    A. flat
    B. round
    C. figure eight
    D. basketweave

23. The material that would be used to seal around a window frame is

    A. oakum   B. litharge   C. grout   D. calking

24. The function of a window sill is MOST NEARLY the same as that of a

    A. jamb   B. coping   C. lintel   D. buck

25.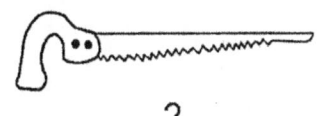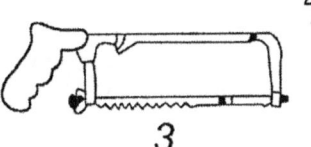

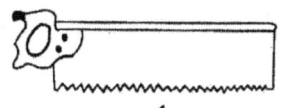

The saw that is used PRINCIPALLY where curved cuts are to be made is numbered

A. 1   B. 2   C. 3   D. 4

KEY (CORRECT ANSWERS)

1. C		11. D	
2. B		12. D	
3. A		13. A	
4. A		14. B	
5. C		15. C	
6. C		16. C	
7. C		17. D	
8. A		18. A	
9. B		19. A	
10. C		20. B	

21. B
22. A
23. D
24. B
25. B

EXAMINATION SECTION
TEST 1

DIRECTIONS: Each question or incomplete statement is followed by several suggested answers or completions. Select the one that BEST answers the question or completes the statement. *PRINT THE LETTER OF THE CORRECT ANSWER IN THE SPACE AT THE RIGHT.*

1. A requisition for nails was worded as follows: *100 lbs., 10d, 3 inch, common wire nails, galvanized.*
   The UNNECESSARY information in this requisition is

   A. 100 lbs.   B. common   C. galvanized   D. 3 inch

   1.____

2. Of the following, the MOST important advantage of a ratchet wrench as compared to an open-end wrench is that the ratchet wrench

   A. is adjustable
   B. cannot strip the threads of a nut
   C. can be used in a limited space
   D. measures the force applied

   2.____

3. One advantage of plywood is that it

   A. is cheaper than soft pine
   B. does not contain any glue
   C. never splinters
   D. resists warping

   3.____

4. When floor beams are to be supported by nailing to vertical supports, then the STRONGEST arrangement would be provided by the method shown in

   4.____

   A. Beam / Vertical support
   B.
   C.
   D. Wood block

5. Wood is LEAST likely to split when a nail is driven through it if the wood

   A. is very thin
   B. is very hard
   C. has been bleached white by the sun
   D. is soft

   5.____

6. The side support for steps or stairs is called a

   A. ledger board   B. runner
   C. stringer   D. riser

   6.____

7. A gouge is a tool used for

   A. planing wood smooth   B. grinding metal
   C. drilling steel   D. chiseling wood

   7.____

8. A router is used PRINCIPALLY to

   A. clean pipe
   B. cut grooves in wood
   C. bend electric conduit
   D. sharpen tools

9. The principle of operation of a sabre saw is MOST similar to that of a _____ saw.

   A. circular
   B. radial
   C. swing
   D. jig

10. A staircase has twelve risers, each 6 3/4" high. The TOTAL rise of the staircase is

    A. 6'2 1/4"
    B. 6'9"
    C. 7'0"
    D. 7'3 3/4"

11. A twenty-foot straight ladder placed at an angle against a wall should be at a distance from the wall equal to _____ feet.

    A. 3
    B. 5
    C. 7
    D. 9

12. The leverage that can be obtained with a wrench is determined MAINLY by the

    A. material of which the wrench is made
    B. gripping surface of the jaw
    C. length of the handle
    D. thickness of the wrench

13. Of the following, the MAIN reason why flashing is used in the building trade is to make an area

    A. decorative
    B. watertight
    C. level
    D. heat-resistant

14. A spandrel beam will USUALLY be found

    A. at the wall
    B. around stairs
    C. at the peak of a roof
    D. underneath a column

15. The MAIN reason for using oil on an oilstone is to

    A. make the surface of the stone smoother
    B. prevent clogging of the pores of the stone
    C. reduce the number of times the stone has to be *dressed*
    D. prevent gouging of the stone's surface

16. End grain of a post can be MOST easily planed by use of a _____ plane.

    A. rafter
    B. jack
    C. fore
    D. block

17. A butt gauge is used when

    A. hanging doors
    B. laying out stairs
    C. making rafter cuts
    D. framing studs

18. Assume that you have been asked to remove a door knob. You inspect the door and find that it has a mortise lock, and that the door knob is fastened with a set screw. Which of the following is the FIRST step that you should take in removing the door knob?

A. Unscrew the set screw on the slimmest part of the knob
B. Saw off the knob at its thinnest point
C. Turn the knob repeatedly to the right and to the left until it finally falls off
D. Use a pinchbar to spring the lock

19. To *shim a hinge* means to

   A. swing the hinge from side to side
   B. paint the hinge
   C. polish the hinge
   D. raise up the hinge

20. To hold work that is being planed, sawed, drilled, shaped, sharpened, or riveted, you should use a

   A. punch   B. rasp   C. reamer   D. vise

21. In the wood frame shown at the right, whose corners are all square, the TOTAL length of one-inch boards is _____ inches.

   A. 42
   B. 43
   C. 44
   D. 45

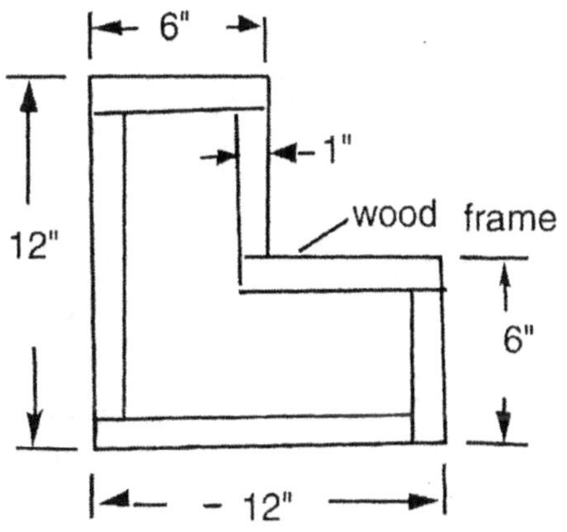

22. Clutch-head, offset, Phillips, and spiral-ratchet are all different types of

   A. drills   B. files
   C. wrenches   D. screwdrivers

23. Of the following, the MOST important reason for keeping tools in perfect working order is to make sure

   A. the proper tool is being used for the required work
   B. the tools can be operated safely
   C. each employee can repair a variety of building defects
   D. no employee uses a tool for his private use

24. In order to properly hang a door, shims are frequently inserted under the hinges. These shims are MOST often made of

   A. cardboard
   B. sheet steel
   C. bakelite
   D. the same materials as the hinges

25. Flooring nails are USUALLY _____ nails. 25.____

   A. casing B. common C. cut D. clinch

KEY (CORRECT ANSWERS)

1. D
2. C
3. D
4. B
5. D

6. C
7. D
8. B
9. D
10. B

11. B
12. C
13. B
14. A
15. B

16. D
17. A
18. A
19. D
20. D

21. C
22. D
23. B
24. A
25. C

TEST 2

DIRECTIONS: Each question or incomplete statement is followed by several suggested answers or completions. Select the one that BEST answers the question or completes the statement. *PRINT THE LETTER OF THE CORRECT ANSWER IN THE SPACE AT THE RIGHT.*

1. A non-bearing wall unit between columns enclosing a structure is known as a _____ wall.

    A. panel B. curtain C. apron D. spandrel

    1._____

2. *Drywall* is installed by

    A. carpenters B. lathers
    C. plasterers D. masons

    2._____

3. A cantilever beam would MOST likely be used in connection with a

    A. floor opening B. balcony
    C. warehouse floor D. roof opening

    3._____

4. A floor is designed as a reinforced concrete floor with a hardwood surface. A section through the floor would MOST likely be

    4._____

    A. hardwood floor / subfloor / sleeper / concrete
    B. hardwood floor / sleeper / concrete
    C. hardwood floor / concrete
    D. hardwood floor / subfloor / anchor floor / concrete

5. With respect to flooring, shrinkage in a wood joist is MOST serious in

    A. length B. width
    C. depth D. all of the above

    5._____

6. A *screw pitch gauge* measures only the

    A. looseness of threads
    B. tightness of threads
    C. number of threads per inch
    D. gauge number

    6._____

7. An offset screwdriver is MOST useful for turning a wood screw when

    A. a strong force needs to be applied
    B. the screw head is marred
    C. space is limited
    D. speed is desired

    7._____

25

8. Specifications which contain the term *kiln dried* would MOST likely refer to

   A. asphalt shingles
   B. brick veneer
   C. paint lacquer
   D. lumber

9. Headers and stretchers are used in the construction of

   A. floors   B. walls   C. ceilings   D. roofs

10. Construction of a dormer window does NOT usually involve

    A. cut rafters
    B. rafter headers
    C. trimmer rafters
    D. hip rafters

11. A frame building with 2x4 studding has an interior partition with 2x6 studding. The MOST probable reason for the heavier studding is to provide

    A. heat insulation
    B. sound insulation
    C. room for a soil stack
    D. room for steam pipes

12. The length of a 20 penny nail is MOST NEARLY _____ inches.

    A. 2½   B. 3   C. 3½   D. 4

13. Of the following, which is the HIGHEST grade of lumber?

    A. Construction
    B. Utility
    C. Standard
    D. Run of the mill

14. In a stairway, the number of

    A. treads and risers is the same
    B. treads is one more than the number of risers
    C. risers is one more than the number of treads
    D. treads is two more than the number of risers

15. Lumber is usually sold by the board foot, and a board foot is defined as a board one foot square and one inch thick.
    If the price of one board foot of lumber is $1.80 and you need 20 feet of lumber 6 inches wide and 1 inch thick, the cost of the 20 feet of lumber is

    A. $18.00   B. $24.00   C. $36.00   D. $48.00

16. When an unusually high degree of accuracy is required with woodwork, lines should be marked with a

    A. pencil ground to a chisel point
    B. pencil line over a crayon line
    C. sharp knife point
    D. scriber

17. The two planes which make up the MOST useful combination for general carpentry work are the _____ plane and the _____ plane.

    A. jack; jointer
    B. jack; block
    C. smooth; block
    D. fore; jointer

18. The terms *plank, scantling, heavy joists,* when used in connection with lumber, refer to

    A. dimensions
    B. use
    C. grade
    D. finish

19. Of the following woods, the one that is the HARDEST is

    A. douglas fir
    B. sitka spruce
    C. southern pine
    D. hickory

20. A specification on finished hardware refers to roses and escutcheon plates. These are MOST likely to be installed on

    A. desks
    B. blackboards
    C. windows
    D. doors

21. Wall sheathing can be installed either diagonally or horizontally on the studs. When installed diagonally, the wall is

    A. cheaper
    B. smoother
    C. more weatherproof
    D. more rigid

22. A wall of a building which supports any load other than its own weight is called a _____ wall.

    A. curtain
    B. retaining
    C. parapet
    D. bearing

23. Soffits are USUALLY located in

    A. the roofing
    B. bathrooms
    C. stairways
    D. the flooring

24. A specification on carpentry for a housing project calls for the use of a nail set. Of the following, the BEST reason for this requirement is that

    A. certain nails are to be removed
    B. the points of certain nails are to be bent over for better anchorage
    C. the heads of certain nails are to be sunk
    D. certain nails are to be spaced at a specified interval

25. Of the following grades of lumber, the one that is MOST likely to be specified for interior finish which is to be painted is Grade

    A. No. 1 Common
    B. No. 2 Common
    C. No. 1 Clear
    D. D, Select

KEY (CORRECT ANSWERS)

1. B
2. A
3. B
4. A
5. C

6. C
7. C
8. D
9. B
10. D

11. C
12. D
13. A
14. C
15. A

16. C
17. B
18. A
19. D
20. D

21. D
22. D
23. C
24. C
25. C

TEST 3

DIRECTIONS: Each question or incomplete statement is followed by several suggested answers or completions. Select the one that BEST answers the question or completes the statement. *PRINT THE LETTER OF THE CORRECT ANSWER IN THE SPACE AT THE RIGHT.*

1. A four-foot mason's level is USUALLY used to determine whether the top of a wall is level and whether it is   1.____

    A. square B. plumb C. rigid D. in line

2. To match a tongue in a board, the matching board MUST have a   2.____

    A. rabbet B. chamfer C. bead D. groove

3. When driving screws in close quarters, the BEST type of screwdriver to use is a(n)   3.____

    A. Phillips B. offset C. butt D. angled

4. Panel doors may have horns which must be cut off before the door is hung. In the sketch at the right, the arrow which indicates a horn is labeled number   4.____

    A. 1
    B. 2
    C. 3
    D. 4

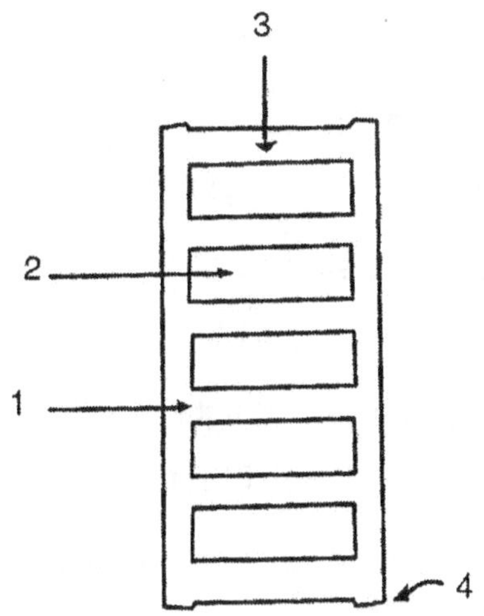

5. In carpentry work, the MOST commonly used hand saw is the _____ saw.   5.____

    A. hack B. rip C. buck D. cross-cut

6. The device which USUALLY keeps a doorknob from rotating on the spindle is a   6.____

    A. cotter pin   B. tapered key
    C. set screw   D. stop screw

7. The one of the following types of nails that USUALLY requires the use of a tool known as a nail set is the _____ nail.   7.____

    A. finishing B. sheetrock C. 6-penny D. cut

8. To locate a point on a floor directly under a point on the ceiling, the PROPER tool to use is a   8.____

    A. square   B. line level
    C. height gauge   D. plumb bob

9. A *fire cut* is *made* on

   A. timber posts B. rafters
   C. floor joists D. lathing

10. The one of the following items that is LEAST related to the others is

    A. joist hanger B. pintle
    C. bridle iron D. stirrup

11. The PROPER order of nailing subflooring and bridging is

    A. top of bridging, bottom of bridging, subflooring
    B. bottom of bridging, subflooring, top of bridging
    C. top of bridging, subflooring, bottom of bridging
    D. bottom of bridging, top of bridging, subflooring

12. Sleepers would be found in

    A. walls B. doors C. footings D. floors

13. The one of the following woods that is MOST commonly used for finish flooring is

    A. hemlock B. cypress C. larch D. oak

14. Spacing of studs in a stud partition is MOST frequently _____ " o.c.

    A. 12 B. 14 C. 16 D. 18

15. A wood screw which can be tightened by a wrench is known as a _____ screw.

    A. lag B. Phillips C. carriage D. monkey

16. Of the following kinds of lumber, the one that is MOST likely to be specified for finish flooring for a gymnasium is

    A. spruce B. hemlock C. pine D. maple

17. Ninety 2" x 4"s, 16' long, S4S are needed.
    The number of board feet required is MOST NEARLY

    A. 840 B. 960 C. 1080 D. 1200

18. Of the following, the wood section that is NOT commonly used for siding is

    A. tongue and groove B. shiplap
    C. splined plank D. clapboard

19. If the allowable load on a wooden scaffold is 60 pounds per square foot and the scaffold surface area is 3 feet by 12 feet, then the MAXIMUM total distributed load that is permitted on the scaffold is _____ pounds.

    A. 720 B. 1800 C. 2160 D. 2400

20. A piece of lumber with a cross-section as shown at the right is used in connection with 20.____

   A. stairs
   B. baseboards
   C. doors
   D. windows

Questions 21-25.

DIRECTIONS: For each item in the sketch shown below, labelled 21 to 25, select that letter that MOST NEARLY identifies the item and print that letter in the space next to the number of the item.

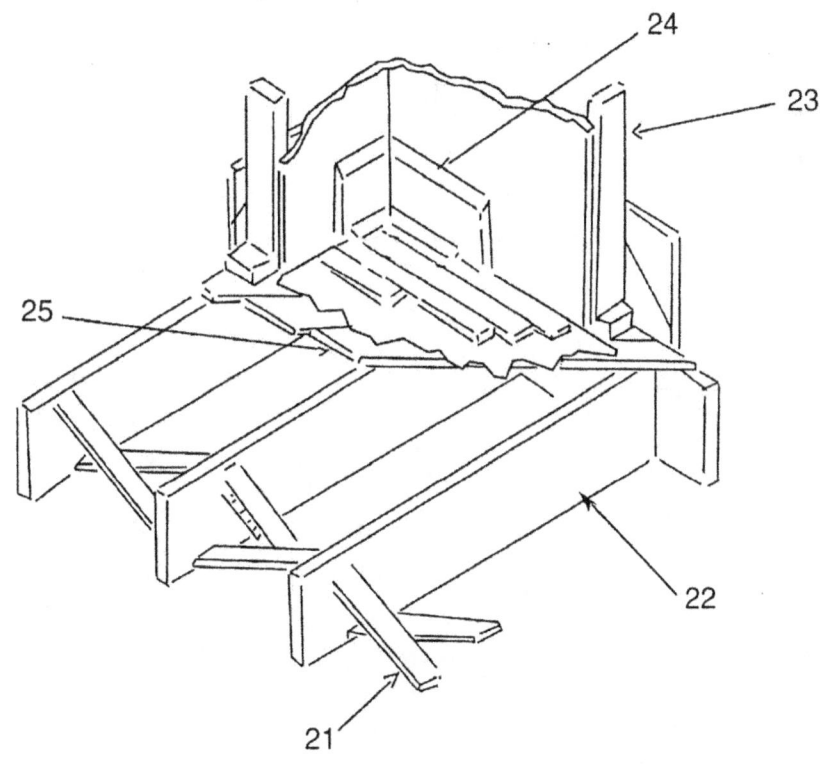

A. Sheathing	H. Header	21.____
B. Finish flooring	I. Sole	22.____
C. Paper	J. Cap	23.____
D. Subflooring	K. Bridging	24.____
E. Baseboard	L. Wainscoting	25.____
F. Shoe	M. Stud	
G. Joist	N. Ledger	

KEY (CORRECT ANSWERS)

1. B
2. D
3. B
4. D
5. D

6. C
7. A
8. D
9. C
10. B

11. C
12. D
13. D
14. C
15. A

16. D
17. B
18. C
19. C
20. C

21. K
22. G
23. M
24. E
25. D

EXAMINATION SECTION
TEST 1

DIRECTIONS: Each question or incomplete statement is followed by several suggested answers or completions. Select the one that BEST answers the question or completes the statement. *PRINT THE LETTER OF THE CORRECT ANSWER IN THE SPACE AT THE RIGHT.*

1. A lintel is MOST closely associated with a
   - A. wall opening
   - B. floor opening
   - C. roof opening
   - D. fire escape

   1.____

2. An apron is MOST closely associated with a
   - A. door
   - B. window
   - C. yard
   - D. bulkhead

   2.____

3. Of the following, the one which is NOT usually classified as interior wood trim is
   - A. apron
   - B. ribbon
   - C. jamb
   - D. base mold

   3.____

4. Single-strength glass would MOST likely be found in
   - A. single light sash
   - B. doors in fire walls
   - C. doors in fire partitions
   - D. multi-light sash

   4.____

5. The one of the following items that is LEAST related to the others is
   - A. newel
   - B. riser
   - C. nosing
   - D. sill

   5.____

6. Sixteen pieces of 2 x 4 lumber, each 10'6" long, contain a TOTAL of _____ FBM.
   - A. 110
   - B. 111
   - C. 112
   - D. 113

   6.____

7. In multiple dwellings, handrails must be provided on each side of a stairway if the stairway exceeds a certain
   - A. height
   - B. width
   - C. steepness
   - D. tread-riser ratio

   7.____

8. The base composition of *drywall* is
   - A. vermiculite
   - B. perlite
   - C. gypsum
   - D. Portland cement

   8.____

9. The specifications for a construction job state: Furnish and erect chair rail of birch with continuous kerfing where required by room finish schedule.
   Kerfing means MOST NEARLY
   - A. planing
   - B. rounding
   - C. jointing
   - D. grooving

   9.____

10. Headers and trimmers are used in the construction of
    - A. footings
    - B. walls
    - C. floors
    - D. arches

    10.____

11. In the design of stairs, the designer should consider   11.___

    A. maximum height of riser *only*
    B. minimum width of tread *only*
    C. product of riser height by tread width *only*
    D. all of the above

12. A reduction in the required number of columns in a building can be made by using one of   12.___
    the following types of beam.
    Which one?

    A. Floor   B. Girder   C. Cantilever   D. Jack

13. Doors sheathed in metal are known as _____ doors.   13.___

    A. kalamein   B. tin-clad
    C. bethlehem   D. flemish

14. In the wood frame shown at the right,   14.___
    whose corners are all square, the TOTAL
    length of one inch board is _____
    inches.
    A. 40
    B. 42
    C. 44
    D. 46

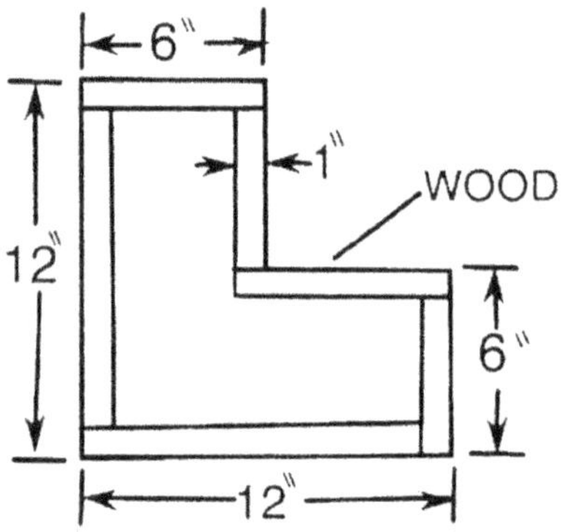

15. Floor beams are sometimes crowned to   15.___

    A. provide arch action
    B. eliminate deflection
    C. strengthen the floor
    D. provide a more nearly level floor than would be provided by straight beams

16. Cracks in lumber due to contraction along annual rings are known as   16.___

    A. checks   B. wanes
    C. pitch pockets   D. dry rot

17. Of the following, the one which would LEAST likely be used in conjunction with the others   17.___
    is

    A. rafter   B. collar beam
    C. ridgeboard   D. tail beam

18. The dimensions of a 2 x 4 when dressed are MOST NEARLY   18.___

    A. 2" x 4"   B. 1½" x 3½"
    C. 1 5/8" x 3 5/8"   D. 1¾" x 3½"

19. A piece of wood covering the plaster below the stool of a window is called a(n)   19._____

    A. apron   B. sill   C. coping   D. trimmer

20. The BEST wood to use for handles of tools such as axes and hammers is   20._____

    A. hemlock   B. pine   C. oak   D. hickory

21. Tongue and groove flooring is shown in Sketch No.   21._____
    A. 1
    B. 2
    C. 3
    D. 4

    FLOORING

    NO.1
    NO.2
    NO.3
    NO.4

Questions 22-25.

DIRECTIONS: Questions 22 through 25 are to be answered on the basis of the label pictured below.

LABEL

BREGSON'S CLEAR GLUE HIGHLY FLAMMABLE A clear quick-drying glue	PRECAUTIONS Use with adequate ventilation
For temporary bonding, apply glue to one surface and join immediately	Close container after use
For permanent bonding, apply glue to both surfaces, permit to dry, and press together	Keep out of reach of children
Use for bonding plastic to plastic, plastic to wood, and wood to wood only	Avoid prolonged breathing of vapors and repeated contact with skin
Will not bond at temperatures below 60°	

22. Assume that you, as a member of a repair crew, have been asked to repair a wood banister in the hallway of a house. Since the heat has been turned off, the hallway is very cold, except for the location where you have to make the repair. Another repair crew worker is working at that same location using a blow torch to solder a pipe in the wall.   22._____

    The temperature at that location is about 67°. According to the instruction on the above label, the use of this glue to make the necessary repair is

A. *advisable;* the glue will bond wood to wood
B. *advisable;* the heat from the soldering will cause the glue to dry quickly
C. *inadvisable;* the work area temperature is too low
D. *inadvisable;* the glue is highly flammable

23. According to the instructions on the above label, this glue should NOT be used for which of the following applications? 23.___

    A. Affixing a pine table leg to a walnut table
    B. Repairing leaks around pipe joints
    C. Bonding a plastic knob to a cedar drawer
    D. Attaching a lucite knob to a lucite drawer

24. According to the instructions on the above label, using this glue to bond ceramic tile to a plaster wall by coating both surfaces with glue, letting the glue dry, and then pressing the tile to the plaster wall is 24.___

    A. *advisable;* the glue is quick drying and clear
    B. *advisable;* the glue should be permanently affixed to the one surface of the tile only
    C. *inadvisable;* the glue is not suitable for bonding ceramic tile to plaster walls
    D. *inadvisable;* the bonding should be a temporary one

25. The precaution described in the above label, *Use with adequate ventilation,* means that 25.___

    A. the area you are working in should be very cold
    B. there should be sufficient fresh air where you are using the glue
    C. you should wear gloves to avoid contact with the glue
    D. you must apply a lot of glue to make a permanent bond

KEY (CORRECT ANSWERS)

1.	A	11.	D
2.	B	12.	C
3.	B	13.	A
4.	D	14.	C
5.	D	15.	D
6.	C	16.	A
7.	B	17.	D
8.	C	18.	C
9.	D	19.	A
10.	C	20.	D

21. A
22. D
23. B
24. C
25. B

TEST 2

DIRECTIONS: Each question or incomplete statement is followed by several suggested answers or completions. Select the one that BEST answers the question or completes the statement. *PRINT THE LETTER OF THE CORRECT ANSWER IN THE SPACE AT THE RIGHT.*

1. A post supporting a handrail is known as a

    A. tread   B. riser   C. newel   D. bevel

    1._____

2. The live load on a floor is 40 pounds per square foot. The floor joists are on a 14'0" span and are spaced 2'6" on centers.
The MAXIMUM live load carried by a joist is, in pounds, MOST NEARLY

    A. 700   B. 933   C. 1167   D. 1400

    2._____

3. Of the following terms, the one LEAST related to the others is

    A. ground   B. purlin
    C. rafter   D. ridge board

    3._____

4. If a hand saw becomes worn so that the teeth are no longer properly set, the

    A. blade will lose its temper
    B. saw will not cut straight
    C. cut will have jagged edges
    D. blade will tend to bind in the cut

    4._____

5. Many portable electric power tools, such as electric drills, have a third conductor in the power lead which is used to connect the case of the tool to a grounded part of the electric outlet.
The reason for this extra conductor is to

    A. have a spare wire in case one power wire should break
    B. strengthen the power lead so it cannot easily be damaged
    C. prevent the user of the tool from being shocked
    D. enable the tool to be used for long periods of time without overheating

    5._____

6. A non-bearing wall in skeleton construction built between columns and wholly supported at each story is a _____ wall.

    A. party   B. partition   C. panel   D. fire

    6._____

7. The part of a window that holds the glass is the

    A. jamb   B. sash   C. casing   D. bead

    7._____

8. A one-panel door has two stiles and _____ rails.

    A. no   B. one   C. two   D. three

    8._____

9. The vertical part of a stair step is a

    A. kick-plate   B. tread
    C. landing   D. riser

    9._____

10. When the joist hanger is used, the joists and girder are fitted together
    A. by notching the joists *only*
    B. by notching the girder *only*
    C. by notching both the joists and the girder
    D. without notching either the joists or girder

    JOIST GIRDER JOIST JOIST HANGER

11. Small wood members which are inserted in a diagonal position between floor joists for the purpose of bracing the joists and spreading loads to adjacent joists are called

    A. struts   B. ties
    C. bridging   D. ledger strips

12. A beam placed perpendicular to joists and to which joists are nailed in framing for a chimney, stairway, or other opening is called a

    A. trimmer joist   B. tail beam
    C. girder   D. header

13. A narrow board let into the studding to provide added support for joists is known as a

    A. sill   B. trimmer   C. ribbon   D. sole plate

14. In the city, metal door frames are USUALLY set in place by

    A. carpenters
    B. structural steel workers
    C. miscellaneous iron workers
    D. masons

15. When inspecting the installation of wood trim, you find that one of the carpenters is leaving the round imprint of his hammer around almost every nail.
    Of the following, the BEST way for you to treat this situation is to

    A. recommend that this carpenter be removed
    B. recommend that the damaged trim be removed
    C. warn the carpenter that he must be more careful
    D. recommend that the specifications be changed to call for a harder wood

16. A casement window is USUALLY a window that

    A. is double hung   B. opens inwardly only
    C. is made of wood   D. is pivoted vertically

Questions 17-25.

DIRECTIONS: Questions 17 through 25 are to be answered SOLELY on the basis of the following instructions for carpentry work on elevated stations. Read these instructions carefully before answering these items.

CARPENTRY WORK ON ELEVATED STATIONS

Joists are to be 3 inches by 10 inches and bridging shall be 2 inches by 4 inches. All joists are to be yellow pine, spaced 20 inches on centers. Joists having a span of from 8 feet to 16 feet are to have one row of cross-bridging while spans of over 16 feet are to have two rows of cross-bridging. Bridging shall be nailed at each end. The joists are fastened to the steel supporting beams with special clips. Wood flooring for train platforms is to be yellow pine, 2 inches by 6 inches, dressed four sides, laid transversely with 1/4-inch open joints and is not to be used in lengths of less than five feet. Service walks (track walks) are to consist of five lengths of slatting laid side by side and continuously. The slatting is to be 2 inches by 6 inches and of random lengths varying upward in multiples of four feet six inches. Slatting is to be fastened to each support by two twenty penny cut nails.

17. Joists are fastened to the supporting beams with

    A. special clips
    B. ordinary nails
    C. twenty penny nails
    D. screws

18. Slatting may be used without cutting if it has a length of

    A. 4 feet
    B. 4 feet 5 inches
    C. 9 feet
    D. 12 feet

19. Joists shall be

    A. 3" x 5" yellow pine
    B. 3" x 10" yellow pine
    C. 3" x 6" spruce
    D. 2" x 8" spruce

20. Wood which is dressed four sides is used for

    A. bridging
    B. joists
    C. service walks
    D. train platform flooring

21. The center spacing of joists is to be

    A. 15 inches
    B. 20 inches
    C. 5 feet 4 inches
    D. 7 feet

22. The number of rows of cross-bridging required for joists having a span of 18 feet is

    A. four   B. three   C. two   D. one

23. Slatting is fastened

    A. to every other joist
    B. with ten penny nails
    C. to each support
    D. with special clips

24. Service walks are to have a width of _____ slats.

    A. 3   B. 4   C. 5   D. 6

25. Wood which is to be 2" x 6" is for

    A. platform flooring and the track walks
    B. the bridging *only*
    C. the track walks and the joists
    D. platform flooring and the bridging

KEY (CORRECT ANSWERS)

1.	C	11.	C
2.	D	12.	D
3.	A	13.	C
4.	D	14.	A
5.	C	15.	B
6.	C	16.	D
7.	B	17.	A
8.	C	18.	C
9.	D	19.	B
10.	D	20.	D

21. B
22. C
23. C
24. C
25. A

TEST 3

DIRECTIONS: Each question or incomplete statement is followed by several suggested answers or completions. Select the one that BEST answers the question or completes the statement. *PRINT THE LETTER OF THE CORRECT ANSWER IN THE SPACE AT THE RIGHT.*

1. Of the following statements relating to the plies in plywood, the one that is CORRECT is: 1.____

    A. The primary difference between exterior and interior plywood is the quality of the exterior plies
    B. Exterior plywood has more plies than interior plywood
    C. Exterior plywood has no surface defects on the outer plies while interior plywood permits surface defects on the outer plies
    D. Plywood has an odd number of plies

2. Of the following, the one that is NOT a principal classification of lumber according to the American Lumber Standards is 2.____

    A. building   B. structural
    C. yard   D. shop

3. Of the following types of lumber, the one that is classified as a hardwood is 3.____

    A. cedar   B. fir   C. pine   D. maple

Questions 4-6.

DIRECTIONS: Questions 4 through 6 are to be answered SOLELY on the basis of the following passage.

A utility plan is a floor plan which shows the layout of a heating, electrical, plumbing, or other utility system. Utility plans are used primarily by the persons responsible for the utilities, but they are important to the craftsman as well. Most utility installations require the leaving of openings in walls, floors, and roofs for the admission or installation of utility features. The craftsman who is, for example, pouring a concrete foundation wall must study the utility plans to determine the number, sizes, and locations of the openings he must leave for piping, electric lines, and the like.

4. The one of the following items of information which is LEAST likely to be provided by a utility plan is the 4.____

    A. location of the joists and frame members around stairwells
    B. location of the hot water supply and return piping
    C. location of light fixtures
    D. number of openings in the floor for radiators

5. According to the above passage, the persons who will MOST likely have the GREATEST need for the information included in a utility plan of a building are those who 5.____

    A. maintain and repair the heating system
    B. clean the premises
    C. paint housing exteriors
    D. advertise property for sale

41

6. According to the above passage, a repair crew member should find it MOST helpful to consult a utility plan when information is needed about the

   A. thickness of all doors in the structure
   B. number of electrical outlets located throughout the structure
   C. dimensions of each window in the structure
   D. length of a roof rafter

7. A piece of lumber with a cross-section as shown at the right is called a

   A. crown moulding   B. panel moulding
   C. shoe moulding   D. quarter round

8. A nut is shown with a wrench placed on it in positions 1 and 2. The numbered arrows show the directions of forces applied to the wrench to turn it.
   In order to tighten the nut, the CORRECT combination of wrench position and direction of applied force is
   A. 1-3
   B. 1-4
   C. 2-5
   D. 2-6

9. The upright finished board in the side of a door opening is called a

   A. batten   B. saddle   C. jamb   D. stile

10. Which one of the following terms is LEAST related to the others?

    A. Stop   B. Jamb   C. Buck   D. Siding

11. Which one of the following terms is LEAST related to the others?

    A. Pipe   B. Riser   C. Tread   D. Nosing

12. Of the following terms, the one which is LEAST related to the others is

    A. baseboard   B. base mold
    C. casing   D. base plate

13. When marking and sawing a timber to a desired length, it is good practice to mark

    A. slightly smaller than the length and saw just outside the line on the waste side
    B. the exact length and cut just outside the line on the waste side
    C. the exact length and cut on the line
    D. slightly larger than the length and cut on the line

14. If the drawing of a carpentry detail is made to a scale of 3/4" to the foot, a scaled measurement of 6" would represent a length of

    A. 3/8 inches   B. 8 inches
    C. 4½ feet   D. 8 feet

15. In order to clear the jamb, the lock-edge of a door must be beveled. The bevel must be GREATEST when the door is

    A. wide and thin
    B. wide and thick
    C. narrow and thin
    D. narrow and thick

16. The saw shown at the right would be used to cut
    A. curved designs in thin wood
    B. strap iron
    C. asphalt tiles to fit against walls
    D. soft lead pipe

17. The timbers that support the rough flooring are called

    A. lintels   B. sills   C. beams   D. studs

18. Wood for the wearing surface of a floor should PREFERABLY be

    A. flat-sawed
    B. quarter-sawed
    C. cross-cut
    D. rip-sawed

19. Wainscoting is

    A. the moulding around a room for hanging pictures
    B. the moulding around a room to protect the plaster from the backs of chairs
    C. panel work covering part or all of a wall
    D. the tile or cement flooring in a kitchen around the stove or range

20. Of the following, the one that is NOT a defect of lumber is

    A. wane   B. plinth   C. check   D. shake

21. A specification reads: Douglas fir shall average on either one end or the other not less than 6 nor more than 20 annual rings per inch over a 3-inch portion of a radial line. The object of this requirement is to secure lumber that is

    A. of beautiful grain
    B. close-grained
    C. free of knots
    D. chiefly heartwood

22. Of the following grades of lumber, the BEST grade is

    A. No. 1 Common
    B. No. 2 Common
    C. Select Grade A
    D. Select Grade B

23. Twist drills ranging in size from 5/16" to 1/2" and having 1/4" shanks are available for use in electric drills. These drills are designed in this manner so that they may be used

    A. in $\frac{1}{4}$" electric drills for high speed drilling of steel
    B. in $\frac{1}{4}$" electric drills for drilling wood
    C. when it is important that, if the twist drill breaks, it does not do so in the hole being drilled
    D. in $\frac{1}{2}$" electric drills in order to increase the peripheral speed of the twist drill

24. The wrench is shown in position to unloosen a tight nut. If the hand is placed on the wrench at A, the force necessary to start the nut as compared to the force necessary if the hand were placed at B would be
   A. 150%
   B. 110%
   C. 85%
   D. 70%

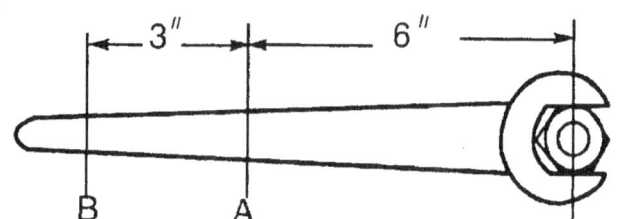

25. The tool that should be used to cut a 1" x 4" plank down to a 3" width is a
   A. hacksaw
   B. crosscut saw
   C. rip saw
   D. backsaw

KEY (CORRECT ANSWERS)

1. D
2. A
3. D
4. A
5. A

6. B
7. D
8. D
9. C
10. D

11. A
12. D
13. B
14. D
15. D

16. A
17. C
18. B
19. C
20. B

21. B
22. C
23. B
24. A
25. C

CARPENTRY

EXAMINATION SECTION
TEST 1

DIRECTIONS: Each question or incomplete statement is followed by several suggested answers or completions. Select the one that BEST answers the question or completes the statement. *PRINT THE LETTER OF THE CORRECT ANSWER IN THE SPACE AT THE RIGHT.*

1. In a ratchet bit brace, the part that holds the bit is called the   1.____
   A. vise   B. chuck   C. pawl   D. cam ring

2. The BEST tool to use as a guide when scribing a line perpendicular to the side of a 2" x 4" stud is a   2.____
   A. T-square   B. Try square
   C. Batter board   D. Parallel bar

3. Of the following planes, the *one* that does NOT have a double plane iron is the   3.____
   A. block plane   B. jack plane
   C. fore plane   D. smooth plane

4. Of the following files, the BEST one to use to sharpen a rip-saw is a   4.____
   A. taper   B. flat bastard   C. mill   D. half round

5. The size of auger bit to select in order to bore a 5/8" hole is   5.____
   A. #5   B. #8   C. #10   D. #12

6. The type of circular saw used for cutting grooves that are *wider* than the cut that can be made by ordinary saws is known as a   6.____
   A. dado set   B. rabbet set
   C. scarf set   D. dove tail set

7. Of the following saws, the *one* that should be used for cutting circular disks out of 5/8" plywood is a   7.____
   A. circular saw   B. buck saw
   C. back saw   D. band saw

8. The saw used in a miter box is a   8.____
   A. compass saw   B. coping saw
   C. back saw   D. hacksaw

9. Of the following, the BEST wood to use for the handle of a claw hammer is   9.____
   A. pine   B. hickory   C. cypress   D. elm

10. A 3" belt sander requires a 3 x 21 belt. The "21" refers to the belt's   10.____
    A. grit number   B. diameter
    C. contact area   D. length

11. In sharpening a paring chisel, a carpenter should grind the bevel at an angle of, *approximately*,

    A. 5° B. 15° C. 25° D. 35°

12. "Dressing" a saw has to do with

    A. lowering the height of the teeth
    B. removing burrs from the side of the teeth
    C. lowering of the tooth gullets
    D. tilting the file upward at the end of the stroke

13. To cut a 1/4-inch chamfer in a piece of wood two feet long, a carpenter should use a

    A. chisel B. plane C. saw D. hone

14. To tighten a lag screw, a Carpenter should use a

    A. mallet
    B. Phillips head screw-driver
    C. wrench
    D. hammer

15. When boring a hole through a thin piece of wood, the bit that will LEAST splinter the backside of the wood is a(n)

    A. center bit
    B. expensive bit
    C. Foerstner bit
    D. countersink bit

16. Shown below is a sketch of a hinge.

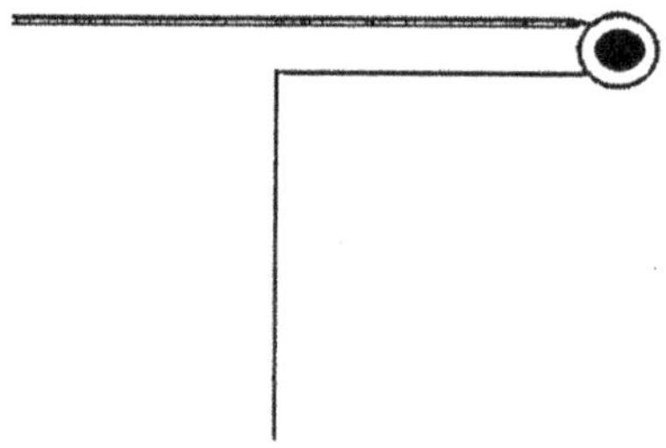

    The hinge is a(n)

    A. T-hinge
    B. strap hinge
    C. piano hinge
    D. offset hinge

17. A hinged strap with a slotted flap that passes over a staple and is secured by a padlock is known as a

    A. hasp B. hamper C. harbinger D. hawk

18. To bend saw teeth to the proper angle, a carpenter should use a

    A. saw screed B. saw tap C. saw bit D. saw set

19. A tool used to make a pilot hole for starting a screw in wood is a(n)

    A. grommet B. cotter pin C. awl D. counter point

20. The tool to use to finish driving a nail into corners and moldings is a nail

    A. set B. punch C. pin D. all

21. Of the following fasteners, the *one* that is LEAST often used in structural wood work is a   21.____

    A. lag screw   B. wood screw   C. nail   D. spike

22. When wood loses moisture, it shrinks in   22.____

    A. thickness and width and expands in length
    B. thickness and expands in width and length
    C. width and length and expands in thickness
    D. thickness, width, and length

23. Of the following types of commercial nails, the *one* that has the GREATEST withdrawal resistance is a   23.____

    A. cement-coated nail   B. galvanized nail
    C. chemically etched nail   D. spirally grooved nail

24. The grit number for a 1/0 sand paper is   24.____

    A. 200   B. 100   C. 80   D. 60

25. The length of a 6d nail is   25.____

    A. 1 3/4"   B. 2"   C. 2 1/4"   D. 2 3/4"

KEYS (CORRECT ANSWERS)

1.	B	11.	B
2.	B	12.	B
3.	A	13.	B
4.	A	14.	C
5.	C	15.	A
6.	A	16.	D
7.	D	17.	A
8.	C	18.	D
9.	B	19.	C
10.	D	20.	A

21. B
22. D
23. D
24. C
25. B

TEST 2

DIRECTIONS: Each question or incomplete statement is followed by several suggested answers or completions. Select the one that BEST answers the question or completes the statement. *PRINT THE LETTER OF THE CORRECT ANSWER IN THE SPACE AT THE RIGHT.*

1. The number of board feet in 15 pieces of lumber 2" x 10" by 12 feet long is 1.___
   A. 30 B. 300 C. 600 D. 900

2. When unpainted wood is left outdoors for a considerable time, the color of the wood *usually* changes to 2.___
   A. brown B. gray C. yellow D. amber

3. When wood is to be in permanent contact with earth, it should be treated with 3.___
   A. creosote B. tri-sodium phosphate
   C. sodium chloride D. sal ammoniac

4. A panic bolt is *most frequently* installed on a 4.___
   A. window B. door C. roof scuttle D. skylight

5. Of the following, the BEST reason for oiling plywood concrete forms is to 5.___
   A. lubricate the concrete during vibration
   B. allow forms to be removed easily
   C. decrease porosity of the plywood
   D. prevent seapage of rain water into the concrete in case it rains while the concrete is setting

6. Of the following species of wood, the *one* that is classified as a SOFT wood is 6.___
   A. chestnut B. white ash C. birch D. cypress

7. S.S. glass means 7.___
   A. Smooth Surface glass B. Silicone Surface glass
   C. Single Strength glass D. Square Sides glass

8. Of the following types of wood, the *one* that is NOT coarsegrained is 8.___
   A. oak B. pine C. walnut D. chestnut

9. The one of the following materials that does NOT contain wood is 9.___
   A. hardboard B. compressed board
   C. particle board D. masonite

10. Plywood sub flooring is used instead of 1" x 6" sub flooring MAINLY because it 10.___
    A. is more sound proof B. is easier to install
    C. is more fire resistant D. makes the floor more rigid

11. Wainscoting paneling would be installed on a 11.___
    A. wall B. floor C. ceiling D. roof

12. According to the building code, galvanized wire staple fasteners in plywood may 12.____
    A. not be used anywhere in buildings
    B. be used on roofs only
    C. be used on wall sheathing only
    D. be used on roofs and wall sheathing

13. Galvanized nails are nails that are coated with 13.____
    A. brass   B. cadmium   C. copper   D. zinc

14. The tip of a Phillips screwdriver is 14.____
    A. elliptical   B. pointed   C. flat   D. concave

15. Putlogs are used PRIMARILY on 15.____
    A. ladders   B. scaffolds   C. horses   D. hatchways

16. The tapered end of a file that fits into a wood handle is called the 16.____
    A. tip   B. heel   C. edge   D. tang

17. Of the following bolts, the type which has a *round* head is the 17.____
    A. machine bolt   B. stud bolt
    C. carriage bolt   D. coupling bolt

18. A metal T-anchor would be used on a 18.____
    A. door   B. window   C. joist   D. stud

19. A lock that is surface mounted on the side of a door is known as a 19.____
    A. rim lock   B. tenon lock
    C. mortise lock   D. flange lock

20. Clapboards are *generally* used for 20.____
    A. stair treads   B. wood siding
    C. window sills   D. roof copings

21. Shown below is a sketch of the floor joists in a building. 21.____

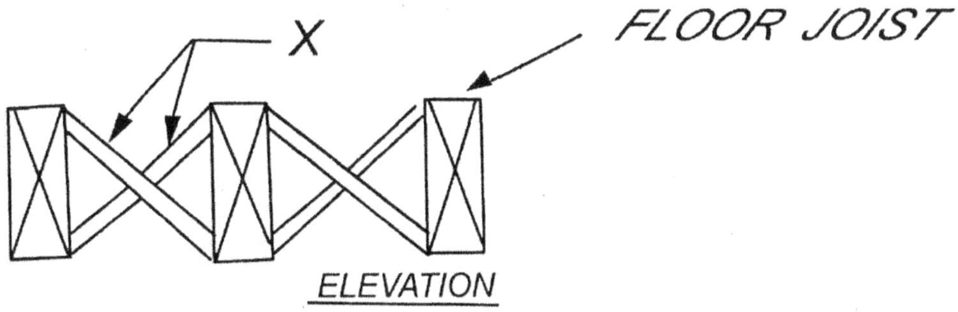

    ELEVATION

    The pieces of wood marked X are known as
    A. bridging   B. bracketing   C. corbeling   D. casing

22. A specification for a belt sander states that it is *UL* approved. The *UL* in the specification 22.___
    is an abbreviation of

    A. Universal Listing   B. Underwriters Laboratories
    C. Unlimited Liability   D. Use Limited

23. Shown below is a sketch of a wood joint. 23.___

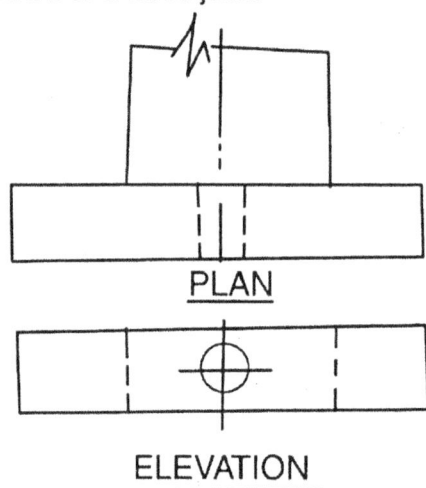

PLAN

ELEVATION

The wood joint is a

    A. peg tenon   B. plain dovetail butt
    C. dovetail half lap   D. blind housed tenon

Questions 24-25.

DIRECTIONS: Questions 24 and 25 refer to the wood form work for concrete shown in the sketch at the top of the next page.

24. The horizontal member X is known as a 24.___

    A. girt   B. soldier   C. pivot   D. waler

25. The horizontal member Y is known as a 25.___

    A. scab   B. ledger   C. kerf   D. putlog

4 (#2)

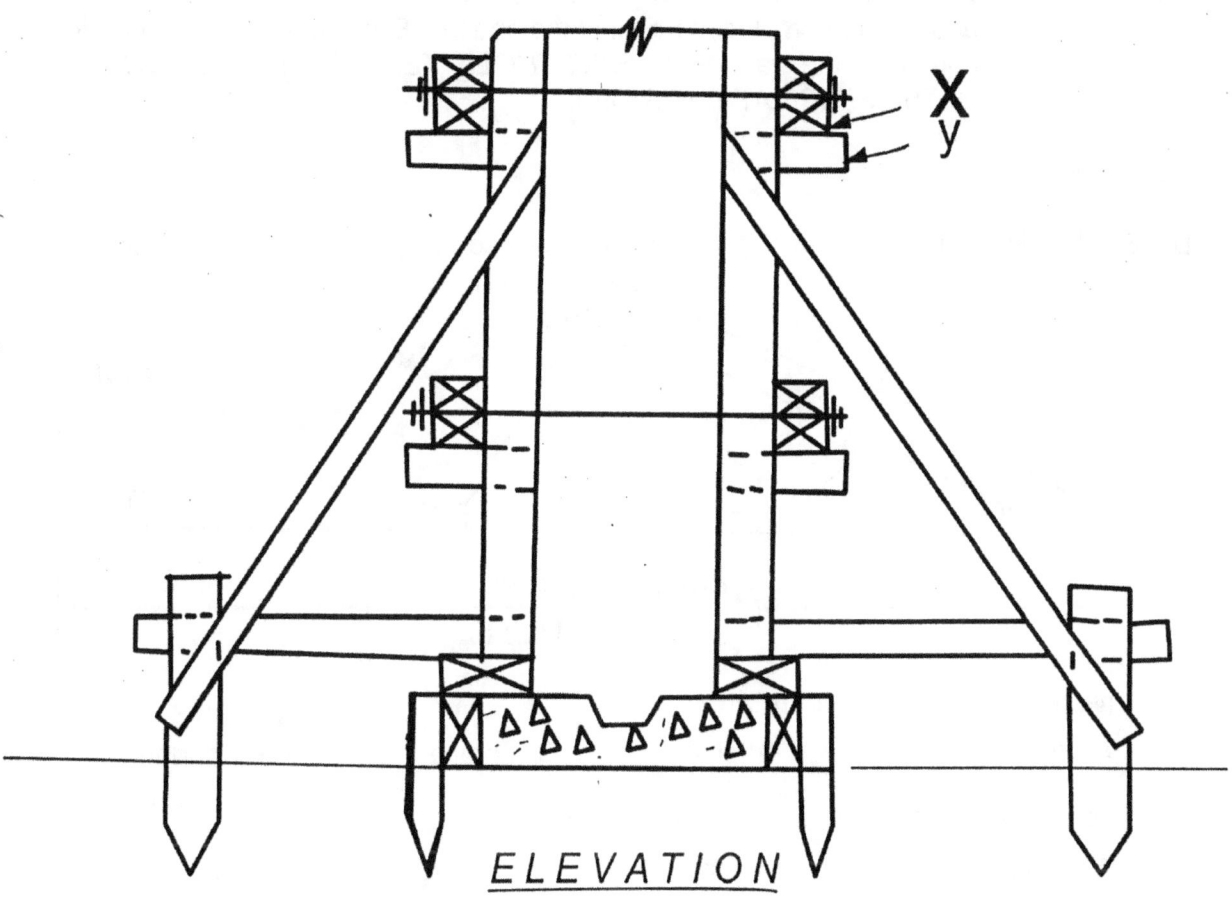

ELEVATION

KEYS (CORRECT ANSWERS)

1.	B	11.	A
2.	B	12.	D
3.	A	13.	D
4.	B	14.	B
5.	B	15.	B
6.	D	16.	D
7.	C	17.	C
8.	B	18.	C
9.	B	19.	A
10.	B	20.	B

21.	A
22.	B
23.	A
24.	D
25.	B

TEST 3

DIRECTIONS: Each question or incomplete statement is followed by several suggested answers or completions. Select the one that BEST answers the question or completes the statement. *PRINT THE LETTER OF THE CORRECT ANSWER IN THE SPACE AT THE RIGHT.*

Questions 1-3.

DIRECTIONS: Questions 1 through 3 refer to the wood truss shown in the sketch below.

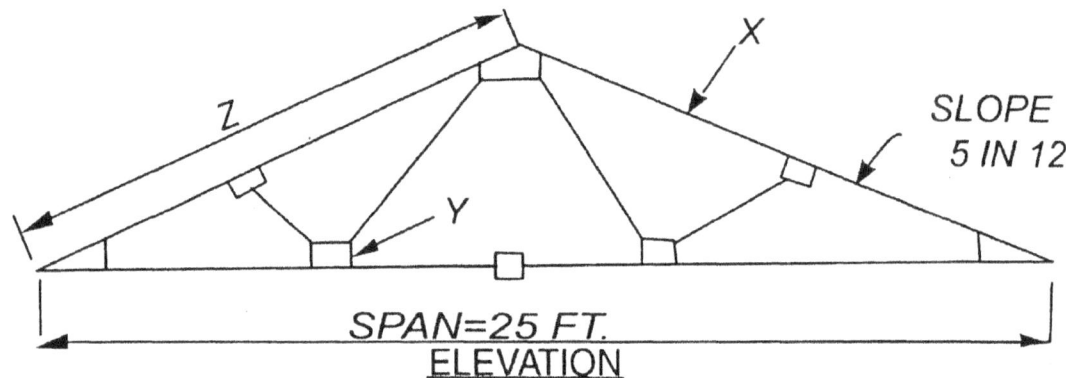

1. The inclined member X is known as a

   A. ridge   B. rafter   C. brace   D. bridge

2. The plate marked Y is known as a(n)

   A. gusset   B. batten   C. spacer   D. anchor

3. The TOTAL distance Z is, *most nearly,*

   A. 13' 2 1/2"
   B. 13' 4 1/2"
   C. 13' 6 1/2"
   D. 13' 8 1/2"

4. Shown in the sketch below is a bolted timber.

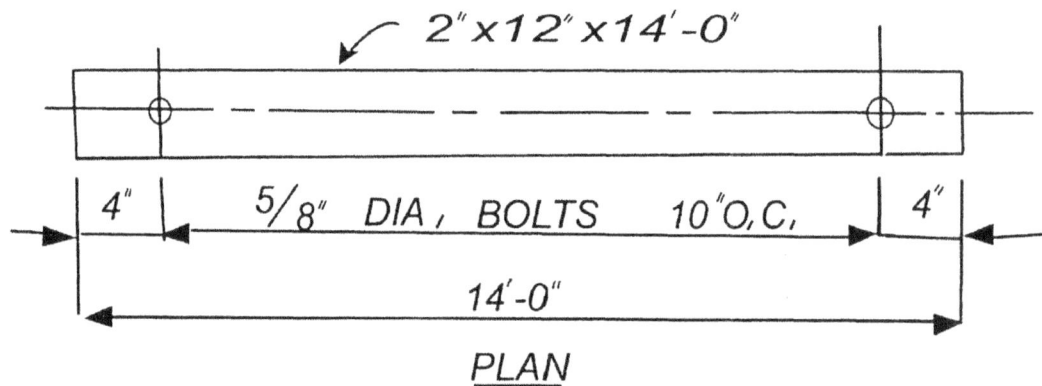

The number of 5/8" diameter bolts required is

   A. 15   B. 16   C. 17   D. 18

1.___

2.___

3.___

4.___

5. Plywood sub flooring 5/8" thick has a Panel Identification Index of 42/20. The "20" indicates the

   A. maximum allowable load in pounds on a square foot of panel
   B. maximum permitted center to center distance in inches between floor joists
   C. weight of a cubic foot of panel
   D. minimum number of 8d nails required per panel

6. An identifying symbol *HDO* G-1 - DFPA - 19 - PS1 - 66 is stamped on the edge of a plywood panel. The *HDO* part of this code stands for

   A. Heavy Duty Outside
   B. High Density Oak
   C. High Density Overlaid
   D. Housing Development Organization

7. Floor plans showing the modification of partitions are drawn to a scale of 1/4" to a foot. If the length of a partition shown on the drawing scales 6 3/8", then the ACTUAL length of the partition would be, *most nearly*,

   A. 2.4' 6"   B. 25' 2"   C. 24' 4"   D. 25' 6"

Questions 8-9.

DIRECTIONS: Questions 8 and 9 refer to the DETAIL shown below.

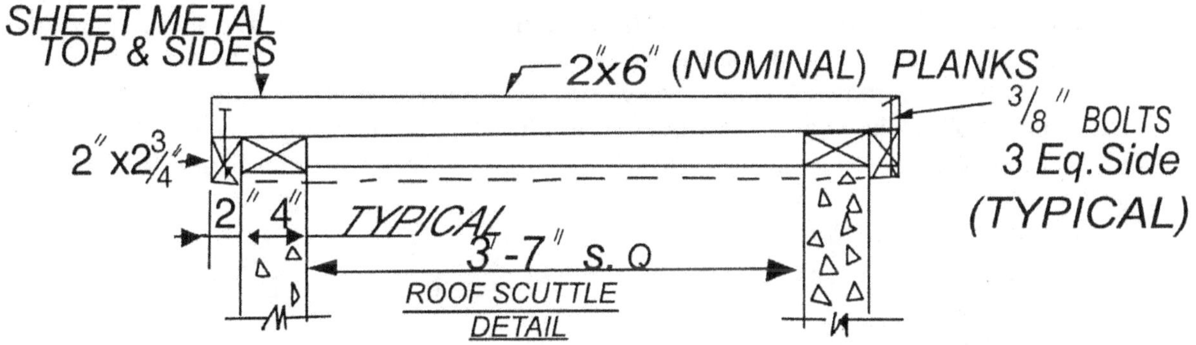

8. The number of 3/8" bolts in the roof scuttle is

   A. 6   B. 8   C. 10   D. 12

9. In the DETAIL shown above, the number of 2" x 6" planks required is

   A. 7   B. 8   C. 9   D. 10

10. On an alteration drawing, the location of *new* partitions would be shown on a(n)

    A. floor plan
    C. frame cross-section
    B. front elevation
    D. end view

11. A drawing specifies "3-1x6-*Fas* - Wh. Oak S4S." *Fas* is an abbreviation for

    A. face all sides
    C. fabricate as specified
    B. finish all sides
    D. firsts and seconds

12.

In the trade mark shown above, the abbreviation DFPA means

A. Designers Fabricated Partition Authority
B. Douglas Fir Plywood Association
C. Developed Fabricated Plyscord Association
D. Durable Federal Product Authority

13. A specification calls for *3/8" x 2"* steel lag screw. In the above specification, the *3/8"* refers to the

A. height of the head
B. root diameter of the thread
C. diameter of the body under the head
D. length of body under the head

14. The following statement is taken from a specification scope of work:
   Except as otherwise specified, furnish, deliver and install all carpentry and millwork, related work and equipment as required by the drawings and specified herein, including, but not necessarily limited to the following:
   All rough carpentry work where shown on the drawings, implied as necessary, specified, or otherwise required including permanent and temporary grounds, blocking, rough framing and *bucks,* nailing strips, furring, plates, under floor sleepers, and the like.
   In the above passage, *bucks* would refer to

A. doors   B. windows   C. scuppers   D. hatchways

15. A specification states the floowing:
    Blind nail T and G flooring.
    In the above specification, the word *blind* means to

A. bend   B. hide   C. extrude   D. offset

16. Narrow strips of wood nailed upon walls and ceilings as a support for the wall or ceiling finish is known as

A. darbying   B. batting   C. heading   D. furring

17. A purlin is *most similar* in function to a

A. stud   B. jamb   C. joist   D. batten

18. If the riser for a stairway is 7 1/2" high, then the *number* of risers required for a flight of stairs 8' 9" high is

A. 11   B. 12   C. 13   D. 14

19. The one of the following that is NOT a common type of wood joint is the   19.____

    A. scarf   B. dovetail   C. chamfer   D. butt

20. A flat hardwood board set on the floor in a doorway between rooms is called a   20.____

    A. mullion   B. jamb   C. jib   D. saddle

21. Shown below is a section of wall and flooring of a building.   21.____

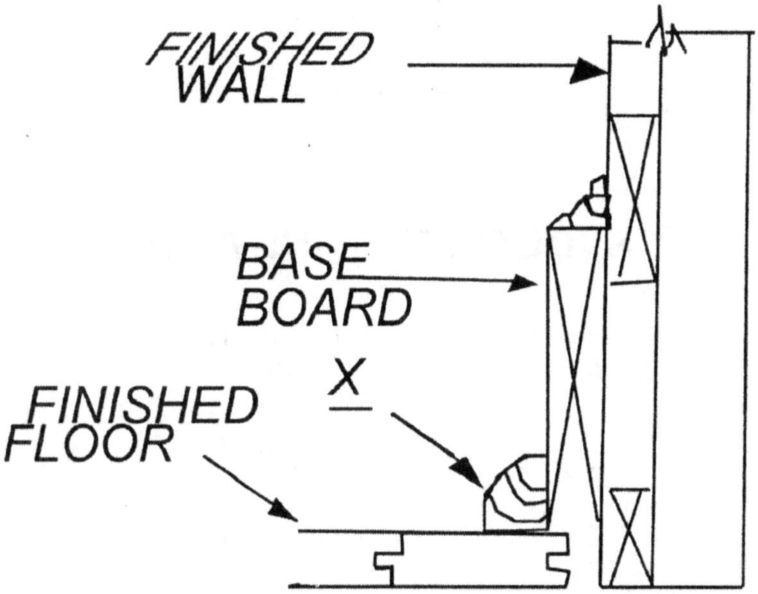

    In the drawing shown above, the molding X represents a

    A. base mold   B. shoe mold   C. bed mold   D. lip mold

22. Shown below is a section through a door.   22.____

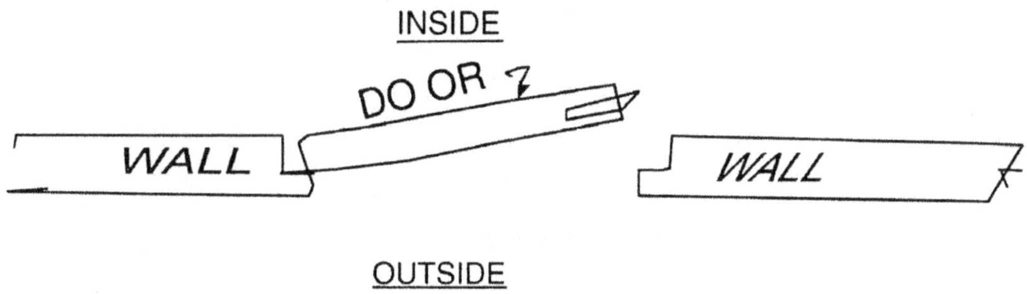

    The hand of the door is

    A. left hand regular   B. left hand reverse
    C. right hand regular   D. right hand reverse

23. A 3/4" thick flooring is to be laid directly on joists.   23.____
    Of the following, the BEST practice is to nail the flooring to

    A. every joist
    B. every third joist
    C. end joists only
    D. end joists and middle joist only

24. The margin which should be left all around between the edges of an 8" x 10" pane of glass and the sides of the rabbet in a wood sash is

    A. none B. 1/16" C. 3/16" D. 5/16"

25. The *horizontal* wood member which supports the load over a window or door is known as a

    A. putlog B. ledger C. collar D. lintel

KEYS (CORRECT ANSWERS)

1. B
2. A
3. C
4. C
5. B
6. C
7. D
8. D
9. D
10. A
11. D
12. B
13. C
14. A
15. B
16. D
17. C
18. D
19. C
20. D
21. B
22. A
23. A
24. B
25. D

TEST 4

DIRECTIONS: Each question or incomplete statement is followed by several suggested answers or completions. Select the one that BEST answers the question or completes the statement. *PRINT THE LETTER OF THE CORRECT ANSWER IN THE SPACE AT THE RIGHT.*

1. Shown below is a section of a wood joint.

    ELEVATION

    The joint shown is a

    A. dove tail joint
    B. double butt joint
    C. shiplap joint
    D. serrated joint

    1.____

2. In the construction of a wood frame building a metal shield is sometimes placed between the top of concrete piers and the wood girder resting on it. Of the following, the BEST reason for the metal shield is to

    A. spread the load over the pier
    B. protect the wood against termites
    C. insulate the building
    D. allow for expansion and contraction of the wood

    2.____

3. Shown below is a section of wood molding.

    The molding is a(n)

    A. reed
    B. center bead
    C. round
    D. astragal

    3.____

4. Wood is *most frequently* fastened to a concrete wall by a(n)

    A. clevis
    B. expansion shield
    C. brad
    D. spike

    4.____

5. A bolt with a spring loaded part used for securing wood to a hollow wall is a(n)

    A. anchor bolt
    B. stud bolt
    C. toggle bolt
    D. toe bolt

    5.____

6. The *number* of plane surfaces in a gambrel roof is

    A. two
    B. three
    C. four
    D. five

    6.____

7. The *vertical* members of a wooden door are known as

   A. rails B. stiles C. struts D. sleepers

8. Driving nails at an angle to the surface of a vertical member in order to get adequate penetration into a horizontal member is known as

   A. clinch nailing B. toe nailing
   C. French nailing D. dog nailing

9. Collar beams are *most often* used on

   A. trusses B. windows C. girders D. doors

10. On a double-hung wood window, the stool rests on the sill *and* a(n)

    A. mullion B. rail C. apron D. stud

11. In a two-story wood frame building, a fascia would be found on the

    A. roof B. stair C. wall D. floor

12. A baluster is a part of a

    A. roof B. wall C. door D. stair

13. Stair treads rest on strips of wood nailed to the inside of stair stringers. These strips of wood are called

    A. shims B. wedges C. stubs D. cleats

14. Shown at the top of the next page is a section through the exterior wall of a building. The member X represents a

    A. wall plate B. ledger
    C. fire stop   D. girder

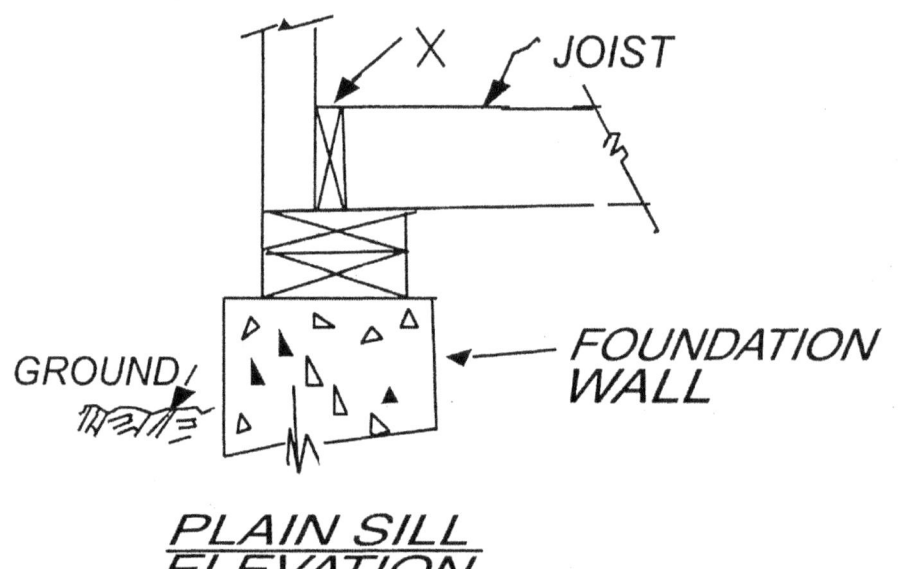

PLAIN SILL ELEVATION

15. The molded projection which finishes the top of the wall of a building is a   15.____

    A. coronet   B. corolla   C. cornice   D. cupola

16. The BEST reason for *not* painting a wood ladder is that   16.____

    A. the paint may conceal cracks
    B. it saves money not to paint the ladder
    C. painted ladder rungs get very slippery when wet
    D. the wood used is difficult to paint and paint spalls readily

17. In case of a fire in the floor below in a building in which a carpenter is making alterations, the BEST action for the carpenter to take is to   17.____

    A. walk quickly to the nearest stairway
    B. walk quickly to the nearest elevator
    C. collect all his tools and run to the nearest stairway
    D. open all the windows and run to the nearest stairway

18. Of the following, the one that should NOT be used as an improvised tourniquet is a   18.____

    A. leather belt   B. Venetian blind cord
    C. stocking   D. scarf

19. Of the following character traits, the BEST trait for a supervisor to have is   19.____

    A. optimism   B. rudeness   C. punctuality   D. decisiveness

20. Assume that you are acting in charge of a group of carpenters in the field installing partitions. You receive a telephone call from the office that they need a carpenter in the shop to do a rush job.   20.____
    Of the following, the BEST action to take is to

    A. send the senior carpenter
    B. send the most capable carpenter
    C. ask for volunteers
    D. send the least capable carpenter

21. In assigning additional work to carpenters, a supervisor should FIRST consider the carpenter's   21.____

    A. seniority   B. previous output
    C. current work load   D. attendance record

22. In checking the daily work of several carpenters at different locations, a good supervisor should visit the men   22.____

    A. according to each man's seniority
    B. at random hours each day
    C. according to location of nearest man first and farthest man last
    D. according to priority of when jobs have to be completed

23. Of the following jobs, the *one* that usually requires WRITTEN orders instead of ORAL orders is a job where   23.___

    A. progress can be easily checked
    B. emergency exists
    C. a mistake will be of little consequence
    D. many details are involved

24. To obtain cooperation from subordinates, a supervisor should   24.___

    A. complain about it   B. practice it
    C. demand it   D. suggest it

25. The BEST way to *temporarily* store oily sawdust in a carpenter shop before discarding the sawdust is in a   25.___

    A. metal can with a perforated metal cover
    B. metal can without a cover
    C. metal can with an air-tight metal cover
    D. perforated metal can with an air-tight cover

KEYS (CORRECT ANSWERS)

1. C	11. A
2. B	12. D
3. D	13. D
4. B	14. C
5. C	15. C
6. C	16. A
7. B	17. A
8. B	18. B
9. A	19. D
10. C	20. B

21. C
22. B
23. D
24. B
25. C

TEST 5

DIRECTIONS: For questions 1 through 11, the item referred to is shown to the right of the question.

1. The bolt shown should be used
    A. in foundations
    B. in cement curbs
    C. to connect rails
    D. to connect girders

    1.____

2. The screw shown is called a
    A. set screw
    B. anchor screw
    C. lag screw
    D. toggle screw

    2.____

3. The anchor shown should be used in a
    A. wood post
    B. concrete wall
    C. plaster wall
    D. gypsum block wall

    3.____

4. The wrench shown is called a(n)
    A. monkey wrench
    B. Allen wrench
    C. "L" wrench
    D. socket wrench

    4.____

5. The anchor shown should be used in a
    A. concrete wall
    B. veneer wall
    C. plaster wall
    D. brick wall

    5.____

6. The cutter shown should be used on
    A. pipes
    B. cables
    C. re-bars
    D. bolts

    6.____

7. The saw shown is called a
    A. coping saw
    B. cross-cut saw
    C. hack saw
    D. back saw

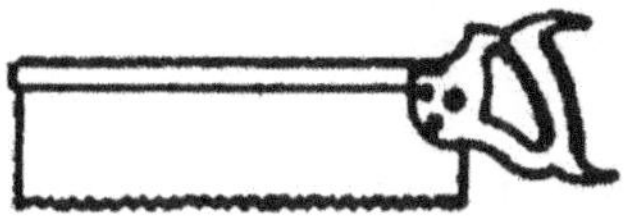

    7.____

8. The tool shown is a
    A. "D" clamp
    B. "C" clamp
    C. pipe vise
    D. metal vise

    8.____

9. The tool shown is a
   A. hawk
   B. trowel
   C. screed
   D. joiner

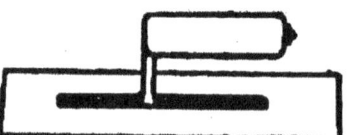

10. The tool shown is called a
    A. try square
    B. T-bevel
    C. miter box
    D. miter square

11. The tool shown should be used to
    A. make grooves in side walks
    B. turn lead bends
    C. make copper bends
    D. finish brick joints

KEYS (CORRECT ANSWERS)

1.	A	6.	A
2.	C	7.	D
3.	B	8.	B
4.	B	9.	B
5.	C	10.	C
		11.	A

EXAMINATION SECTION
TEST 1

DIRECTIONS: Each question or incomplete statement is followed by several suggested answers or completions. Select the one that BEST answers the question or completes the statement. *PRINT THE LETTER OF THE CORRECT ANSWER IN THE SPACE AT THE RIGHT.*

1. Concrete platforms in the subway are finished off with wooden edging strips. This design feature is of interest to the maintenance of way department because these strips

    A. perform a useful function under emergency conditions
    B. serve as markers to outline the platform edge
    C. are easier and less costly to maintain than a concrete edge
    D. make a more durable edge than concrete

    1._____

2. In order to select a bit to drill a 5/8" hole from a set of auger bits, you should

    A. look for one marked 5/8" on the shank
    B. check diameters with a caliper set at 5/8"
    C. look for one marked 10 on the tang
    D. pick out the likely one by eye and check size by a scrap piece of wood

    2._____

3. A number of different woods are used for fine interior finishes.
However, a wood which would most likely NOT be used for this purpose is

    A. birch   B. chestnut   C. red gum   D. ash

    3._____

4. The cleats that are fastened to the sides of a girder to help support the joists that frame into it are called

    A. ledger boards   B. cripples
    C. verge boards   D. toe-holts

    4._____

5. A 2 foot long carpenter's level was used to check a wood sill on top of one side of a concrete foundation wall. The sill was found to be out of level by 1/8".
If the length of the sill was 30'6", the sill would have to be shimmed a maximum amount of APPROXIMATELY

    A. 1/8"   B. 3/4"   C. 1 7/8"   D. 3 3/4"

    5._____

6. A price inquiry was made of two lumberyards on 100 2x4's - 10 ft. and 100 2x10's - 12 ft. Yard A quoted a price of 10¢ per linear foot for the 2x4's and 25¢ per linear foot for the 2x10's. Yard B quoted a price of 15¢ per board-foot for both items.
It can, therefore, be calculated that the price of yard A is

    A. cheaper than yard B for the 2x4's but dearer for the 2x10's
    B. dearer than yard B for the 2x4's but cheaper for the 2x10's
    C. the same as yard B for the 2x4's but dearer for the 2x10's
    D. the same as yard B for both items

    6._____

7. The nail-holding power of hardwoods, compared to that of softwoods, is

   A. about double
   B. about the same
   C. about one-half
   D. greater or smaller, depending on the particular species being compared

8. The sizes of hand saws which make up the most useful combination for general carpentry work are the _____ crosscut and the _____ rip.

   A. 16-inch, 10-point; 24-inch, 10-point
   B. 20-inch, 10-point; 26-inch, 8-point
   C. 22-inch, 9-point; 20-inch, 9-point
   D. 26-inch, 8-point; 26-inch, 5 ½-point

9. A 3" x 6" timber used as a beam between supports 12 feet apart will safely support a uniform load of 80 pounds per linear foot.
   If the same beam is used between supports which are only 6 feet apart, the uniform load per linear foot can safely be increased by _____ pounds.

   A. 80   B. 160   C. 240   D. 320

10. If the subfloor is laid diagonally, the finish flooring can be laid parallel to either dimension of the room because the

    A. finish floor will have a stronger foundation
    B. shrinkage of the subfloor will not noticeably affect the finish floor
    C. irregularities of the subfloor will then be equalized
    D. shrinkage of the subfloor will help pull the finish flooring together

11. A maintainer requests a special privilege because of certain unusual circumstances, and his gang foremen grants the request because he feels it to be definitely justified. Shortly thereafter, a helper requests the same privilege and gives as his only reason the fact that the maintainer had been granted this privilege.
    The gang foreman should, in the helper's case,

    A. grant the request because all men should be treated the same regardless of title
    B. grant the request to avoid a charge of discriminating against helpers
    C. deny the request and explain why it was granted to the maintainer
    D. tell him that the request will be granted if a better reason is furnished

12. Two long boards are to be glued together, edge to edge.
    The two edges are BEST trued-up by the use of a _____ plane.

    A. block   B. smoothing   C. jack   D. fore

13. When filing saw teeth, it should be kept in mind that

    A. a rip saw is filed straight across but a crosscut saw is filed at a 45° angle
    B. both rip saws and crosscut saws are filed straight across
    C. a rip saw is filed at a 45° angle but a crosscut saw is filed straight across
    D. both rip saws and crosscut saws are filed at a 45° angle

14. Unless otherwise specified, finish flooring will be supplied *standard matched*. This means that the

    A. distance from the top surface to the center of the tongue and groove is greater than the distance from the bottom surface to this center
    B. distance from the top surface to the center of the tongue and groove is less than the distance from the bottom surface to this center
    C. flooring is flat-grain and the grain is matched within prescribed limits
    D. flooring is edge-grain and the grain is in the same direction through each piece of flooring

Questions 15-20.

DIRECTIONS: Questions 15 through 20, inclusive, are based on the sketch shown on the following page, representing the floor plan of a one-story frame structure. Consult this drawing when answering these questions.

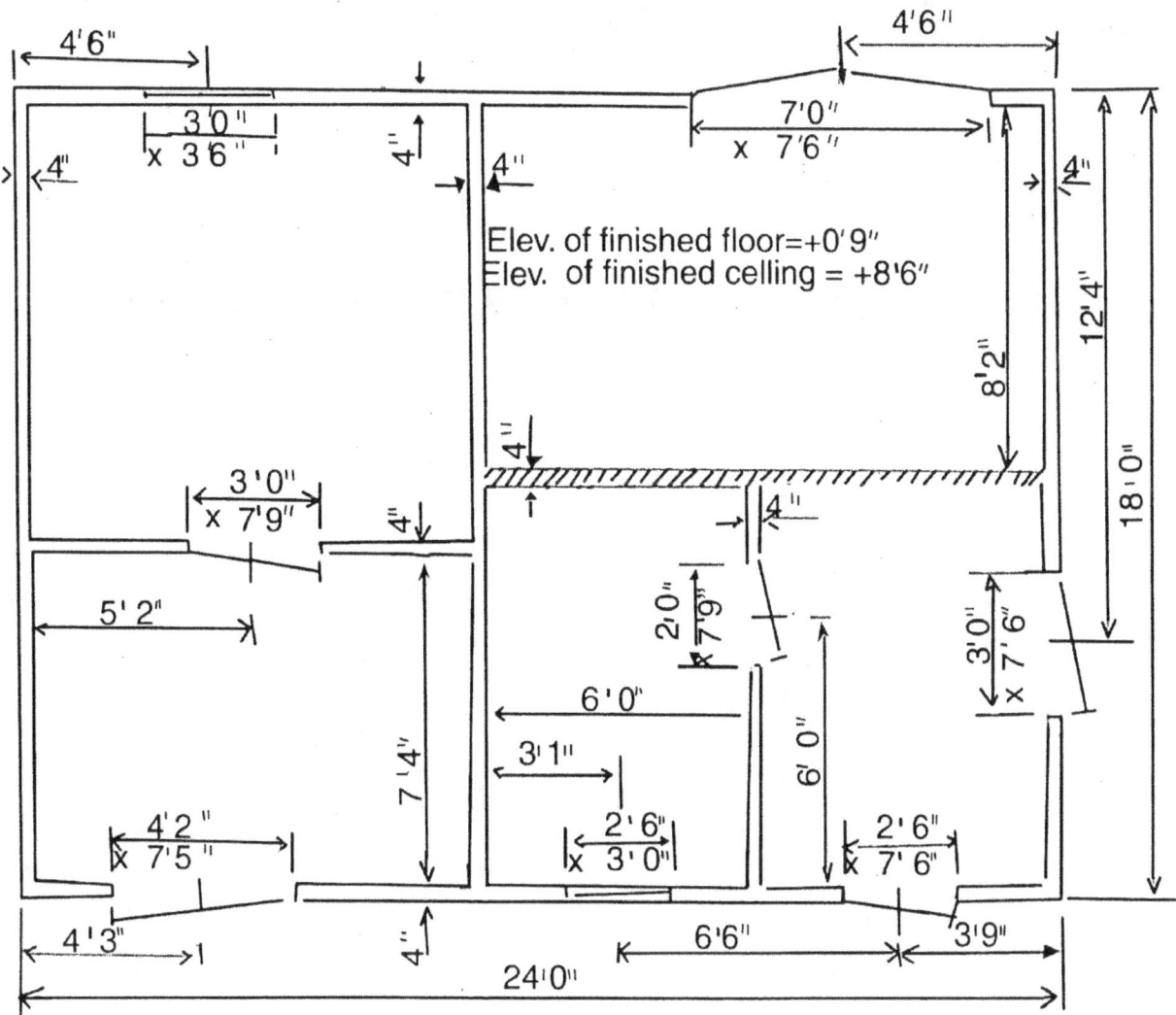

15. The number of linear feet of interior partitions required will be MOST NEARLY

    A. 44'2"   B. 46'6"   C. 49'2"   D. 51'6"

16. The total area of exterior openings in square feet will be MOST NEARLY

   A. 125   B. 143   C. 164   D. 182

17. The total exterior perimeter of the building, exclusive of door openings, will be MOST NEARLY

   A. 54'0"   B. 61'10"   C. 67'4"   D. 84'0"

18. The net floor area of the only corner room not provided with an exterior door is about _____ square feet.

   A. 53   B. 59   C. 97   D. 106

19. The dimensions of the largest room are

   A. 9'8" x 13'0"
   B. 8'2" x 13'0"
   C. 8'10" x 13'0"
   D. 10'0" x 17'4"

20. If 2" x 3" studs are placed at 14" o.c., the cross-hatched interior partition will require _____ studs.

   A. 10   B. 11   C. 12   D. 13

KEY (CORRECT ANSWERS)

1.	C	11.	C
2.	C	12.	D
3.	D	13.	A
4.	A	14.	A
5.	C	15.	A
6.	D	16.	B
7.	A	17.	C
8.	D	18.	C
9.	C	19.	B
10.	B	20.	C

TEST 2

DIRECTIONS: Each question or incomplete statement is followed by several suggested answers or completions. Select the one that BEST answers the question or completes the statement. *PRINT THE LETTER OF THE CORRECT ANSWER IN THE SPACE AT THE EIGHT.*

1. The MOST important reason for the use of furring on masonry surfaces is to provide   1.____

    A. a backing on which to nail lath
    B. a space for electric wiring
    C. thermal insulation
    D. increased structural strength for the finished plastered surface

2. If the drawing of a carpentry detail is made to a scale of 3/4" to the foot, a scaled measurement of 6" would represent a length of   2.____

    A. 3/8 inches B. 8 inches
    C. 4½ feet   D. 8 feet

3. When the end of a wood joist is set in a brick wall, it should be   3.____

    A. cut on a bevel   B. set on a pilaster
    C. cut square   D. set on a corbel

4. A rectangular form can be checked for squareness by taking the necessary measurements using only a tape, or by checking the necessary number of corners using only a steel square, or by taking certain measurements with a tape combined with the checking of certain corners with a steel square.
The form CANNOT be correctly checked by using a   4.____

    A. tape and finding the opposite sides equal and the diagonals of the same length
    B. steel square and finding that three corners are each 90 degrees
    C. steel square and finding that two diagonally opposite corners are each 90 degrees
    D. tape and finding the opposite sides equal, then using a steel square and finding one corner is 90 degrees

5. With respect to shrinking and swelling of wood, it is NOT true that   5.____

    A. wood which shrinks considerably when drying will swell considerably when moistened
    B. a flat-grain board will shrink more in width than an edge-grain board
    C. settlement occurring in a building where studs are supported on top of joists is due to shrinkage in the studs
    D. any beam will shrink more in depth than in length

6. An IMPORTANT reason for installing grounds is to   6.____

    A. provide a dead air space for better heat insulation
    B. get a tight joint between the back of the interior trim and the finished plaster
    C. prevent chipping of the finished plaster surface
    D. give increased structural support for the finished plastered surface

7. When it is necessary to install rows of cross bridging between floor joists, it is good practice to make the distance between the rows no more than _____ feet.

   A. 4   B. 8   C. 12   D. 16

8. An adjustable bit gauge will commonly be used on an auger bit to

   A. countersink the holes
   B. obtain equal diameter holes
   C. eliminate the need for center punching
   D. drill a number of holes to the same depth

9. If a certain type of structural timber is said to have a factor of safety of 4, it means that

   A. it should be used to carry no more than one-fourth of its design load
   B. it can safely carry four times its design load
   C. only one-quarter of the ultimate strength of a perfect piece is used for design purposes
   D. it is four times as strong as any other type of structural timber

10. All of the following groups of terms are used in pattern-making EXCEPT

    A. draft and core
    B. pattern and shrinkage
    C. splitter and mandrill
    D. cope and drag

11. The STIFFEST floor beam, of those listed, would be a

    A. 2" x 12" long leaf pine
    B. 3" x 8" spruce
    C. 2" x 12" hemlock
    D. 3" x 8" fir

12. In jointing a ½" x 6" x 10' white pine board on a 6-foot jointer, one finds that the material comes out concave (hollow).
    This is PROBABLY caused by the

    A. rear table being low on the far end
    B. rear table being low on the cutter end (middle of machine)
    C. cutter head being higher than the front and rear tables
    D. material being thin and long

13. Seasoning of wood under conditions of controlled temperature and humidity is known as

    A. dry seasoning
    B. dehydrating
    C. kiln drying
    D. demoisturizing

14. The PROPER thinner for varnish is

    A. alcohol
    B. toluene
    C. turpentine
    D. benzine

15. In general, gluing pressures should be

    A. *light* for softwoods, *heavy* for hardwoods
    B. *light* for thick glue, *heavy* for thin glue
    C. *light* for hardwoods, *heavy* for softwoods
    D. *always* as heavy as possible, with the exception of balsa

16. The material MOST commonly used in *drywall* construction is   16._____

    A. rock lath   B. wood lath and plaster
    C. wire (*rib*) lath   D. gypsum board

17. Veneer and plywood can be PROPERLY defined as follows: 17._____

    A. Both veneer and plywood are really the same
    B. Veneer is the name given to thin plywood
    C. Veneer is a single thin sheet of wood; plywood is made of several sheets with the grain parallel
    D. Veneer is a single thin sheet of wood; plywood is made of several sheets at angles to each other

18. In general, the BEST single criterion in judging the strength of lumber is its   18._____

    A. rings per inch   B. weight
    C. method of sawing   D. moisture content

19. The CHIEF advantage of plywood is its   19._____

    A. economy
    B. high strength
    C. resistance to abrasion and splitting
    D. uniformity of strength

20. The LEAST expensive and MOST common type of sandpaper used by home mechanics is   20._____

    A. garnet   B. flint or quartz
    C. aluminum oxide   D. silicon carbide

KEY (CORRECT ANSWERS)

1. A	11. A
2. D	12. A
3. A	13. C
4. C	14. C
5. C	15. A
6. B	16. D
7. B	17. D
8. D	18. B
9. C	19. B
10. C	20. B

EXAMINATION SECTION
TEST 1

DIRECTIONS: Each question or incomplete statement is followed by several suggested answers or completions. Select the one that BEST answers the question or completes the statement. *PRINT THE LETTER OF THE CORRECT ANSWER IN THE SPACE AT THE RIGHT.*

1. *Dimension lumber* is used MAINLY for

    A. door and sash cuttings
    B. exterior trim
    C. interior trim
    D. studding

    1._____

2. *Blind nailing* is the term used to describe nailing

    A. when it is not known into what material the nails are driven
    B. done with finishing nails
    C. done with assorted size nails
    D. done in such a way that the heads are not visible on the face of the work

    2._____

3. If two 2 x 4's are to be securely nailed to make one 4x4 (approximately) and the nail points are not to come through, of the following, the BEST size nails to use is _____ penny.

    A. 20   B. 10   C. 8   D. 6

    3._____

4. Lumber used in building construction should be well-seasoned because this

    A. makes it more fire-resistant
    B. helps prevent shakes
    C. prevents damage by termites
    D. prevents shrinkage and warping

    4._____

5. Timber that has been pressure creosoted is MOST likely to be used as

    A. beams in buildings to support heavy loads
    B. columns in buildings to support heavy loads
    C. rafters in a roof truss
    D. piles in wet ground

    5._____

6. Toe nailing is illustrated in the sketch marked

    6._____

A   B   C   D

71

7. A ribband or ribbon is a horizontal strip of wood notched into the studs. It is used ONLY in _____ -frame construction.

   A. balloon B. braced C. platform D. western

8. The bracing between wood floor beams is called

   A. internal bracing B. bridging
   C. reinforcing D. cross-bracing

9. The MAXIMUM allowable spacing for the bracing described in the preceding question, according to the Building Code, is _____ feet.

   A. 6 B. 8 C. 10 D. 12

10. In wooden floor construction, the bracing described above is used PRIMARILY to

    A. prevent the joists from turning over before the flooring is placed
    B. transfer load from the joist directly under a load on the floor to adjacent joists
    C. keep a uniform spacing of the joists
    D. eliminate the need for header and trimmer beams at floor openings

11. In floor construction, the bracing described in the same question should

    A. be nailed at the top and the lower ends left loose until the sub-flooring is nailed in position
    B. be nailed at both ends before the sub-flooring is placed in position
    C. not be nailed at all until after the sub-flooring is nailed in position
    D. not be nailed until after the sub-flooring is nailed and the finished flooring placed

12. Of the following, the wood that is MOST commonly used today for floor joists is

    A. long leaf yellow pine B. douglas fir
    C. oak D. birch

13. Quarter-sawed lumber is preferred for the best finished flooring PRINCIPALLY because it

    A. has the greatest strength
    B. shrinks the least
    C. is the easiest to nail
    D. is the easiest to handle

14. A tool used in hanging doors is a

    A. miter gauge B. line level
    C. try square D. butt gauge

15. Of the following, the MAXIMUM height that would be considered acceptable for a stair riser is _____ inches.

    A. 6½ B. 7½ C. 8½ D. 9½

16. The PRINCIPAL reason for *cross banding* the layers of wood in a plywood panel is to _____ of the panel.

    A. reduce warping
    B. increase the strength
    C. reduce the cost
    D. increase the beauty

17. The part of a tree that will produce the DENSEST wood is the _____ wood.

    A. spring   B. summer   C. sap   D. heart

18. Casing nails MOST NEARLY resemble _____ nails.

    A. common   B. roofing   C. form   D. finishing

19. In woodwork, countersinking is MOST often done for

    A. lag screws
    B. carriage bolts
    C. hanger bolts
    D. flat head screws

20. Bridging is MOST often used in connection with

    A. door frames
    B. window openings
    C. floor joists
    D. stud walls

21. A saddle is part of a

    A. doorway
    B. window
    C. stairwell
    D. bulkhead

22. To make it easier to drive screws into hard wood, it is BEST to

    A. use a screwdriver that is longer than that used for soft wood
    B. rub the threads of the screw on a bar of soap
    C. oil the screw threads
    D. use a square shank screwdriver assisted by a wrench

23. In using a doweled joint to make a repair of a wooden door, it is IMPORTANT to remember that

    A. the dowel hole must be smaller in diameter than the dowel so that there is a tight fit
    B. the dowel hole must be longer than the dowel to provide a room for excess glue
    C. the dowel must be of the same type of wood as the door frame
    D. the dowel must be held in place by a small screw while waiting for the glue to set

24. The edges of MOST finished wood flooring are

    A. tongue and groove
    B. mortise and tenon
    C. bevel and miter
    D. lap and scarf

25. For the SMOOTHEST finish, sanding of wood should be done

    A. in a circular direction
    B. diagonally against the grain
    C. across the grain
    D. parallel with the grain

KEY (CORRECT ANSWERS)

1. D
2. D
3. B
4. D
5. D

6. A
7. A
8. B
9. B
10. B

11. A
12. B
13. B
14. D
15. B

16. A
17. D
18. D
19. D
20. C

21. A
22. B
23. B
24. A
25. D

TEST 2

DIRECTIONS: Each question or incomplete statement is followed by several suggested answers or completions. Select the one that BEST answers the question or completes the statement. *PRINT THE LETTER OF THE CORRECT ANSWER IN THE SPACE AT THE RIGHT.*

Questions 1-5.

DIRECTIONS: Questions 1 through 5 refer to the following specification for wood flooring. In answering these questions, refer to this specification.

    2" x 4" wood sleepers laid flat @ 16" o.c.
    1" x 6" sub-flooring, laid diagonally; cut at butt joints with parallel cuts; joints at center of sleepers, well staggered, no two joints side by side. Not less than 1/8" space between boards.
    One layer of 15# asphalt felt on top of sub-floor.
    Finish floor – North Rock Maple, T & G, laid perpendicular to sleepers; 8d nails not more than 12" apart; end joints well scattered with at least 2 flooring strips between joints.
    Flooring 25/32" x 2 1/4" face - 1st quality.

1. It is MOST likely that the floor referred to in the specification is to be laid

   A. directly on the ground
   B. on a concrete base
   C. on wood joists
   D. on steel beams

2. The BEST reason for specifying that the sub-flooring be parallel cut at butt joints is that this

   A. requires less material
   B. provides staggered joints
   C. provides more nailing surface
   D. allows the joint to fall between sleepers

3. The BEST reason for specifying a minimum space between the sub-floor boards is that it

   A. saves on material
   B. reduces creaking
   C. allows for expansion
   D. prevents dry rot

4. The BEST reason for specifying at least 2 flooring strips between joints in the finish flooring is that

   A. it looks better
   B. it is more economical
   C. each board is supported by two adjoining boards
   D. each finish board is supported by at least two sub-floor boards

5. The BEST reason for placing asphalt felt on top of the sub-floor is to

   A. deaden noise
   B. preserve the wood
   C. reduce dampness
   D. permit movement

6. The number of board feet in a piece of lumber is equal to the cross-sectional area in square inches divided by 12 and multiplied by the length of the piece in feet. Therefore, among four different pieces of lumber of equal length, the GREATEST number of board feet would be in the piece whose other two dimensions are

    A. 1" x 12"   B. 2" x 10"   C. 3" x 8"   D. 4" x 4"

7. When sandpapering wood by hand, the sanding should be done

    A. with the grain
    B. across the grain
    C. diagonally to the grain
    D. with a circular motion

8. A drift pin is used to

    A. line up holes
    B. set nails
    C. enlarge holes
    D. keep a nut from turning

Questions 9-13.

DIRECTIONS: In Questions 9 through 13, for each figure in Column I, representing a cross-section of a piece of lumber, select the letter preceding the term in Column II which is MOST closely associated with figure.
NOTE: These figures are not to scale.

COLUMN I   COLUMN II

A. Flooring
B. Siding
C. Baseboard
D. Window steel
E. Threshold
F. Shingle

14. Lumber in quantity is ordered by

   A. cubic feet
   B. foot board measure
   C. lineal feet
   D. weight and length

15. The ends of a joist in a brick building are cut to a bevel. This is done PRINCIPALLY to prevent damage to a

   A. joist   B. floor   C. sill   D. wall

16. Of the following terms, all of which refer to tools, the one which is LEAST related to the others is

   A. back   B. box-end   C. cross-cut   D. rip

17. Of the following tools, the one which is LEAST like the others is

   A. brace and bit
   B. draw-knife
   C. plane
   D. spoke-shave

18. When wood splits easily, it is advisable to drill a hole for each nail. The hole for the nail should be _____ the nail.

   A. larger in diameter than
   B. smaller in diameter than
   C. exactly the same diameter as
   D. less than one-quarter the length of

19. The length of a 10-penny nail is, in inches,

   A. $2\frac{1}{2}$ B. 3   C. $3\frac{1}{2}$ D. 4

20. The decimal equivalent of 31/64 of an inch is MOST NEARLY

   A. 0.45   B. 0.46   C. 0.47   D. 0.48

21. Of the following, the one which is BEST classified as an abrasive is

   A. a saw   B. a chisel   C. graphite   D. sandpaper

22. A claw hammer is PROPERLY used for

   A. driving a cold chisel
   B. driving brads
   C. setting rivets
   D. flattening a ¼" metal bar

23. It is POOR practice to hold a piece of wood in the hands or lap when tightening a screw in the wood because

   A. sufficient leverage cannot be obtained
   B. the screwdriver may bend
   C. the wood will probably split
   D. personal injury is likely to result

24. Open-end wrenches are made with the sides of the jaws at about a 15° angle to the line of the handle.
This angle

    A. is useful when working the wrench in close quarters
    B. increases the strength of the jaws
    C. prevents extending the handle with a piece of pipe
    D. serves only to improve the appearance of the wrench

24.___

25. When laying tongue and groove flooring, each piece is laid with the tongue to the front and the groove fitted to the tongue of the previously laid piece.
In order to make this a tight fit before nailing into place, it is good practice when laying each piece to

    A. temporarily toe-nail through its tongue to draw it up tight
    B. fit a small piece of scrap flooring to it and strike the scrap piece
    C. strike it only on the middle of the tongue
    D. pull it into place using a chisel as a pry bar

25.___

KEY (CORRECT ANSWERS)

1.	B	11.	E
2.	C	12.	A
3.	C	13.	B
4.	C	14.	B
5.	C	15.	D
6.	C	16.	B
7.	A	17.	A
8.	A	18.	B
9.	C	19.	B
10.	D	20.	D

21.	D
22.	B
23.	D
24.	A
25.	B

TEST 3

DIRECTIONS: Each question or incomplete statement is followed by several suggested answers or completions. Select the one that BEST answers the question or completes the statement. *PRINT THE LETTER OF THE CORRECT ANSWER IN THE SPACE AT THE RIGHT.*

1. The MAIN purpose of bridging in building floor construction is to

    A. spread floor loads evenly to joists
    B. reduce the number of joists required
    C. permit use of thinner subflooring
    D. reduce noise passage through floors

    1.____

2. Of the following, the material MOST commonly used for subflooring is

    A. rock lath
    B. insulation board
    C. plywood
    D. transite

    2.____

3. In connection with stair construction, the one of the following that is LEAST related to the others is

    A. tread   B. cap   C. nosing   D. riser

    3.____

4. The type of nail MOST commonly used in flooring is

    A. common   B. cut   C. brad   D. casing

    4.____

5. The edge joint of flooring boards is COMMONLY

    A. mortise and tenon
    B. shiplap
    C. half lap
    D. tongue and groove

    5.____

6. The purpose of a ridge board in building construction is to

    A. locate corners of a building
    B. keep plaster work smooth
    C. support the ends of roof rafters
    D. conceal openings at the eaves

    6.____

7. Holes are USUALLY countersunk when installing

    A. carriage bolts
    B. lag screws
    C. flathead screws
    D. square nuts

    7.____

8. Of the following, the tool that is LEAST easily broken is a

    A. file
    B. pry bar
    C. folding rule
    D. hacksaw blade

    8.____

9. The wood joint which is a mortise and tenon is

    9.____

10. Of the following, the saw MOST frequently employed by a carpenter is a _____ saw. 10._____

    A. keyhole   B. jig   C. crosscut   D. miter

11. Of the following, a chain saw would MOST likely be used to cut 11._____

    A. bevelled edges   B. tongue and groove joints
    C. heavy timbers   D. long thin wood members

12. Wire for other than electrical work is USUALLY specified by 12._____

    A. number of mils   B. gauge number
    C. number of circular mils   D. weight per foot

13. Lumber that has NOT been seasoned properly 13._____

    A. is brittle   B. has a tendency to rot
    C. will have pitch pockets   D. will tend to warp

14. The specifications state that an 8-penny common nail is required as a fastener. Such nail should measure, in inches, MOST NEARLY 14._____

    A. 2   B. $2\frac{1}{2}$ C. 3   D. $3\frac{1}{2}$

15. To drill a hole 1 1/2 inches in diameter, a carpenter would MOST likely use a(n) 15._____

    A. 1 1/2" diameter drill   B. keyhole saw
    C. expansion bit   D. doall saw

16. A newel is part of a 16._____

    A. stairway   B. door   C. window   D. skylight

17. The area occupied by the building in the sketch at the right, in square feet, is MOST NEARLY 17._____

    A. 3300
    B. 4200
    C. 15,000
    D. 4050

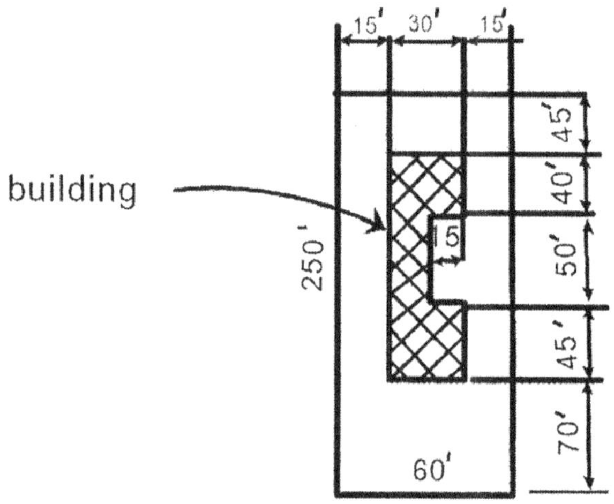

18. When timbers are bolted together, a flat washer is GENERALLY used under the head of the bolt to 18._____

    A. prevent the bolt from turning
    B. increase the strength of the bolt
    C. reduce crushing of the wood when the bolt is tightened
    D. make it easier to turn the bolt

19. The sketch at the right shows a gauge used to
    A. measure the depth of a hole
    B. determine if a board has been smoothly planed
    C. check the width of a brick
    D. scribe a line on a board parallel to its edge

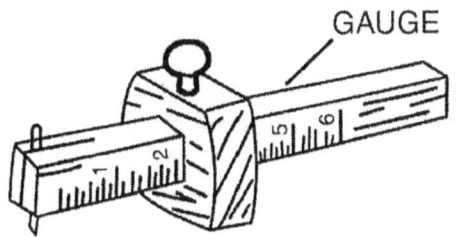

20. The joints in long vertical supporting timbers of wooden scaffolds are made with the timbers butted, rather than lapped, PRINCIPALLY because this results in
    A. better appearance
    B. more resistance to the weather
    C. lighter timbers
    D. less strain on the nails

KEY (CORRECT ANSWERS)

1.	A	11.	C
2.	C	12.	B
3.	B	13.	D
4.	B	14.	B
5.	D	15.	C
6.	C	16.	A
7.	C	17.	A
8.	B	18.	C
9.	B	19.	D
10.	C	20.	D

EXAMINATION SECTION
TEST 1

DIRECTIONS: Each question or incomplete statement is followed by several suggested answers or completions. Select the one that BEST answers the question or completes the statement. *PRINT THE LETTER OF THE CORRECT ANSWER IN THE SPACE AT THE RIGHT.*

1. The specification states: *The value of each change order shall be computed separately by cost of labor and materials, plus equipment allowance, plus overhead and profit.* The MOST probable value of overhead and profit is _____% of the cost of labor and materials plus equipment allowance.

    A. 5   B. 15   C. 34   D. 55

2. In the specifications is an item: *Equipment Allowance: Shall include rental of necessary equipment plus 9% of this rental.*
   According to the above specification, if a piece of equipment rents for $35 per day, Equipment Allowance for this equipment rented for 11 days is MOST NEARLY

    A. $484.00   B. $378.42   C. $385.00   D. $419.65

3. A supplier quotes a list price of $172.00 less 15 and 10 percent for twelve tools. The ACTUAL cost for these twelve tools is MOST NEARLY

    A. $146   B. $132   C. $129   D. $112

4. Which one of the following is the PRIMARY object in drawing up a set of specifications for materials to be purchased?

    A. Control of quality
    B. Outline of intended use
    C. Establishment of standard sizes
    D. Location and method of inspection

5. In order to avoid disputes over payments for extra work in a contract for construction, the BEST procedure to follow would be to

    A. have contractor submit work progress reports daily
    B. insert a special clause in the contract specifications
    C. have a representative on the job at all times to verify conditions
    D. allocate a certain percentage of the cost of the job to cover such expenses

6. You wish to order sponges in the most economical manner. Keeping in mind that large sponges can be cut up into many smaller sizes, the one of the following that has the LEAST cost per cubic inch of sponge is _____ sponges @ _____.

    A. 2" x 4" x 6"; $.24
    B. 4" x 8" x 12"; $1.44
    C. 4" x 6" x 36"; $4.80
    D. 6" x 8" x 32"; $9.60

7. The cost of a certain job is broken down as follows:
   - Materials $375
   - Rental of equipment 120
   - Labor   315

   The percentage of the total cost of the job that can be charged to materials is MOST NEARLY _____%.

   A. 40   B. 42   C. 44   D. 46

8. Partial payments to outside contractors are USUALLY based on the

   A. breakdown estimate submitted after the contract was signed
   B. actual cost of labor and material plus overhead and profit
   C. estimate of work completed which is generally submitted periodically
   D. estimate of material delivered to the job

9. Building contracts usually require that estimates for changes made in the field be submitted for approval before the work can start.
   The MAIN reason for this requirement is to

   A. make sure that the contractor understands the change
   B. discourage such changes
   C. keep the contractor honest
   D. enable the department to control its expenses

10. If the cost of a broom went up from $4.00 to $6.00, the percent INCREASE in the original cost is

    A. 20   B. 25   C. 33 1/3   D. 50

11. The AVERAGE of the numbers 3, 5, 7, 8, 12 is

    A. 5   B. 6   C. 7   D. 8

12. The cost of 100 bags of cotton cleaning cloths, 89 pounds per bag, at 7 cents per pound is

    A. $549.35   B. $623.00   C. $700.00   D. $890.00

13. If 5 1/2 bags of sweeping compound cost $55,00, then 6 1/2 bags would cost

    A. $60.00   B. $62.50   C. $65.00   D. $67.00

14. The cost of cleaning supplies in a project averaged $330.00 a month during the first 8 months of the year.
    How much can be spent each month for the last four months if the total amount that can be spent for cleaning supplies for the year is $3,880?

    A. $124   B. $220   C. $310   D. $330

15. The cost of rawl plugs is $2.75 per gross. The cost of 2,448 rawl plugs is

    A. $46.75   B. $47.25   C. $47.75   D. $48.25

16. A caretaker received $70.00 for having worked from Monday through Friday, 9 A.M. to 5 P.M. with one hour a day for lunch.
The number of hours the caretaker would have to work to earn $12.00 is

    A. 10
    B. 6
    C. 70 divided by 12
    D. 70 minus 12

17. Assume that an employee is paid at the rate of $5.43 per hour with time and a half for overtime past 40 hours in a week.
If he works 43 hours in a week, his gross weekly pay is

    A. $217.20   B. $219.20   C. $229.59   D. $241.64

18. Kerosene costs 36 cents a quart.
At that rate, two gallons would cost

    A. $1.44   B. $2.16   C. $2.88   D. $3.60

Questions 19-21.

DIRECTIONS: Questions 19 through 21 are to be answered on the basis of the following table.

	Man Days Borough 1		Man Days Borough 2		Man Days Borough 3		Man Days Borough 4	
	Oct.	Nov.	Oct.	Nov.	Oct.	Nov.	Oct.	Nov.
Carpenter	70	100	35	180	145	205	120	85
Plumber	95	135	195	100	70	130	135	80
House Painter	90	90	120	80	85	85	95	195
Electrician	120	110	135	155	120	95	70	205
Blacksmith	125	145	60	180	205	145	80	125

19. In accordance with the above table, if the average daily pay of the five trades listed above is $47.50, the approximate labor cost of work done by the five trades during the month of October for Borough 1 is MOST NEARLY

    A. $22,800   B. $23,450   C. $23,750   D. $26,125

20. In accordance with the above table, the Borough which MOST NEARLY made up 22.4% of the total plumbing work force for the month of November is Borough

    A. 1   B. 2   C. 3   D. 4

21. In accordance with the above table, the average man days per month per Borough spent on electrical work for all Boroughs combined is MOST NEARLY

    A. 120   B. 126   C. 130   D. 136

22. When preparing an estimate for a certain repair job, you determine that $125 worth of materials and 220 man-hours are required to complete the job.
If your man-hour cost is $5.25 per hour, the TOTAL cost of this repair job is

    A. $1,030   B. $1,155   C. $1,280   D. $1,405

23. Assume that in determining the total cost of a repair job, a 15% shop cost is to be added to the costs of material and labor.
    For a repair job which cost $200 in materials and $600 in labor, the shop cost is

    A. $30   B. $60   C. $90   D. $120

24. Assume that in quantity purchases, the city receives a discount of 33 1/3%.
    If a one gallon can of paint retails at $5.33 per gallon, the cost of 375 gallons of this paint is MOST NEARLY

    A. $1,332.50   B. $1,332.75   C. $1,333.00   D. $1,333.25

25. Assume that eight barrels of cement together weigh a total of 3004 lbs. and 12 oz.
    If there are four bags of cement per barrel, then the weight of one bag of cement is HOST NEARLY _____ lbs.

    A. 93.1   B. 93.5   C. 93.9   D. 94.3

26. Lumber is usually sold by the board foot, and a board foot is defined as a board one foot square and one inch thick.
    If the price of one board foot of lumber is 18 cents and you need 20 feet of lumber 6 inches wide and 1 inch thick, the cost of the 20 feet of lumber is

    A. $1.80   B. $2.40   C. $3.60   D. $4.80

27. Assume that a trench is 42" wide, 5' deep, and 100' long. If the unit price of excavating the trench is $35 per cubic yard, the cost of excavating the trench is MOST NEARLY

    A. $2,275   B. $5,110   C. $7,000   D. $21,000

28. No single activity has a very large effect on the final price of the complete housing structure and, therefore, the total cost is not affected appreciably by the price policy of any component.
    From the above statement, you may conclude that

    A. we cannot hope for substantial reductions in housing costs
    B. the builder must assume responsibility for the high cost of construction
    C. a 10% reduction in the cost of materials would result in much less than a 10% reduction in the cost of housing
    D. federal government financing would reduce the city's cost of public housing

29. Four board feet of lumber, listed at $350 per M, will cost

    A. $3.50   B. $1.40   C. $1.80   D. $4.00

30. The cost of material is approximately 3/8ths of the total cost of a certain job.
    If the total cost of the job is $127.56, then the cost of material is MOST NEARLY

    A. $47.83   B. $48.24   C. $48.65   D. $49.06

31. It takes four men six days to do a certain job. Working at the same speed, the number of days it will take three men to do this job is

    A. 7   B. 8   C. 9   D. 10

32. A contractor on a large construction project USUALLY receives partial payments based on

    A. estimates of completed work
    B. actual cost of materials delivered and work completed
    C. estimates of material delivered and not paid for by the contractor
    D. the breakdown estimate submitted after the contract was signed and prorated over the estimated duration of the contract

33. In estimating the cost of a reinforced concrete structure, the contractor would be LEAST concerned with

    A. volume of concrete
    B. surface area of forms
    C. pounds of reinforcing steel
    D. type of coarse aggregate

34. Assume that an employee is paid at the rate of $6.25 per hour with time and a half for overtime past 40 hours in a week.
    If she works 45 hours in a week, her gross weekly pay is

    A. $285.49   B. $296.88   C. $301.44   D. $325.49

35. Cleaning fluid costs $1.19 a quart.
    If there is a 10% discount for purchases over 5 gallons, how much will 8 gallons cost?

    A. $34.28   B. $38.08   C. $42.28   D. $43.43

KEY (CORRECT ANSWERS)

1. B	11. C	26. A
2. D	12. B	27. A
3. B	13. C	28. C
4. A	14. C	29. B
5. C	15. A	30. A
6. B	16. B	31. B
7. D	17. D	32. A
8. C	18. C	33. D
9. D	19. C	34. B
10. D	20. B	35. A
	21. B	
	22. C	
	23. D	
	24. A	
	25. C	

TEST 2

DIRECTIONS: Each question or incomplete statement is followed by several suggested answers or completions. Select the one that BEST answers the question or completes the statement. *PRINT THE LETTER OF THE CORRECT ANSWER IN THE SPACE AT THE RIGHT.*

1. When windows are mounted side by side, the vertical piece between them is called the

   A. muntin   B. casement   C. sash   D. mullion

2. Approximately how many pounds of 16d nails would be required for 1,000 square feet of floor framing area?

   A. 4-5   B. 7-8   C. 8-10   D. 10-12

3. What is represented by the electrical symbol shown at the right?

   A. Transformer   B. Buzzer
   C. Telephone   D. Bell

4. Which of the following structures would typically require a relatively higher grade of lumber?

   A. Vertical stud   B. Joist
   C. Column   D. Mud sill

5. A dump truck with a capacity of 10-12 cubic yards must load, drive, dump, and reposition itself over a 1-mile haul distance.
   What average amount of time should be estimated for this sequence?

   A. 15 minutes   B. 30 minutes
   C. 1 hour   D. 2 hours

6. The stripping of forms that are to be reused should be charged as

   A. common labor   B. masonry labor
   C. carpentry labor   D. material credit

7. What type of brick masonry unit is represented by the drawing shown at the right?
   A. Modular
   B. Norwegian
   C. 3 core
   D. Economy

   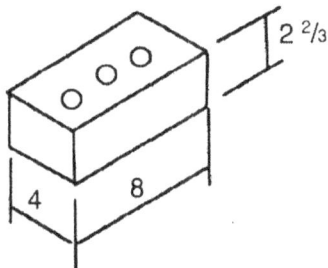

8. Which of the following would be a typical thickness of a crushed-rock base course for an area of asphalt paving?

   A. 2"   B. 5"   C. 7"   D. 10"

9. Which of the following wood floor materials would be MOST expensive to install?

   A. Unfinished plank
   B. Walnut parquet
   C. Maple strip
   D. Oak parquet

10. When calculating the air-conditioning needs for a building, a loss factor of _____ should be used for the exposure of walls to common heated surfaces.

    A. 2.0
    B. 3.5
    C. 6.0
    D. 7.5

11. Approximately how many linear feet of moldings, door and window trim, handrails, or similar parts can a carpenter install in a typical work day?

    A. 100
    B. 250
    C. 400
    D. 500

12. Which of the following constructions is NOT typically found in bathroom lavatories?

    A. Enameled pressed steel
    B. Cast iron
    C. Cast ceramic
    D. Stainless steel

13. What size reinforcing bar is typically used for masonry walls?

    A. 3
    B. 4
    C. 7
    D. 9

14. Which of the following would NOT be a typical source for a cost-per-square-foot estimate?

    A. Architect
    B. Engineer
    C. Appraiser
    D. Building contractor

15. Approximately how many stair treads with risers can a carpenter install in an average work day?

    A. 5-8
    B. 10-12
    C. 15-18
    D. 21-25

16. Each of the following materials is commonly used as sheet metal flashing for roof waterproofing EXCEPT

    A. lead
    B. galvanized steel
    C. copper
    D. zinc

17. The MOST commonly used type of metal lath for wall support is

    A. self-furring
    B. flat rib
    C. flat diamond mesh
    D. 3/8" rib

18. Approximately how long will it take to install a non-mortised lockset?

    A. 15 minutes
    B. 30 minutes
    C. 1 hour
    D. 2 hours

19. What is represented by the architectural symbol shown at the right?

    A. Cut stone
    B. Concrete block
    C. Rubble stone
    D. Brick

20. What type of nails are typically used for installing floor sheathing?

    A. 4d
    B. 8d
    C. 12d
    D. 16d

21. Each of the following is considered *finish* electrical work EXCEPT

    A. outlet boxes
    B. light fixtures
    C. connection of fixtures to wiring
    D. switches

22. Which component of cost estimating typically presents the GREATEST difficulty?

    A. Materials
    B. Overhead
    C. Profit
    D. Labor

23. Approximately how many hours will it take to install and caulk a typical sliding shower door assembly?

    A. 2   B. 4   C. 6   D. 8

24. What is represented by the electrical symbol shown at the right?

    A. Single pole switch
    B. Lock or key switch
    C. Service weather head
    D. Main switch

25. Approximately how many exterior square feet can one painter cover, applying a primer coat and two coats of finish paint, in an average work day?

    A. 100   B. 250   C. 350   D. 500

KEY (CORRECT ANSWERS)

1. D		11. B	
2. B		12. D	
3. C		13. B	
4. B		14. C	
5. B		15. C	
6. C		16. A	
7. A		17. C	
8. B		18. B	
9. B		19. A	
10. B		20. B	

21. A
22. D
23. B
24. A
25. D

TEST 3

DIRECTIONS: Each question or incomplete statement is followed by several suggested answers or completions. Select the one that BEST answers the question or completes the statement. *PRINT THE LETTER OF THE CORRECT ANSWER IN THE SPACE AT THE RIGHT.*

1. Irregular shapes and narrow lites typically reduce the rate of glass installation by _____%. 1.____
   A. 10-20 B. 25-35 C. 30-50 D. 55-75

2. What is represented by the electrical symbol shown at the right? 2.____
   A. Exposed wiring
   B. Fusible element
   C. Three-way switch
   D. Circuit breaker

3. Approximately how many square feet of siding can be installed by a crew in a typical work day? 3.____
   A. 250 B. 500 C. 750 D. 1,000

4. What is the construction term for hinges used on doors? 4.____
   A. Gables B. Butts C. Hips D. Plates

5. Floor joists are typically spaced about _____ apart. 5.____
   A. 16" B. 2 feet C. 3 feet D. 4 feet

6. Which of the following paving materials is generally MOST expensive? 6.____
   A. Brick on sand bed
   B. Random flagstone
   C. Asphalt
   D. Concrete

7. Approximately how long should it take a 2-person crew to install floor joists for a 100 square-foot area of floor space? 7.____
   A. 30 minutes
   B. 1 hour
   C. 3 hours
   D. 1 work day

8. A _____ is represented by the mechanical symbol shown at the right. 8.____
   A. pressure-reducing valve
   B. motor-operated valve
   C. lock and shield valve
   D. globe valve

9. On average, labor costs for a job will be about _____% of the total job cost. 9.____
   A. 15 B. 35 C. 55 D. 85

10. Most exterior paint averages a coverage of about _____ square feet per gallon. 10.____
    A. 100 B. 250 C. 400 D. 550

11. What type of window includes two sashes which slide vertically?

    A. Double-hung B. Screen
    C. Casement   D. Sliding

12. Approximately how many linear feet of drywall tape can be applied during an average work day?

    A. 250   B. 400   C. 750   D. 1,000

13. What is used to join lengths of copper pipe?

    A. Molten solder
    B. Threaded ends and sealer
    C. Nipples
    D. Lead-and-oakum seal

14. Typically, one gallon of prepared wallpaper paste will supply adhesive for _____ full rolls of wall covering.

    A. 8   B. 12   C. 24   D. 36

15. What is represented by the electrical symbol shown at the right?

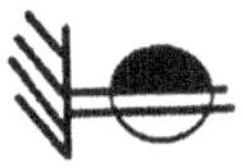

    A. Range outlet
    B. Wall bracket light fixture
    C. Split-wired receptacle
    D. Special purpose outlet

16. What size is MOST wire used in residential work?

    A. 6   B. 8   C. 12   D. 16

17. Most fire codes require fire-resistant floor underneath fireplace units which extends to at least _____ inches beyond the unit.

    A. 6   B. 12   C. 18   D. 24

18. If a building is constructed without a basement, _____ are typically used as footings.

    A. joists   B. staked caissons
    C. grade beams   D. mud sills

19. What is the MOST commonly used size range for flashing and gutter sheet metal?

    A. 8-12   B. 14-18   C. 22-26   D. 24-30

20. Approximately how many square feet of interior wall space can one painter, using a brush, cover in an hour?

    A. 25-50   B. 100   C. 175-200   D. 250

21. Which of the following downspout materials would be MOST expensive?

    A. Copper   B. Aluminum
    C. Zinc   D. Stainless steel

22. What is represented by the mechanical symbol shown at the right?   22.____

    A. Expansion valve   B. Floor drain
    C. Shower   D. Scale trap

23. Approximately how much lead (pounds) is required per joint in one sewer line lead-and-oakum seal?   23.____

    A. 1/4   B. 1/2   C. 1 1/2   D. 3

24. Which of the following caulking materials is MOST expensive?   24.____

    A. Neoprene   B. Butyl
    C. Polyurethane   D. Latex

25. The assembly inside a tank toilet that controls the water supply is the   25.____

    A. P trap   B. bell-and-spigot
    C. gating   D. ball cock

KEY (CORRECT ANSWERS)

1.	C	11.	A
2.	B	12.	A
3.	A	13.	A
4.	B	14.	B
5.	A	15.	C
6.	D	16.	C
7.	C	17.	B
8.	D	18.	C
9.	A	19.	C
10.	C	20.	B

21. A
22. A
23. A
24. B
25. C

EXAMINATION SECTION
TEST 1

DIRECTIONS: Each question or incomplete statement is followed by several suggested answers or completions. Select the one that BEST answers the question or completes the statement. *PRINT THE LETTER OF THE CORRECT ANSWER IN THE SPACE AT THE RIGHT.*

1. A supervisor was given a booklet that showed a new work method that could save time. He didn't tell his men because he thought that they would get the booklet anyway.
   For the supervisor to have acted like this is a
   A. *good* idea, because he saves time and both of talking to the men
   B. *bad* idea, because he should make sure his men know about better work methods
   C. *good* idea, because the men would rather read about it themselves
   D. *bad* idea, because a supervisor should always show his men every memo he gets from higher authority

   1.____

2. A supervisor found it necessary to discipline two subordinates. One man had been operating his equipment in a wrong way, while the other man came to work late for three days in a row. The supervisor decided to talk to both men together.
   For the supervisor to deal with the problems in this way is a
   A. *good* idea because each man will learn about the difficulties of the other person and how to solve such difficulties
   B. *bad* idea because the supervisor should wait until he can bring a larger group together and save time in discussing such questions
   C. *good* idea because he will be able to get the men to see that their problems are related
   D. *bad* idea because he should meet with each man separately and give him his full attention

   2.____

3. A supervisor should try to make his men feel their jobs are important in order to
   A. get the men to say good things about their supervisor to his own superior
   B. get the men to think in terms of advancing to better jobs
   C. let higher management in the agency know that the supervisor is efficient
   D. help the men to be able to work more efficiently and enthusiastically

   3.____

4. A supervisor should know approximately how long it takes to do a particular kind of job CHIEFLY because he
   A. will know how much time to take if he has to do it himself
   B. will be able to tell his men to do it even faster
   C. can judge the performance of the person doing the job
   D. can retrain experienced employees in better work habits

   4.____

5. Supervisors often get their employees' opinions about better work methods because
    A. the men will know that they are respected
    B. the men would otherwise lose all their confidence in the supervisor
    C. the supervisor might find in this way a good suggestion he could use
    D. this is the best method for improvement of work methods

6. Right after you have trained your subordinates in doing a new job, you find that they seem to be doing all right, but that it will take them several days to finish. You also have several groups of men working at other locations.
    The MOST efficient way for you to make sure that the men continue doing the new job properly is to
    A. stay on that job with the men until it is finished just in case trouble develops
    B. visit the men every half hour until the job is done
    C. stay away from their job that day and visit the men the next day to ask them if they had any problems
    D. visit the men a few times each day until they finish the new job

7. Assume that one of your new employees is older than you are. You also think that he may be hard to get along with because he is older than you.
    The BEST way for you to avoid any problems with the older worker is for you to
    A. lay down the law immediately and tell the man he better not cause you any trouble
    B. treat the man just the way you would any other worker
    C. always ask the older worker for advice in the presence of all the men
    D. ignore the man entirely until he realizes that you are the boss

8. Assume that you have tried a new method suggested by one of your employees and find that it is easier and cheaper than the method you had been using.
    The PROPER thing for you to do NEXT is to
    A. say nothing to anyone but train your men to use the new method
    B. train your men to use the new method and tell your crew that you got the idea from one of the men
    C. continue using the old method because a supervisor should not use suggestions of his men
    D. have your crew learn the new method and take credit for the idea since you are the boss

9. Suppose you are a supervisor and your superior tells you that the way your men are doing a certain procedure is wrong and that you should re-train our men as soon as possible.
    When you begin to re-train the men, the FIRST thing you should do is to
    A. tell your men that a wrong procedure had been used and that a new method must be learned as a result
    B. train your employees in the new method with no explanation since you are the boss

C. tell the crew that your superior has just decided that everyone should learn a new method
D. tell the crew that your superior says your method is wrong but that you don't agree with this

10. It is BAD practice to criticize a man in front of the other men because
    A. people will think you are too strict
    B. it is annoying to anyone who walks by
    C. it is embarrassing to the man concerned
    D. it will antagonize the other men

10.____

11. A supervisor decides not to put his two best men on a work detail because he knows that they won't like it.
    For the supervisor to make the work assignment this way is a
    A. *good* idea because it is only fair to give your best men a break once in a while
    B. *bad* idea because you should treat all of your me fairly and not show favoritism
    C. *good* idea because you save the strength of these men for another job
    D. *bad* idea because more of the men should be exempted from the assignment

11.____

12. Suppose you are a supervisor and you find it inconvenient to obey an established procedure set by your agency. You think another procedure would be better.
    The BEST thing to do first about this procedure that you don't like is for you to
    A. obey the procedure even if you don't to and suggest your idea to your own supervisor
    B. disregard the procedure because a supervisor is supposed to have some privileges
    C. follow the procedure some of the time but ignore it when the men are not watching
    D. organize a group of other supervisors to get the procedure changed

12.____

13. A supervisor estimated that it would take his crew one workday per week to do a certain job each week. However, after a month he noticed that the job averaged two and a half days a week and this delayed other jobs that had to be done.
    The FIRST thing that the supervisor should do in this case is to
    A. call him men together and warn them that they will get a poor work evaluation if they do not work harder
    B. talk to each man personally, asking him to work harder on the job
    C. go back and study the maintenance job by himself to see if more men should be assigned to the job
    D. write his boss a report describing in detail how much time it is taking the men to do the job

13.____

14. An employee complains to you that some of the work assignments are too difficult to do alone.
    Which of the following is the BEST way for you to handle this complaint?
    A. Go with him to see exactly what he does and why he finds it so difficult
    B. Politely tell the man that he has to do the job or be brought up on charges
    C. Tell the man to send his complaint to the head of your agency
    D. Sympathize with the man and give him easier jobs

15. The BEST way for a supervisor to keep control of his work assignments is to
    A. ask the men to report to him immediately when their jobs are finished
    B. walk around the buildings once a week and get a first-hand view of what is being done
    C. keep his ears open for problems and complaints, but leave the men aloe to do the work
    D. write up a work schedule and check it periodically against the actual work done

16. A supervisor made a work schedule for his men. At the bottom of it, he wrote, *No changes or exceptions will be made in this schedule for any reason.*
    For the supervisor to have made this statement is
    A. *good*, because the men will respect the supervisor for his attitude
    B. *bad*, because there are emergencies and special situations that occur
    C. *good*, because each man will know exactly what is expected of him
    D. *bad*, because the men should expect that no changes will ever be made in the work schedule without written permission

17. Which one of the following would NOT be a result of a well-planned work schedule?
    The schedule
    A. makes efficient use of the time of the staff
    B. acts as a checklist for an important job that might be left out
    C. will give an idea of the work to a substitute supervisor
    D. shows at a glance who the best men are

18. A new piece of equipment you have ordered is delivered. You are familiar with it, but the men under you who will use it do not know the equipment.
    Of the following methods, which is the BEST to take in explaining to them how to operate this equipment?
    A. Ask the men to watch other crews using the equipment
    B. Show one reliable man how to operate the equipment and ask him to teach the other men
    C. Ask the men to read the instructions in the manual for the equipment
    D. Call the men together and show them how to operate the equipment

19. One supervisor assigns work to his men by calling his crew together each week and describing what has to be done that week. He then tells them to arrange individual assignments among themselves and to work as a team during the week.

This method of scheduling work is a
- A. *good* idea because this guarantees that the men will work together
- B. *bad* idea because responsibility for doing the job is poorly fixed
- C. *good* idea because the men will finish the job in less time, working together
- D. *bad* idea because the supervisor should always stay with his men

20. Suppose that an employee came to his supervisor with a problem concerning his assignment.
    For the supervisor to listen to his problem is a
    - A. *good* idea because a supervisor should always take time off to talk when one of his men wants to talk
    - B. *bad* idea because the supervisor should not be bothered during the work day
    - C. *good* idea because it is the job of the supervisor to deal with problems of job assignment
    - D. *bad* idea because the employee could start annoying the supervisor with all sorts of problems

20.____

21. Suppose that on the previous afternoon you were looking for an experienced employee in order to give him an emergency job and he was missing from his job location. The next morning, he tells you that he got sick suddenly and had to go home, but could not tell you since you were not around. He has never done this before.
    What should you do?
    - A. Tell the man he is excused and that in such circumstances he did the wisest thing
    - B. Bring the man up on charges because whatever he says he could still have notified you
    - C. Have the man examined by a doctor to see if he really was sick the day before
    - D. Explain to the mean that he should make every effort to tell you or to get a message to you if he must leave

21.____

22. An employee had a grievance and went to his supervisor about it. The employee was not satisfied with the way the supervisor tried to help him and told him so. Yet, the supervisor had done everything he could under the circumstances.
    The PROPER action for the supervisor to take at this time is to
    - A. politely tell the employee that there is nothing more for the supervisor to do about the problem
    - B. let the employee know how he can bring his complaint to a higher authority
    - C. tell the employee that he must solve the problem on his own since he did not want to follow the supervisor's advice
    - D. suggest to the employee that he ask for another supervisor for assistance

22.____

23. In which of the following situations is it BEST to give your men spoken rather than written orders? 23.____
    A. You want your men to have a record of the instructions.
    B. Spoken instructions are less likely to be forgotten.
    C. An emergency situation has arisen in which there is no time to write up instructions.
    D. There are instructions on time and leave regulations which are complicated.

24. One of your employees tells you that a week ago he had a small accident on the job but he did not bother telling you because he was able to continue working. 24.____
    For the employee not to have told his supervisor about the accident was
    A. *good*, because the accident was a small one
    B. *bad*, because all accidents should be reported, no matter how small
    C. *good*, because the supervisor should be bothered only for important matters
    D. *bad*, because having an accident is one way to get excused for the day

25. For a supervisor to deal with each of his subordinate in exactly the same manner is 25.____
    A. *poor*, because each man presents a different problem and there is no one way of handling all problems
    B. *good*, because once a problem is handled with one man, he can handle another man with the same problem
    C. *poor*, because the men will resent it if they are not handled each in a better way than others
    D. *good*, because this assures fair and impartial treatment of each subordinate

KEY (CORRECT ANSWERS)

1.	B		11.	B
2.	D		12.	A
3.	D		13.	C
4.	C		14.	A
5.	C		15.	D
6.	D		16.	B
7.	B		17.	D
8.	B		18.	D
9.	A		19.	B
10.	C		20.	C

21. D
22. B
23. C
24. B
25. A

TEST 2

DIRECTIONS: Each question or incomplete statement is followed by several suggested answers or completions. Select the one that BEST answers the question or completes the statement. *PRINT THE LETTER OF THE CORRECT ANSWER IN THE SPACE AT THE RIGHT.*

1. Jim Johnson has been on your staff for over four years. He has always been a conscientious and productive worker. About a month ago, his wife died; and since that time, his work performance has been very poor.
   As his supervisor, which one of the following is the BEST way for you to deal with this situation?
   A. Allow Jim as much time as he needs to overcome his grief and hope that his work performance improves
   B. Meet with Jim to discuss ways to improve his performance
   C. Tell Jim directly that you are more concerned with his work performance than with his personal problem
   D. Prepare disciplinary action on Jim as soon as possible

   1.____

2. You are responsible for the overall operation of a storehouse which is divided into two sections. Each section has its own supervisor. You have decided to make several complex changes in the storekeeping procedures which will affect both sections.
   Of the following, the BEST way to make sure that these changes are understood by the two supervisors is for you to
   A. meet with both supervisors to discuss the changes
   B. issue a memorandum to each supervisor explaining the changes
   C. post the changes where the supervisors are sure to see them
   D. instruct one supervisor to explain the changes to the other supervisor

   2.____

3. You have called a meeting of all your subordinates to tell them what has to be done on a new project in which they will all be involved. Several times during the meeting, you ask if there are any questions about what you have told them.
   Of the following, to ask the subordinates whether there are any questions during the meeting can BEST be described as
   A. *inadvisable*, because it interferes with their learning about the new project
   B. *advisable*, because you will find out what they don't understand and have a chance to clear up any problems they may have
   C. *inadvisable*, because it makes the meeting too long and causes the subordinates to lose interest in the new project
   D. *advisable*, because it gives you a chance to learn which of your subordinates are paying attention to what you say

   3.____

4. As a supervisor, you are responsible for seeing to it that absenteeism does not become a problem among your subordinates.
   Which one of the following is NOT an acceptable way of controlling the problem of excessive absences?

   4.____

A. Distribute a written statement to your staff on the policies regarding absenteeism in your organization
B. Arrange for workers who have the fewest absences to talk to those workers who have the most absences
C. Let your subordinates know that a record is being kept of all absences
D. Arrange for counseling of those employees who are frequently absent

5. One of your supervisors has been an excellent worker for the past two years. There are no promotion opportunities for this worker in the foreseeable future. Due to the city's present budget crisis, a salary increase is not possible.
Under the circumstances, which one of the following actions on your part would be MOST likely to continue to motivate this worker?
   A. Tell the worker that times are bad all over and jobs are hard to find
   B. Give the worker less work and easier assignments
   C. Tell the worker to try to look for a better paying job elsewhere
   D. Seek the worker's advice often and show that the suggestions provided are appreciated

6. As a supervisor in a warehouse, it is important that you use your available work force to its fullest potential.
Which one of the following actions on your part is MOST likely to increase the effectiveness of your work force?
   A. Assigning more workers to a job than the number actually needed
   B. Eliminating all job training to allow more time for work output
   C. Using your best workers on jobs that average workers can do
   D. Making sure that all materials and equipment used are maintained in good working order

7. You learn that your storage area will soon be undergoing changes which will affect the work of your subordinates. You decide not to tell your subordinates about what is to happen.
Of the following, your action can BEST be described as
   A. *wise*, because your subordinates will learn of the changes for themselves
   B. *unwise*, because your subordinates should be advised about what is to happen
   C. *wise*, because it is better for your subordinates to continue working without being disturbed by such news
   D. *unwise*, because the work of your subordinates will gradually slow down

8. In making plans for the operation of your unit, you are MOST likely to see these plans carried out successfully if you
   A. allow your staff to participate in developing these plans
   B. do not spend any time on the minor details of these plans
   C. base these plans on the past experiences of others
   D. allow these plans to interact with outside activities in other units

9. As a supervisor in charge of the total operation of a food supply warehouse, you find vandalism to be a potentially serious problem. On occasion, trespassers have gained entrance into the facility by climbing over an unprotected 8-foot fence surrounding the warehouse whose dimensions measure 100 feet by 100 feet.
Assuming that all of the following would be equally effective ways in preventing these breaches in security in the situation described above, which one would be LEAST costly?
    A. Using two trained guard dogs to roam freely throughout the facility at night
    B. Hiring a security guard to patrol the facility after working hours
    C. Installing tape razor wire on top of the fence surrounding the facility
    D. Installing an electronic burglar alarm system requiring the installation of a new fence

10. The area for which you have program responsibility has undergone recent changes. Your staff is now required to perform many new tasks, and morale is low.
The LEAST effective way for you to improve long-term staff morale would be to
    A. develop support groups to discuss problems
    B. involve staff in job development
    C. maintain a comfortable social environment within the group
    D. adequately plan and give assignments in a timely manner

11. As a supervisor in a large office, one of your subordinate supervisors stops you in the middle of the office and complains loudly that he is being treated unfairly. The rest of the staff ceases work and listens to the complaint.
The MOST appropriate action for you to take in this situation is to
    A. ignore this unprofessional behavior and continue on your way
    B. tell the supervisor that his behavior is unprofessional and he should learn how to conduct himself
    C. explain to the supervisor why you believe he is not being treated unfairly
    D. ask the supervisor to come to your office at a specific time to discuss the matter

12. You are told that one of your subordinates is distributing literature which attempts to recruit individuals to join a particular organization. Several workers complain that their rights are being violated.
Of the following, the BEST action for you to take FIRST is to
    A. ignore the situation because no harm is being done
    B. discuss the matter further with your supervisor
    C. ask the worker to stop distributing the literature
    D. tell the workers that they do not have to read the material

13. You have been assigned to develop a short training course for a recently issued procedure.
In designing this course, which of the following statements is the LEAST important for you to consider?

A. The learning experience must be interesting and meaningful in terms of the staff member's job.
B. The method of teaching must be strictly followed in order to develop successful learning experiences.
C. The course content should incorporate the rules and regulations of the agency.
D. The procedure should be consistent with the agency's objectives.

14. As a supervisor, there are several newly-promoted employees under your supervision. Each of these employees is subject to a probationary period PRIMARILY to
    A. assess the employee's performance to see if the employee should be retained or removed from the position
    B. give the employee the option to return to his former employment if the employee is unhappy in the new position
    C. give the employee an opportunity to learn the duties and responsibilities of the position
    D. judge the employee's potential for upward mobility in the future

14._____

15. An employee under your supervision rushes into your office to tell you he has just received a telephone bomb threat.
    As the administrative supervisor, the FIRST thing you should do is
    A. evacuate staff from the floor
    B. call the police and building security
    C. advise your administrator
    D. do a preliminary search

15._____

16. After reviewing the Absence Control form for a unit under your supervision, you find that one of your staff members has a fifth undocumented sick leave within a six-month period.
    In this situation, the FIRST action you should take is to
    A. discuss the seriousness of the matter with the staff member when he returns to work and fully document the details of the discussion
    B. review the case with the location director and warn the staff member that future use of sick leave will be punished
    C. submit the proper disciplinary forms to ensure that the staff member is penalized for excessive absences
    D. request that the timekeeper put the staff member on doctor's note restriction

16._____

17. A subordinate supervisor recently assigned to your office begins his first conference with you by saying that he has learned something that another supervisor is doing that you should know about.
    After hearing this statement, of the following, the BEST approach for you to take is to
    A. explain to the supervisor that the conference is to discuss his work and not that of his co-workers
    B. tell the supervisor that you do not encourage a spy system among the staff you supervise

17._____

C. tell the supervisor that you will listen to his report only if the other supervisor is present
D. allow the supervisor to continue talking until you have enough information to make a decision on how best to respond

18. Assume that you are a supervisor recently assigned to a new unit. You notice that, for the past few days, one of the employees in your unit whose work is about average has been stopping work at about four o'clock and has been spending the rest of the afternoon relaxing at his desk.
The BEST of the following actions for you to take in this situation is to
   A. assign more work to this employee since it is apparent that he does not have enough work to keep him busy
   B. observe the employee's conduct more closely for about ten days before taking any more positive action
   C. discuss the matter with the employee, pointing out to him how he can use the extra hour daily to raise the level of his job performance
   D. question the previous supervisor in charge of the unit in order to determine whether he had sanctioned such conduct when he supervised that unit

18.____

19. A new supervisor was assigned to your program four months ago. Although he tries hard, he has been unable to meet certain standards because he still has a lot to learn. As his supervisor, you are required to submit performance evaluations within a few days.
How would you rate this employee on the tasks where he fails to meet standards because of lack of experience?
   A. Satisfactory   B. Conditional
   C. Unsatisfactory   D. Unratable

19.____

20. You find that there is an important procedural error in a memo which you distributed to your staff several days ago.
The BEST approach for you to take at this time is to
   A. send a corrected memo to the staff, indicating what prior error was made
   B. send a corrected memo to the staff without mentioning the prior error
   C. tell the staff about the error at the next monthly staff meeting
   D. place the corrected memo on the office bulletin board

20.____

21. Your superior asks you, a supervisor, about the status of the response to a letter from a public official concerning a client's case. When you ask the subordinate who was assigned to prepare the response to give you the letter, the subordinate denies that it was given to him. You are certain that the subordinate has the letter, but is withholding it because the response has not yet been prepared.
Of the following, in order to secure the letter from the subordinate, you should FIRST
   A. accuse the subordinate of lying and demand that the letter be given to you immediately
   B. say that you would consider it a personal favor if the subordinate would find the letter

21.____

C. continue to question the subordinate until he admits to having been given the letter
D. offer a face-saving solution, such as asking the subordinate to look again for the letter

22. As a supervisor, you have been assigned to write a few paragraphs to be included in the agency's annual report, describing a public service agency department this year as compared to last year.
Which of the following elements basic to the agency is LEAST likely to have changed since last year?
   A. Mission   B. Structure   C. Technology   D. Personnel

23. As a supervisor, you have been informed that a grievance has been filed against you, accusing you of assigning a subordinate to out-of-title tasks.
Of the following, the BEST approach for you to take is to
   A. waive the grievance so that it will proceed to a Step II hearing
   B. immediately change the subordinate's assignment to avoid future problems
   C. respond to the grievance, giving appropriate reasons for the assignment
   D. review the job description to ensure that the subordinate's tasks are not out-of-title

24. Which of the following is NOT a correct statement about agency group training programs in a public service agency?
   A. Training sessions continue for an indefinite period of time.
   B. Group training sessions are planned for designated personnel.
   C. Training groups are organized formally through administrative planning.
   D. Group training is task-centered and aimed toward accomplishing specific educational goals.

25. As a supervisor, you have submitted a memo to your superior requesting a conference to discuss the performance of a manager under your supervision. The memo states that the manager has a good working relationship with her staff; however, she tends to interpret agency policy too liberally and shows poor administrative skills by missing some deadlines and not keeping proper controls.
Which of the following steps should NOT be taken in order to prepare for this conference with your superior?
   A. Collect and review all your notes regarding the manager's prior performance.
   B. Outline your agenda so that you will have sufficient time to discuss the situation.
   C. Tell the manager that you will be discussing her performance with your superior.
   D. Clearly define objectives which will focus on improving the manager's performance.

KEY (CORRECT ANSWERS)

1.	B	11.	D
2.	A	12.	C
3.	B	13.	B
4.	B	14.	A
5.	D	15.	B
6.	D	16.	A
7.	B	17.	D
8.	A	18.	C
9.	C	19.	B
10.	C	20.	A

21.	D
22.	A
23.	C
24.	A
25.	C

EXAMINATION SECTION
TEST 1

DIRECTIONS: Each question or incomplete statement is followed by several suggested answers or completions. Select the one that BEST answers the question or completes the statement. *PRINT THE LETTER OF THE CORRECT ANSWER IN THE SPACE AT THE RIGHT.*

1. Which of the following is the MOST likely action a supervisor should take to help establish an effective working relationship with his departmental superiors?
    A. Delay the implementation of new procedures received from superiors in order to evaluate their appropriateness.
    B. Skip the chain of command whenever he feels that it is to his advantage
    C. Keep supervisors informed of problems in his area and the steps taken to correct them
    D. Don't take up superiors' time by discussing anticipated problems but wait until the difficulties occur

   1.____

2. Of the following, the action a supervisor could take which would generally be MOST conducive to the establishment of an effective working relationship with employees includes
    A. maintaining impersonal relationships to prevent development of biased actions
    B. treating all employees equally without adjusting for individual differences
    C. continuous observation of employees on the job with insistence on constant improvement
    D. careful planning and scheduling of work for your employees

   2.____

3. Which of the following procedures is the l FAST likely to establish effective working relationships between employees and supervisors?
    A. Encouraging two-way communication with employees
    B. Periodic discussion with employees regarding their job performance
    C. Ignoring employees' gripes concerning job difficulties
    D. Avoiding personal prejudices in dealing with employees

   3.____

4. Criticism can be used as a tool to point out the weak areas of a subordinate's work performance.
   Of the following, the BEST action for a supervisor to take so that his criticism will be accepted is to
    A. focus his criticism on the act instead of on the person
    B. exaggerate the errors in order to motivate the employee to do better
    C. pass judgment quickly and privately without investigating the circumstances of the error
    D. generalize the criticism and not specifically point out the errors in performance

   4.____

5. In trying to improve the motivation of his subordinates, a supervisor can achieve the BEST results by taking action based upon the assumption that most employees
   A. have an inherent dislike of work
   B. wish to be closely directed
   C. are more interested in security than in assuming responsibility
   D. will exercise self-direction without coercion

6. When there are conflicts or tensions between top management and lower-level employees in any department, the supervisor should FIRST attempt to
   A. represent and enforce the management point of view
   B. act as the representative of the workers to get their ideas across to management
   C. serve as a two-way spokesman, trying to interpret each side to the other
   D. remain neutral, but keep informed of changes in the situation

7. A probationary period for new employees is usually provided in many agencies. The MAJOR purpose of such a period is usually to
   A. allow a determination of employee's suitability for the position
   B. obtain evidence as to employee's ability to perform in a higher position
   C. conform to requirements that ethnic hiring goals be met for all positions
   D. train the new employee in the duties of the position

8. An effective program of orientation for new employees usually includes all of the following EXCEPT
   A. having the supervisor introduce the new employee to his job, outlining his responsibilities and how to carry them out
   B. permitting the new worker to tour the facility or department so he can observe all parts of it in action
   C. scheduling meetings for new employees, at which the job requirements are explained to them and they are given personnel manuals
   D. testing the new worker on his skills and sending him to a centralized in-service workshop

9. In-service training is an important responsibility of many supervisors. The MAJOR reason for such training is to
   A. avoid future grievance procedures because employees might say they were not prepared to carry out their jobs
   B. maximize the effectiveness of the department by helping each employee perform at his full potential
   C. satisfy inspection teams from central headquarters of the department
   D. help prevent disagreements with members of the community

10. There are many forms of useful in-service training. Of the following, the training method which is NOT an appropriate technique for leadership development is to
    A. provide special workshops or clinics in activity skills
    B. conduct institutes to familiarize new workers with the program of the department and with their roles

C. schedule team meetings for problem-solving, including both supervisors and leaders
D. have the leader rate himself on an evaluation form periodically

11. Of the following techniques of evaluating work training programs, the one that is BEST is to
    A. pass out a carefully designed questionnaire to the trainees at the completion of the program
    B. test the knowledge that trainees have both at the beginning of training and at its completion
    C. interview the trainees at the completion of the program
    D. evaluate performance before and after training for both a control group and an experimental group

11.____

12. Assume that a new supervisor is having difficulty making his instructions to subordinates clearly understood.
    The one of the following which is the FIRST step he should take in dealing with this problem is to
    A. set up a training workshop in communication skills
    B. determine the extent and nature of the communications gap
    C. repeat both verbal and written instructions several times
    D. simplify his written and spoken vocabulary

12.____

13. A director has not properly carried out the orders of his assistant supervisor on several occasions to the point where he has been successively warned, reprimanded, and severely reprimanded.
    When the director once again does not carry out orders, the PROPER action for the assistant supervisor to take is to
    A. bring the director up on charges of failing to perform his duties properly
    B. have a serious discussion with the director, explaining the need for the orders and the necessity for carrying them out
    C. recommend that the director be transferred to another district
    D. severely reprimand the director again, making clear that no further deviation will be countenanced

13.____

14. A supervisor with several subordinates becomes aware that two of these subordinates are neither friendly nor congenial.
    In making assignments, it would be BEST for the supervisor to
    A. disregard the situation
    B. disregard the situation in making a choice of assignment but emphasize the need for teamwork
    C. investigate the situation to find out who is at fault and give that individual the less desirable assignments until such time as he corrects his attitude
    D. place the unfriendly subordinates in positions where they have as little contact with one another as possible

14.____

15. A DESIRABLE characteristic of a good supervisor is that he should   15.____
    A. identify himself with his subordinates rather than with higher management
    B. inform subordinates of forthcoming changes in policies and programs only when they directly affect the subordinates' activities
    C. make advancement of the subordinates contingent on personal loyalty to the supervisor
    D. make promises to subordinates only when sure of the ability to keep them

16. The supervisor who is MOST likely to be successful is the one who   16.____
    A. refrains from exercising the special privileges of his position
    B. maintains a formal attitude toward his subordinates
    C. maintains an informal attitude toward his subordinates
    D. represents the desires of his subordinate to his superiors

17. Application of sound principles of human relations by a supervisor may be   17.____
    expected to _____ the need for formal discipline.
    A. decrease   B. have no effect on
    C. increase   D. obviate

18. The MOST important generally approved way to maintain or develop high   18.____
    morale in one's subordinates is to
    A. give warnings and reprimands in a jocular way
    B. excuse from staff conferences those employees who are busy
    C. keep them informed of new developments and policies of higher management
    D. refrain from criticizing their faults directly

19. In training subordinates, an IMPORTANT principle for the supervisor to   19.____
    recognize is that
    A. a particular method of instruction will be of substantially equal value for all employees in a given title
    B. it is difficult to train people over 50 years of age because they have little capacity for learning
    C. persons undergoing the same course of training will learn at different rates of speed
    D. training can seldom achieve its purpose unless individual instruction is the chief method used

20. Over an extended period of time, a subordinate is MOST likely to become and   20.____
    remain most productive if the supervisor
    A. accords praise to the subordinate whenever his work is satisfactory, withholding criticism except in the case of very inferior work
    B. avoids both praise and criticism except for outstandingly good or bad work performed by the subordinate
    C. informs the subordinate of his shortcomings, as viewed by management, while according praise only when highly deserved
    D. keeps the subordinate informed of the degree of satisfaction with which his performance of the job is viewed by management.

KEY (CORRECT ANSWERS)

1.	C	11.	D
2.	D	12.	B
3.	C	13.	A
4.	A	14.	D
5.	D	15.	D
6.	C	16.	D
7.	A	17.	A
8.	D	18.	C
9.	B	19.	C
10.	D	20.	D

TEST 2

DIRECTIONS: Each question or incomplete statement is followed by several suggested answers or completions. Select the one that BEST answers the question or completes the statement. *PRINT THE LETTER OF THE CORRECT ANSWER IN THE SPACE AT THE RIGHT.*

1. A supervisor has just been told by a subordinate, Mr. Jones, that another employee, Mr. Smith, deliberately disobeyed an important rule of the department by taking home some confidential departmental material.
   Of the following courses of action, it would be MOST advisable for the supervisor FIRST to
   A. discuss the matter privately with both Mr. Jones and Mrs. Smith at the same time
   B. call a meeting of the entire staff and discuss the matter generally without mentioning any employee by name
   C. arrange to supervise Mr. Smith's activities more closely
   D. discuss the matter privately with Mr. Smith

   1.____

2. The one of the following actions which would be MOST efficient and economical for a supervisor to take to minimize the effect of periodical fluctuations in the workload of his unit is to
   A. increase his permanent staff until it is large enough to handle the work of the busy loads
   B. request the purchase of time- and labor-saving equipment to be used primarily during the busy loads
   C. lower, temporarily, the standards for quality of work performance during peak loads
   D. schedule for the slow periods work that is not essential to perform during the busy periods

   2.____

3. Discipline of employees is usually a supervisor's responsibility. There may be several useful forms of disciplinary action.
   Of the following, the form that is LEAST appropriate is the
   A. written reprimand or warning
   B. involuntary transfer to another work setting
   C. demotion or suspension
   D. assignment of added hours of work each week

   3.____

4. Of the following, the MOST effective means of dealing with employee disciplinary problems is to
   A. give personality tests to individuals to identify their psychological problems
   B. distribute and discuss a policy manual containing exact rules governing employee behavior
   C. establish a single, clear penalty to be imposed for all wrongdoing irrespective of degree
   D. have supervisors get to know employees well through social mingling

   4.____

5. A recently developed technique for appraising work performance is to have the supervisor record on a continual basis all significant incidents in each subordinate's behavior that indicate unsuccessful action and those that indicate poor behavior.
Of the following, a MAJOR disadvantage of this method of performance appraisal is that it
   A. often leads to overly close supervision
   B. results in competition among those subordinates being evaluated
   C. tends to result in superficial judgments
   D. lacks objectivity for evaluating performance

6. Assume that you are a supervisor and have observed the performance of an employee during a period of time. You have concluded that his performance needs improvement.
In order to improve his performance, it would, therefore, be BEST for you to
   A. note your findings in the employee's personnel folder so that his behavior is a matter of record
   B. report the findings to the personnel officer so he can take prompt action
   C. schedule a problem-solving conference with the employee
   D. recommend his transfer to simpler duties

7. When an employee's absences or latenesses seem to be nearing excessiveness, the supervisor should speak with him to find out what the problem is.
Of the following, if such a discussion produces no reasonable explanation, the discussion usually BEST serves to
   A. affirm clearly the supervisor's adherence to proper policy
   B. alert other employees that such behavior is unacceptable
   C. demonstrate that the supervisor truly represents higher management
   D. notify the employee that his behavior is being observed and evaluated

8. Assume that an employee willfully and recklessly violates an important agency regulation. The nature of the violation is of such magnitude that it demands immediate action, but the facts of the case are not entirely clear. Further, assume that the supervisor is free to make any of the following recommendations.
The MOST appropriate action for the supervisor to take is to recommend that the employee be
   A. discharged   B. suspended
   C. forced to resign   D. transferred

9. Although employees' titles may be identical, each position in that title may be considerably different.
Of the following, a supervisor should carefully assign each employee to a specific position based PRIMARILY on the employee's
   A. capability   B. experience   C. education   D. seniority

10. The one of the following situations where it is MOST appropriate to transfer an employee to a similar assignment is one in which the employee
    A. lacks motivation and interest
    B. experiences a personality conflict with his supervisor
    C. is negligent in the performance of his duties
    D. lacks capacity or ability to perform assigned tasks

10.____

11. The one of the following which is LEAST likely to be affected by improvements in the morale of personnel is employee
    A. skill
    B. absenteeism
    C. turnover
    D. job satisfaction

11.____

12. The one of the following situations in which it is LEAST appropriate for a supervisor to delegate authority to subordinates is where the supervisor
    A. lacks confidence in his own abilities to perform certain work
    B. is overburdened and cannot handle all his responsibilities
    C. refers all disciplinary problems to his subordinate
    D. has to deal with an emergency or crisis

12.____

13. Assume that it has come to your attention that two of your subordinates have shouted at each other and have almost engaged in a fist fight. Luckily, they were separated by some of the other employees.
    Of the following, your BEST immediate course of action would generally be to
    A. reprimand the senior of the two subordinates since he should have known better
    B. hear the story from both employees and any witnesses and then take needed disciplinary action
    C. ignore the matter since nobody was physically hurt
    D. immediately suspend and fine both employees pending a departmental hearing

13.____

14. You have been delegating some of your authority to one of your subordinates because of his leadership potential.
    Which of the following actions is LEAST conducive to the growth and development of this individual for a supervisory position?
    A. Use praise only when it will be effective
    B. Give very detailed instructions and supervise the employee closely to be sure that the instructions ae followed precisely
    C. Let the subordinate proceed with his planned course of action even if mistakes, within a permissible range, are made
    D. Intervene on behalf of the subordinate whenever an assignment becomes difficult for him

14.____

15. A rumor has been spreading in your department concerning the possibility of layoffs due to decreased revenues.
    As a supervisor, you should GENERALLY
    A. deny the rumor, whether it is true or false, in order to keep morale from declining

15.____

B. inform the men to the best of your knowledge about this situation and keep them advised of any new information
C. tell the men to forget about the rumor and concentrate on increasing their productivity
D. ignore the rumor since it is not authorized information

16. Within an organization, every supervisor should know to whom he reports and who reports to him.
The one of the following which is achieved by use of such structured relationships is
    A. unity of command
    B. confidentiality
    C. esprit de corps
    D. promotion opportunities

16.____

17. Almost every afternoon, one of your employees comes back from his break ten minutes late without giving you any explanation.
Which of the following actions should you take FIRST in this situation?
    A. Assign the employee to a different type of work and observe whether his behavior changes
    B. Give the employee extra work to do so that he will have to return on time
    C. Ask the employee for an explanation for his lateness
    D. Tell the employee he is jeopardizing the break for everyone

17.____

18. When giving instructions to your employees in a group, which one of the following should you make certain to do?
    A. Speak in a casual, off-hand manner
    B. Assume that your employees fully understand the instructions
    C. Write out your instructions beforehand and read them to the employees
    D. Tell exactly who is to do what

18.____

19. A fist fight develops between two men under your supervision.
The MOST advisable course of action for you to take FIRST is to
    A. call the police
    B. have the other workers pull them apart
    C. order them to stop
    D. step between the two men

19.____

20. You have assigned some difficult and unusual work to one of your most experienced and competent subordinates.
If you notice that he is doing the work incorrectly, you should
    A. assign the work to another employee
    B. reprimand him in private
    C. show him immediately how the work should be done
    D. wait until the job is completed and then correct his errors

20.____

KEY (CORRECT ANSWERS)

1.	D	11.	A
2.	D	12.	C
3.	D	13.	B
4.	B	14.	B
5.	A	15.	B
6.	C	16.	A
7.	D	17.	C
8.	B	18.	D
9.	A	19.	C
10.	B	20.	C

EXAMINATION SECTION
TEST 1

DIRECTIONS: Each question or incomplete statement is followed by several suggested answers or completions. Select the one that BEST answers the question or completes the statement. *PRINT THE LETTER OF THE CORRECT ANSWER IN THE SPACE AT THE RIGHT.*

1. Of the following, the one MOST important quality required of a good supervisor is 1.____
   A. ambition   B. leadership   C. friendliness   D. popularity

2. It is often said that a supervisor can delegate authority but never responsibility. This means MOST NEARLY that 2.____
   A. a supervisor must do his own work if he expects it to be done properly
   B. a supervisor can assign someone else to do his work, but in the last analysis, the supervisor himself must take the blame for any actions followed
   C. authority and responsibility are two separate things that cannot be borne by the same person
   D. it is better for a supervisor never to delegate his authority

3. One of your men who is a habitual complainer asks you to grant him a minor privilege. 3.____
   Before granting or denying such a request, you should consider
   A. the merits of the case
   B. that it is good for group morale to grant a request of this nature
   C. the man's seniority
   D. that to deny such a request will lower your standing with the men

4. A supervisory practice on the part of a foreman which is MOST likely to lead to confusion and inefficiency is for him to 4.____
   A. give orders verbally directly to the man assigned to the job
   B. issue orders only in writing
   C. follow up his orders after issuing them
   D. relay his orders to the men through co-workers

5. It would be POOR supervision on a foreman's part if he 5.____
   A. asked an experienced maintainer for his opinion on the method of doing a special job
   B. make it a policy to avoid criticizing a man in front of his co-workers
   C. consulted his assistant supervisor on unusual problems
   D. allowed a cooling-off period of several days before giving one of his men a deserved reprimand

6. Of the following behavior characteristics of a supervisor, the one that is MOST likely to lower the morale of the men he supervises is
   A. diligence
   B. favoritism
   C. punctuality
   D. thoroughness

7. Of the following, the BEST method of getting an employee who is not working up to his capacity to produce more work is to
   A. have another employee criticize his production
   B. privately criticize his production but encourage him to produce more
   C. criticize his production before his associates
   D. criticize his production and threaten to fire him

8. Of the following, the BEST thing for a supervisor to do when a subordinate has done a very good job is to
   A. tell him to take it easy
   B. praise his work
   C. reduce his workload
   D. say nothing because he may become conceited

9. Your orders to your crew are MOST likely to be followed if you
   A. explain the reasons for these orders
   B. warn that all violators will be punished
   C. promise easy assignments to those who follow these orders best
   D. say that they are for the good of the department

10. In order to be a good supervisor, you should
    A. impress upon your men that you demand perfection in their work at all times
    B. avoid being blamed for your crew's mistakes
    C. impress your superior with your ability
    D. see to it that your men get what they are entitled to

11. In giving instructions to a crew, you should
    A. speak in as loud a tone as possible
    B. speak in a coaxing, persuasive manner
    C. speak quietly, clearly, and courteously
    D. always use the word *please* when giving instructions

12. Of the following factors, the one which is LEAST important in evaluating an employee and his work is his
    A. dependability
    B. quantity of work done
    C. quality of work done
    D. education and training

13. When a District Superintendent first assumes his command, it is LEAST important for him at the beginning to observe
    A. how his equipment is designed and its adaptability
    B. how to reorganize the district for greater efficiency
    C. the capabilities of the men in the district
    D. the methods of operation being employed

14. When making an inspection of one of the buildings under your supervision, the BEST procedure to follow in making a record of the inspection is to
    A. return immediately to the office and write a report from memory
    B. write down all the important facts during or as soon as you complete the inspection
    C. fix in your mind all important facts so that you can repeat them from memory if necessary
    D. fix in your mind all important facts so that you can make out your report at the end of the day

15. Assume that your superior has directed you to make certain changes in your established procedure. After using this modified procedure on several occasions, you find that the original procedure was distinctly superior and you wish to return to it.
    You should
    A. let your superior find this out for himself
    B. simply change back to the original procedure
    C. compile definite data and information to prove your case to your superior
    D. persuade one of the more experienced workers to take this matter up with your superior

16. An inspector visited a large building under construction. He inspected the soil lines at 9 A.M., water lines at 10 A.M., fixtures at 11 A.M., and did his office work in the afternoon. He followed the same pattern daily for weeks.
    This procedure was
    A. *good*, because it was methodical and he did not miss anything
    B. *good*, because it gave equal time to all phases of the plumbing
    C. *bad*, because not enough time was devoted to fixtures
    D. *bad*, because the tradesmen knew when the inspection would occur

17. Assume that one of the foremen in a training course, which you are conducting, proposes a poor solution for a maintenance problem.
    Of the following, the BEST course of action for you to take is to
    A. accept the solution tentatively and correct it during the next class meeting
    B. point out all the defects of this proposed solution and wait until somebody thinks of a better solution
    C. try to get the class to reject this proposed solution and develop a better solution
    D. let the matter pass since somebody will present a better solution as the class work proceeds

18. As a supervisor, you should be seeking ways to improve the efficiency of shop operations by means such as changing established work procedures.
    The following are offered as possible actions that you should consider in changing established work procedures:
    I. Make changes only when your foremen agree to them
    II. Discuss changes with your supervisor before putting them into practice

III. Standardize any operation which is performed on a continuing basis
IV. Make changes quickly and quietly in order to avoid dissent
V. Secure expert guidance before instituting unfamiliar procedures
Of the following suggested answers, the one that describes the actions to be taken to change established work procedures is
   A. I, IV, V   B. II, III, V   C. III, IV, V   D. All of the above

19. A supervisor determined that a foreman, without informing his superior, delegated responsibility for checking time cards to a member of his gang. The supervisor then called the foreman into his office where he reprimanded the foreman.
This action of the supervisor in reprimanding the foreman was
   A. *proper*, because the checking of time cards is the foreman's responsibility and should not be delegated
   B. *proper*, because the foreman did not ask the supervisor for permission to delegate responsibility
   C. *improper*, because the foreman may no longer take the initiative in solving future problems
   D. *improper*, because the supervisor is interfering in a function which is not his responsibility

20. A capable supervisor should check all operations under his control.
Of the following, the LEAST important reason for doing this is to make sure that
   A. operations are being performed as scheduled
   B. he personally observes all operations at all times
   C. all the operations are still needed
   D. his manpower is being utilized efficiently

21. A supervisor makes it a practice to apply fair and firm discipline in all cases of rule infractions, including those of a minor nature.
This practice should PRIMARILY be considered
   A. *bad*, since applying discipline for minor violations is a waste of time
   B. *good*, because not applying discipline for minor infractions can lead to a more serious erosion of discipline
   C. *bad*, because employees do not like to be disciplined for minor violations of the rules
   D. *good*, because violating any rule can cause a dangerous situation to occur

22. A maintainer would PROPERLY consider it poor supervisory practice for a foreman to consult with him on
   A. which of several repair jobs should be scheduled first
   B. how to cope with personal problems at home
   C. whether the neatness of his headquarters can be improved
   D. how to express a suggestion which the maintainer plans to submit formally

23. Assume that you have determined that the work of one of your foremen and the men he supervises is consistently behind schedule. When you discuss this situation with the foreman, he tells you that his men are poor workers and then complains that he must spend all of his time checking on their work.
The following actions are offered for your consideration as possible ways of solving the problem of poor performance of the foreman and his men:
   I. Review the work standards with the foreman and determine whether they are realistic.
   II. Tell the foreman that you will recommend him for the foreman's training course for retraining.
   III. Ask the foreman for the names of the maintainers and then replace them as soon as possible.
   IV. Tell the foreman that you expect him to meet a satisfactory level of performance.
   V. Tell the foreman to insist that his men work overtime to catch up to the schedule.
   VI. Tell the foreman to review the type and amount of training he has given the maintainers.
   VII. Tell the foreman that he will be out of a job if he does not produce on schedule.
   VIII. Avoid all criticism of the foreman and his methods.
Which of the following suggested answers CORRECTLY lists the proper actions to be taken to solve the problem of poor performance of the foreman and his men?
   A. I, II, IV, VI   B. I, III, V, VII   C. II, III, VI, VIII   D. IV, V, VI, VIII

24. When a conference or a group discussion is tending to turn into a *bull session* without constructive purpose, the BEST action to take is to
   A. reprimand the leader of the bull session
   B. redirect the discussion to the business at hand
   C. dismiss the meeting and reschedule it for another day
   D. allow the bull session to continue

25. Assume that you have been assigned responsibility for a program in which a high production rate is mandatory. From past experience, you know that your foremen do not perform equally well in the various types of jobs given to them. Which of the following methods should you use in selecting foremen for the specific types of work involved in the program?
   A. Leave the method of selecting foremen to your supervisor
   B. Assign each foreman to the work he does best
   C. Allow each foreman to choose his own job
   D. Assign each foreman to a job which will permit him to improve his own abilities

KEY (CORRECT ANSWERS)

1.	B	11.	C
2.	B	12.	D
3.	A	13.	B
4.	D	14.	B
5.	D	15.	C
6.	B	16.	D
7.	B	17.	C
8.	B	18.	B
9.	A	19.	A
10.	D	20.	B

21. B
22. A
23. A
24. B
25. B

TEST 2

DIRECTIONS: Each question or incomplete statement is followed by several suggested answers or completions. Select the one that BEST answers the question or completes the statement. *PRINT THE LETTER OF THE CORRECT ANSWER IN THE SPACE AT THE RIGHT.*

1. A foreman who is familiar with modern management principles should know that the one of the following requirements of an administrator which is LEAST important is his ability to
   A. coordinate work
   B. plan, organize, and direct the work under his control
   C. cooperate with others
   D. perform the duties of the employees under his jurisdiction

   1.____

2. When subordinates request his advice in solving problems encountered in their work, a certain chief occasionally answers the request by first asking the subordinate what he thinks should be done.
   This action by the chief is, on the whole,
   A. *desirable*, because it stimulates subordinates to give more thought to the solution of problems encountered
   B. *undesirable*, because it discourages subordinates from asking questions
   C. *desirable*, because it discourages subordinates from asking questions
   D. *undesirable*, because it undermines the confidence of subordinates in the ability of their supervisor

   2.____

3. Of the following factors that may be considered by a unit head in dealing with the tardy subordinate, the one which should be given LEAST consideration is the
   A. frequency with which the employee is tardy
   B. effect of the employee's tardiness upon the work of other employees
   C. willingness of the employee to work overtime when necessary
   D. cause of the employee's tardiness

   3.____

4. The MOST important requirement of a good inspectional report is that it should be
   A. properly addressed   B. lengthy
   C. clear and brief   D. spelled correctly

   4.____

5. Building superintendents frequently inquire about departmental inspectional procedures.
   Of the following, it is BEST to
   A. advise them to write to the department for an official reply
   B. refuse as the inspectional procedure is a restricted matter
   C. briefly explain the procedure to them
   D. avoid the inquiry by changing the subject

   5.____

6. Reprimanding a crew member before other workers is a
   A. *good* practice; the reprimand serves as a warning to the other workers
   B. *bad* practice; people usually resent criticism made in public
   C. *good* practice; the other workers will realize that the supervisor is fair
   D. *bad* practice; the other workers will take sides in the dispute

7. Of the following actions, the one which is LEAST likely to promote good work is for the group leader to
   A. praise workers for doing a good job
   B. call attention to the opportunities for promotion for better workers
   C. threaten to recommend discharge of workers who are below standard
   D. put into practice any good suggestion made by crew members

8. A supervisor notices that a member of his crew has skipped a routine step in his job.
   Of the following, the BEST action for the supervisor to take is to
   A. promptly question the worker about the incident
   B. immediately assign another man to complete the job
   C. bring up the incident the next time the worker asks for a favor
   D. say nothing about the incident but watch the worker carefully in the future

9. Assume you have been told to show a new worker how to operate a piece of equipment.
   Your FIRST step should be to
   A. ask the worker if he has any questions about the equipment
   B. permit the worker to operate the equipment himself while you carefully watch to prevent damage
   C. demonstrate the operation of the equipment for the worker
   D. have the worker read an instruction booklet on the maintenance of the equipment

10. Whenever a new man was assigned to his crew, the supervisor would introduce him to all other crew members, take him on a tour of the plant, tell him about bus schedules and places to eat.
    This practice is
    A. *good*; the new man is made to feel welcome
    B. *bad*; supervisors should not interfere in personal matters
    C. *good*; the new man knows that he can bring his personal problems to the supervisor
    D. *bad*; work time should not be spent on personal matters

11. The MOST important factor in successful leadership is the ability to
    A. obtain instant obedience to all orders
    B. establish friendly personal relations with crew members
    C. avoid disciplining crew members
    D. make crew members want to do what should be done

12. Explaining the reasons for departmental procedure to workers tends to
    A. waste time which should be used for productive purposes
    B. increase their interest in their work
    C. make them more critical of departmental procedures
    D. confuse them

13. If you want a job done well do it yourself.
    For a supervisor to follow this advice would be
    A. *good*; a supervisor is responsible for the work of his crew
    B. *bad*; a supervisor should train his men, not do their work
    C. *good*; a supervisor should be skilled in all jobs assigned to his crew
    D. *bad*; a supervisor loses respect when he works with his hands

14. When a supervisor discovers a mistake in one of the jobs for which his crew is responsible, it is MOST important for him to find out
    A. whether anybody else knows about the mistake
    B. who was to blame for the mistake
    C. how to prevent similar mistakes in the future
    D. whether similar mistakes occurred in the past

15. A supervisor who has to explain a new procedure to his crew should realize that questions from the crew USUALLY show that they
    A. are opposed to the new practice
    B. are completely confused by the explanation
    C. need more training in the new procedure
    D. are interested in the explanation

16. A good way for a supervisor to retain the confidence of his or her employees is to
    A. say as little as possible
    B. check work frequently
    C. make no promises unless they will be fulfilled
    D. never hesitate in giving an answer to any question

17. Good supervision is ESSENTIALLY a matter of
    A. patience in supervising workers   B. care in selecting workers
    C. skill in human relations   D. fairness in disciplining workers

18. It is MOST important for an employee who has been assigned a monotonous task to
    A. perform this task before doing other work
    B. ask another employee to help
    C. perform this task only after all other work has been completed
    D. take measures to prevent mistakes in performing the task

19. One of your employees has violated a minor agency regulation.
The FIRST thing you should do is
    A. warn the employee that you will have to take disciplinary action if it should happen again
    B. ask the employee to explain his or her actions
    C. inform your supervisor and wait for advice
    D. write a memo describing the incident and place it in the employee's personnel file

20. One of your employees tells you that he feels you give him much more work than the other employees, and he is having trouble meeting your deadlines.
You should
    A. ask if he has been under a lot of non-work related stress lately
    B. review his recent assignments to determine if he is correct
    C. explain that this is a busy time, but you are dividing the work equally
    D. tell him that he is the most competent employee and that is why he receives more work

21. A supervisor assigns one of his crew to complete a portion of a job. A short time later, the supervisor notices that the portion has not been completed.
Of the following, the BEST way for the supervisor to handle this is to
    A. ask the crew member why he has not completed the assignment
    B. reprimand the crew member for not obeying orders
    C. assign another crew member to complete the assignment
    D. complete the assignment himself

22. Supposes that a member of your crew complains that you are *playing favorites* in assigning work.
Of the following, the BEST method of handling the complaint is to
    A. deny it and refuse to discuss the matter with the worker
    B. take the opportunity to tell the worker what is wrong with his work
    C. ask the worker for examples to prove his point and try to clear up any misunderstanding
    D. promise to be more careful in making assignments in the future

23. A member of your crew comes to you with a complaint. After discussing the matter with him, it is clear that you have convinced him that his complaint was not justified.
At this point, you should
    A. permit him to drop the matter
    B. make him admit his error
    C. pretend to see some justification in his complaint
    D. warn him against making unjustified complaints

24. Suppose that a supervisor has in his crew an older man who works rather slowly. In other respects, this man is a good worker; he is seldom absent, works carefully, never loafs, and is cooperative.

The BEST way for the supervisor to handle this worker is to
- A. try to get him to work faster and less carefully
- B. give him the most disagreeable job
- C. request that he be given special training
- D. permit him to work at his own speed

25. Suppose that a member of your crew comes to you with a suggestion he thinks will save time in doing a job. You realize immediately that it won't work. Under these circumstances, your BEST action would be to
    - A. thank the worker for the suggestion and forget about it
    - B. explain to the worker why you think it won't work
    - C. tell the worker to put the suggestion in writing
    - D. ask the other members of your crew to criticize the suggestion

25._____

KEY (CORRECT ANSWERS)

1.	D	11.	D
2.	A	12.	B
3.	C	13.	B
4.	C	14.	C
5.	C	15.	D
6.	B	16.	C
7.	C	17.	C
8.	A	18.	D
9.	C	19.	B
10.	A	20.	B

21. A
22. C
23. A
24. D
25. B

READING COMPREHENSION
UNDERSTANDING AND INTERPRETING WRITTEN MATERIAL

EXAMINATION SECTION
TEST 1

DIRECTIONS: Each question or incomplete statement is followed by several suggested answers or completions. Select the one that BEST answers the question or completes the statement. *PRINT THE LETTER OF THE CORRECT ANSWER IN THE SPACE AT THE RIGHT.*

Questions 1-4.

DIRECTIONS: Questions 1 through 4 refer to the following paragraph.

Hot hide glue is an excellent adhesive, but it is generally not used by the home handyman. You can buy hide glue in cake, flake, or ground forms. Soak the glue in lukewarm water overnight, following the manufacturer's instructions. Use glass ovenware or metal containers, double-boiler fashion, to keep it below 150° F. and apply hot. Heat only the quantity needed; frequent reheating weakens the glue. It sets fast, but requires tight clamping and matched joints for proper bonding.

1. According to the paragraph, the number of forms in which hide glue can be bought is   1.____

   A. 2   B. 3   C. 4   D. 5

2. According to the above paragraph, hide glue should   2.____

   A. be used only by the home handyman
   B. be boiled twice
   C. never be used by the home handyman
   D. be prepared according to manufacturer's instructions

3. According to the above paragraph, frequent reheating of hide glue   3.____

   A. makes it set fast   B. weakens it
   C. keeps it below 150° F   D. is desirable

4. The one of the following which is the MOST appropriate title for the above paragraph is   4.____

   A. TIPS FOR THE HOME HANDYMAN
   B. PREPARATION AND USE OF HIDE GLUE
   C. WHAT IS HIDE GLUE?
   D. REPAIR OF GLASS OVENWARE AND METAL CONTAINERS

Questions 5-9.

DIRECTIONS: Questions 5 through 9 are based on the paragraph below. Use only the information contained in this paragraph in answering these questions.

Common nails and brads are designated by the letter *d*, indicating *penny*; thus 8d = 8 penny. In order to determine the length required of a nail in pennies, the thickness of the board to be penetrated, for example, 25/32 of an inch, is multiplied by 8. Then, 11/2 is added to the result, which in this instance indicates an 8d nail: (25/32 x 8 = 61/4 + 11/2=73/4= 8).

To reverse the computation, when only the penny size is known, to determine the length in inches (up to 10d), the penny size is divided by 4 then 1/2 is added. For example, an 8d nail measures 2 1/2 inches because 8 ÷ 4 = 2 + 1/2=2 1/2.

5. The letter used to designate common nails and brads is

   A. a   B. b   C. c   D. d

6. To penetrate a board 15/16" thick, the length of nail required, in pennies, is

   A. 8   B. 9   C. 10   D. 11

7. The length of a 6 penny nail, in inches, is

   A. 2   B. 3   C. 4   D. 5

8. The word *penetrated,* as used in the above paragraph, means MOST NEARLY

   A. congealed   B. dulled
   C. hanged   D. pierced

9. The word *designated,* as used in the above paragraph, means MOST NEARLY

   A. considered   B. driven
   C. named   D. probed

Questions 10-17.

DIRECTIONS: Questions 10 through 17 are based on the paragraph below. Use only the information contained in this paragraph in answering these questions.

Lumber is measured according to a system known as board measure (bm). The unit is a board foot, which is equal in volume to a board 1 foot wide, 1 foot long, and 1 inch thick, or 144 cubic inches. To compute board measure, if the board is less than 1 inch thick, consider the fraction as a full inch. If it is thicker than 1 inch, however, figure the inches and fractions of an inch exactly. Thus, a 1/2 inch board is considered as 1 inch thick bm, but a 1 1/2 inch board as 1 1/2 inches. To compute board feet, multiply the length of the board, in feet, by the width, in feet, and multiply this product by the thickness in inches.

10. The unit of measuring lumber is a

   A. ampere   B. board foot
   C. milligram   D. pound per square inch

11. Lumber is measured according to a system known as

   A. board measure   B. cubic capacity
   C. linear feet   D. logarithms

12. A board foot is equal to

    A. 144 cubic inches
    B. 3 linear feet
    C. 4 by 8 feet
    D. 72 cubic inches

13. If a piece of lumber is 3/4" thick, in computing board measure, its thickness will be considered as

    A. 4"   B. 3/4"   C. 1"   D. 1 1/2"

14. If a piece of lumber is 1 3/4" thick, in computing board measure, its thickness will be considered as

    A. 1/2"   B. 1"   C. 1 1/2"   D. 1 3/4"

15. The number of board feet in a board 12 feet long by 18 inches wide by 1/2 inch thick is

    A. 9   B. 18   C. 108   D. 216

16. The number of board feet in a board 12 feet long by 18 inches wide by 1 3/4 inches thick is

    A. 18   B. 31.5   C. 216   D. 270

17. The word *compute*, as used in the above paragraph, means MOST NEARLY

    A. add   B. calculate   C. divide   D. subtract

Questions 18-24.

DIRECTIONS: Questions 18 through 24 are based on the paragraph below. Use only the information contained in this paragraph in answering these questions.

Screws can be purchased in lengths varying fro1/4" to 6". Lengths from 1/4" to 1" increase by 1/8" units; those from 1" to 3" by 1/4" units; and from 3" to 5" by 1/2" units. They come with flat, round, or oval heads, the flat head type being used for countersinking. Soaping the screw first will facilitate driving it in, especially when working with hardwood.

18. Of the following, the kind of head with which screws do NOT come is

    A. flat   B. round   C. oval   D. square

19. The one of the following lengths of screws which can be purchased is

    A. 1/8"   B. 3/16"   C. 5/16"   D. 3/8"

20. The one of the following lengths of screws which CANNOT be purchased is

    A. 1 1/8"   B. 1 1/2"   C. 1 1/2"   D. 13/4"

21. The one of the following lengths of screws which can be purchased is

    A. 3 3/4"   B. 4 1/2"   C. 4 2/4"   D. 4 3/4"

22. The type of screw used for countersinking is the one whose head is

    A. flat   B. round   C. oval   D. square

23. To facilitate driving a screw in, it should FIRST be   23._____

    A. countersunk   B. sanded
    C. soaped   D. varnished

24. The word *facilitate,* as used in the above paragraph, means MOST NEARLY to make   24._____

    A. angular   B. artificial   C. difficult   D. easy

Questions 25.

DIRECTIONS: Question 25 is based on the following statement.

Interior painting may be done at any time, provided that temperature can be kept above 50° F for ordinary paints and above 65° F for enamels and varnishes.

25. According to this statement, the temperature for enameling and varnishing should be   25._____

    A. above 50° F   B. between 50° F and 65° F
    C. below 65° F   D. above 65° F

KEY (CORRECT ANSWERS)

1. B	11. A
2. D	12. A
3. B	13. C
4. B	14. D
5. D	15. B
6. B	16. B
7. A	17. B
8. D	18. D
9. C	19. D
10. B	20. A

21. C
22. A
23. C
24. D
25. D

TEST 2

Questions 1-8.

DIRECTIONS: Each question or incomplete statement is followed by several suggested answers or completions. Select the one that BEST answers the question or completes the statement. *PRINT THE LETTER OF THE CORRECT ANSWER IN THE SPACE AT THE RIGHT.* Questions 1 through 8 are based on the paragraphs below. Use only the information contained in these paragraphs in answering these questions.

Glue may be either hot or cold. Hot glue, an animal product, is purchased in dry flakes or sheets which must be soaked in water, then heated in a glue pot which is similar to a double boiler. Its main advantage is that it sets quickly, in fact so quickly that one must work fast to complete the joint before the glue sets.

There are numerous kinds of cold glue. One of the best is casein glue, which is manufactured from skimmed milk. It comes as a powder, which must be freshly mixed with water for each job, as the mixture will lose its valuable adhesive properties if stored. Cold glue is just as strong as hot glue, and casein glue resists moisture more effectively, but it needs considerable time to set.

1. The MAIN advantage of hot glue is that it

   A. is easily prepared
   B. is inexpensive
   C. resists moisture more effectively than cold glue
   D. sets quickly

2. Hot glue is purchased as

   A. dry flakes or sheets   B. a liquid
   C. a powder   D. wet film

3. Casein glue

   A. does not need to be mixed with water before application
   B. is purchased as a powder dissolved in water
   C. must be freshly mixed with water for each job
   D. should be mixed with water before storing away

4. The strength of cold glue in relation to that of hot glue is

   A. less
   B. the same
   C. greater
   D. variable, depending on type of glue

5. The time in which hot glue sets in relation to the time in which cold glue sets is

   A. shorter
   B. the same
   C. longer
   D. variable, depending on type of glue

6. If casein glue is mixed with water before storing, its adhesive strength will   6.___

   A. be lost
   B. remain the same
   C. increase
   D. increase or diminish, depending on amount of water used

7. Casein glue in relation to hot glue resists moisture   7.___

   A. less effectively
   B. about the same
   C. more effectively
   D. in varying degrees, depending on type of glue

8. The word *adhesive,* as used in the above paragraph, means MOST NEARLY   8.___

   A. costly   B. economical
   C. glowing brightly D. sticking together

Questions 9-25.

DIRECTIONS: Each question consists of a statement. You are to indicate whether the statement is TRUE (T) or FALSE (F). *PRINT THE LETTER OF THE CORRECT ANSWER IN THE SPACE AT THE RIGHT.*

Questions 9-13.

DIRECTIONS: Questions 9 through 13, inclusive, are to be answered in accordance with the paragraph below.

Wood kept constantly dry or continuously submerged in water does not decay, regardless of species or the presence of sapwood. A large *proportion* of wood in use is kept so dry at all times that it lasts indefinitely. Moisture and temperature are the principal factors affecting the rate of decay. When exposed to conditions that favor decay, wood in warm humid areas of the United States deteriorates more rapidly than in cool or dry areas. High altitudes, as a rule, are less favorable to decay than are low altitudes because the *average* temperatures are lower and the growing season for fungi, which cause decay, are shorter.

9. A wooden beam is supporting a pier and is constantly under water. According to the above paragraph, the beam will have a high rate of decay.   9.___

10. According to the above paragraph, the cause of decay in wood is fungi.   10.___

11. According to the above paragraph, the LOWEST rate of decay in wood is found in climates that are warm and humid.   11.___

12. As used in the above paragraph, *proportion* means MOST NEARLY *percent*.   12.___

13. As used in the above paragraph, *average* means MOST NEARLY *lowest*.   13.___

Questions 14-18.

DIRECTIONS: Questions 14 through 18, inclusive, are to be answered in accordance with the paragraph below.

HOW WOOD IS SEASONED

There are two common methods of drying lumber after it has been sawed. These two methods are air seasoning and kiln drying. Some woods may be air dried *satisfactorily* while others must be put through the kiln drying process before the wood can be successfully used for furniture-making. Most soft, non-porous woods are more easily air-dried than the harder woods. In the air drying process, the lumber is stacked carefully in large piles in the open air. Thin strips are laid between each layer of boards to prevent them from *warping* and to allow the air to circulate between them.

14. According to the above paragraph, all wood can be dried by stacking the lumber in the open air.   14.____

15. According to the above paragraph, if the wood in non-porous, it is better to air dry it.   15.____

16. According to the above paragraph, drying of lumber is done after it is cut to size.   16.____

17. As used in the above paragraph, the word *satisfactorily* means *quickly*.   17.____

18. As used in the above paragraph, the word *warping* means *twisting*.   18.____

Questions 19-25.

DIRECTIONS: Questions 19 through 25, inclusive, are to be answered in accordance with the paragraph below.

CARE OF FURNITURE

Furniture, like floors, interior *trim,* and automobiles, requires frequent care to keep its finish in good condition. The finish of new furniture can be kept in good condition for many years if a coat of wax is *applied* to it regularly at least once each year. The coat of wax maintains the luster of the finish, protects the finishing coat from dampness, and aids in preventing the surface from being *marred* easily.

Excessive use of oil polishes should be avoided since they have a tendency to eventually produce a dull, lifeless surface and cause dust to collect on the finish.

If water has been allowed to remain on a finished surface for some time, it often causes the finish to turn white. The natural color of the finish may usually be restored by rubbing the spots lightly with a cloth moistened with alcohol, followed by the application of a small amount of sweet oil or linseed oil. Excessive moisture often collects on the furniture during the winter season as a result of improper ventilation and the use of open-flame gas stoves. This condition effects the joints and finish and causes the furniture to deteriorate rapidly.

A touch-up pencil may be obtained for the purpose of filling and removing deep scratches and other blemishes from a finished surface.

19. According to the above paragraph, one function of a coat of wax on furniture is to prevent penetration of moisture. 19.___

20. According to the above paragraph, water stains can be removed by FIRST applying a small amount of linseed oil. 20.___

21. According to the above paragraph, it is good practice to apply frequent coats of oil polish. 21.___

22. According to the above paragraph, one reason for the excess moisture that collects on furniture in the winter time is poor ventilation. 22.___

23. As used in the above paragraph, the word *trim* means *walls*. 23.___

24. As used in the above paragraph, the word *marred* means *damaged*. 24.___

25. As used in the above paragraph, the word *applied* means *rubbed*. 25.___

KEY (CORRECT ANSWERS)

1.	D	11.	F
2.	A	12.	T
3.	C	13.	F
4.	B	14.	F
5.	A	15.	F
6.	A	16.	T
7.	C	17.	F
8.	D	18.	T
9.	F	19.	T
10.	T	20.	F

21.	F
22.	T
23.	F
24.	T
25.	F

TEST 3

DIRECTIONS: Each question consists of a statement. You are to indicate whether the statement is TRUE (T) or FALSE (F). *PRINT THE LETTER OF THE CORRECT ANSWER IN THE SPACE AT THE RIGHT.*

Questions 1-7.

DIRECTIONS: Questions 1 through 7, inclusive, are to be answered in accordance with the paragraph below.

    There are several types of lines in a blueprint. The solid line that represents edges of surfaces are somewhat heavier than the other lines on the drawing and are known as working lines. These lines may be straight or curved, depending upon the shape and view of the object. Dotted lines are the same as working lines, except that the surface which is represented by dotted lines is hidden from sight when the object is viewed. To show the size of any structure, or part of it, dimension lines are used. These lines are light lines drawn between two working lines to show the dimensions between two points. If the dimension lines cannot readily be placed on view, the working lines are lengthened or extended in order that the dimension lines may be drawn. These lines are known as extension lines. A shaded area of a drawing made by a series of parallel lines drawn close together at any angle to the working lines of the view is sometimes found on a blueprint. These are known as section lines. They represent what would be seen if that part of the view covered by such lines were cut through and a portion removed.

1. The number of different types of blueprint lines described in the above paragraph is 4. 1.____

2. According to the above paragraph, the HEAVIEST lines on a blueprint are usually the working lines. 2.____

3. According to the above paragraph, extension lines are continuations of working lines 3.____

4. The following line appears on a blueprint 6'4". According to the above paragraph, this line is BEST described as a dimension line. 4.____

5. According to the above paragraph, the shaded area of a blueprint represents what would be seen if that part of the view were cut through and a portion removed. 5.____

6. According to the above paragraph, dimension lines may appear between two section lines. 6.____

7. According to the above paragraph, a series of parallel lines drawn close together at an angle to the working lines are the dotted lines. 7.____

Questions 8-14.

DIRECTIONS: Questions 8 through 14, inclusive, are to be answered in accordance with the paragraph below.

    Native species of trees are divided into two *classes*-hardwoods, which have broad leaves, and softwoods, which have scalelike leaves, as the cedars, or needlelike leaves, as the pines. Hardwoods, except in the warmest regions, shed their leaves at the end of each growing season. Native softwoods, except cypress, tamarack and larch, are evergreen. The terms *hardwood* and *softwood* have no direct application to the hardness or softness of the wood. In fact, such hardwood trees as cottonwood and aspen have softer wood than the white pines and true firs, and *certain* softwoods, such as longleaf pine and Douglas-fir, produce wood that is as hard as that of basswood and yellow-poplar.

8. According to the above paragraph, softwoods are differentiated from hardwoods by the types of leaves. 8.___

9. According to the above paragraph, if a tree sheds its leaves in the winter, you can be sure it is a hardwood. 9.___

10. According to the above paragraph, an example of a tree that stays green throughout the year is cypress. 10.___

11. According to the above paragraph, hardwoods are NOT necessarily *harder* than softwoods. 11.___

12. According to the above paragraph, one of the *harder* softwoods is basswood. 12.___

13. As used in the above paragraph, *classes* means *groups*. 13.___

14. As used in the above paragraph, *certain* means *sure*. 14.___

Questions 15-20.

DIRECTIONS: Questions 15 through 20, inclusive, are to be answered in accordance with the paragraph below.

Sometimes it is impossible to scrape and sand out all blemishes and defects in the wood surfaces. Nail holes left where nailheads have been set below the surface, dents, checks, and pits caused by faulty grain, especially in cedar, usually cannot be removed from the surface. It, therefore, is necessary to fill these defects with a special filler. Some of the better types of fillers used for this purpose include colored stick shellac, plastic wood, and various *types* of crack fillers. It is especially important to use a filler that will match the color of the wood when it is finished. It is *usually* best to stain a scrap piece of wood with the stain that is to be used on the finished project and match the color of the filler to it. Stick shellac and plastic wood may be obtained in various colors, but these colors cannot be changed satisfactorily. Crack fillers may be obtained in various colors and may also be colored to match the color of the stain being used.

15. According to the above paragraph, one of the defects often found in wood is knots. 15.___

16. According to the above paragraph, the BEST method of insuring good color match is to first test the color on a piece of scrap wood. 16.___

17. According to the above paragraph, the one of the types of fillers whose color can be changed is *crack filler*. 17.___

18. According to the above paragraph, it is fairly easy to remove defects from the surface of the wood. 18.___

19. As used in the above paragraph, the word *usually* means *frequently*. 19.___

20. As used in the above paragraph, the word *types* means *kinds*.   20._____

Questions 21-25.

DIRECTIONS: Questions 21 through 25, inclusive, are to be answered in accordance with the paragraph below.

By *squaring stock* is meant the process of working all the surfaces of the stock until they have been made smooth and true, until they are at right angles to the adjoining surfaces, and until opposite surfaces are *parallel* to each other. The quality of your finished project will be determined largely by your ability to square stock quickly and accurately. The *process* of squaring stock is the fundamental basis of all woodworking. Each part of the piece should be accurately squared to *dimensions* in order to insure a proper fit when joined with the other parts of the project.

21. According to the above paragraph, one of the reasons for squaring stock is so that the pieces will fit properly when joined.   21._____

22. According to the above paragraph, the quality of the work will depend upon how accurately you can square.   22._____

23. As used in the above paragraph, the word *parallel* means *at right angles*.   23._____

24. As used in the above paragraph, the word *process* means *ability*.   24._____

25. As used in the above paragraph, the word *dimensions* means *sizes*   25._____

KEY (CORRECT ANSWERS)

1. F	11. T
2. T	12. F
3. T	13. T
4. T	14. F
5. T	15. F
6. F	16. T
7. F	17. T
8. T	18. F
9. F	19. F
10. F	20. T

21. T
22. T
23. F
24. F
25. T

SUPERVISION STUDY GUIDE

Social science has developed information about groups and leadership in general and supervisor-employee relationships in particular. Since organizational effectiveness is closely linked to the ability of supervisors to direct the activities of employees, these findings are important to executives everywhere.

IS A SUPERVISOR A LEADER?

First-line supervisors are found in all large business and government organizations. They are the men at the base of an organizational hierarchy. Decisions made by the head of the organization reach them through a network of intermediate positions. They are frequently referred to as part of the management team, but their duties seldom seem to support this description.

A supervisor of clerks, tax collectors, meat inspectors, or securities analysts is not charged with budget preparation. He cannot hire or fire the employees in his own unit on his say-so. He does not administer programs which require great planning, coordinating, or decision making.

Then what is he? He is the man who is directly in charge of a group of employees doing productive work for a business or government agency. If the work requires the use of machines, the men he supervises operate them. If the work requires the writing of reports, the men he supervises write them. He is expected to maintain a productive flow of work without creating problems which higher levels of management must solve. But is he a leader?

To carry out a specific part of an agency's mission, management creates a unit, staffs it with a group of employees and designates a supervisor to take charge of them. Management directs what this unit shall do, from time to time changes directions, and often indicates what the group should not do. Management presumably creates status for the supervisor by giving him more pay, a title, and special privileges.

Management asks a supervisor to get his workers to attain organizational goals, including the desired quantity and quality of production. Supposedly, he has authority to enable him to achieve this objective. Management at least assumes that by establishing the status of the supervisor's position, it has created sufficient authority to enable him to achieve these goals—not his goals, nor necessarily the group's, but management's goals.

In addition, supervision includes writing reports, keeping records of membership in a higher-level administrative group, industrial engineering, safety engineering, editorial duties, housekeeping duties, etc. The supervisor as a member of an organizational network, must be responsible to the changing demands of the management above him. At the same time, he must be responsive to the demands of the work group of which he is a member. He is placed in the difficult position of communicating and implementing new decisions, changed programs and revised production quotas for his work group, although he may have had little part in developing them.

It follows, then, that supervision has a special characteristic: achievement of goals, previously set by management, through the efforts of others. It is in this feature of the supervisor's job that we find the role of a leader in the sense of the following definition: *A leader is that person who <u>most</u> effectively influences group activities toward goal setting and goal achievements.*

This definition is broad. It covers both leaders in groups that come together voluntarily and in those brought together through a work assignment in a factory, store, or government agency. In the natural group, the authority necessary to attain goals is determined by the group membership and is granted by them. In the working group, it is apparent that the establishment of a supervisory position creates a predisposition on the part of employees to accept the authority of the occupant of that position. We cannot, however, assume that mere occupation confers authority sufficient to assure the accomplishment of an organization's goals.

Supervision is different, then, from leadership. The supervisor is expected to fulfill the role of leader but without obtaining a grant of authority from the group he supervises. The supervisor is expected to influence the group in the achieving of goals but is often handicapped by having little influence on the organizational process by which goals are set. The supervisor, because he works in an organizational setting, has the burdens of additional organizational duties and restrictions and requirements arising out of the fact that his position is subordinate to a hierarchy of higher-level supervisors. These differences between leadership and supervision are reflected in our definition: *Supervision is basically a leadership role, in a formal organization, which has as its objective the effective influencing of other employees.*

Even though these differences between supervision and leadership exist, a significant finding of experimenters in this field is that supervisors <u>must</u> be leaders to be successful.

The problem is: How can a supervisor exercise leadership in an organizational setting? We might say that the supervisor is expected to be a natural leader in a situation which does not come about naturally. His situation becomes really difficult in an organization which is more eager to make its supervisors into followers rather than leaders.

LEADERSHIP: NATURAL AND ORGANIZATIONAL

Leadership, in its usual sense of *natural* leadership, and supervision are not the same. In some cases, leadership embraces broader powers and functions than supervision; in other cases, supervision embraces more than leadership. This is true both because of the organization and technical aspects of the supervisor's job and because of the relatively freer setting and inherent authority of the natural leader.

The natural leader usually has much more authority and influence than the supervisor. Group members not only follow his command but prefer it that way. The employee, however, can appeal the supervisor's commands to his union or to the supervisor's superior or to the personnel office. These intercessors represent restrictions on the supervisor's power to lead.

The natural leader can gain greater membership involvement in the group's objectives, and he can change the objectives of the group. The supervisor can attempt to gain employee support only for management's objectives; he cannot set other objectives. In these instances leadership is broader than supervision.

The natural leader must depend upon whatever skills are available when seeking to attain objectives. The supervisor is trained in the administrative skills necessary to achieve management's goals. If he does not possess the requisite skills, however, he can call upon management's technicians.

A natural leader can maintain his leadership, in certain groups, merely by satisfying members' need for group affiliation. The supervisor must maintain his leadership by directing and organizing his group to achieve specific organizational goals set for him and his group by management. He must have a technical competence and a kind of coordinating ability which is not needed by many natural leaders.

A natural leader is responsible only to his group which grants him authority. The supervisor is responsible to management, which employs him, and also to the work group of which he is a member. The supervisor has the exceedingly difficult job of reconciling the demands of two groups frequently in conflict. He is often placed in the untenable position of trying to play two antagonistic roles. In the above instance, supervision is broader than leadership.

ORGANIZATIONAL INFLUENCES ON LEADERSHIP

The supervisor is both a product and a prisoner of the organization wherein we find him. The organization which creates the supervisor's position also obstructs, restricts, and channelizes the exercise of his duties. These influences extend beyond prescribed functional relationships to specific supervisory behavior. For example, even in a face-to-face situation involving one of his subordinates, the supervisor's actions are controlled to a great extent by his organization. His behavior must conform to the organization policy on human relations, rules which dictate personnel procedures, specific prohibitions governing conduct, the attitudes of his own superior, etc. He is not a free agent operating within the limits of his work group. His freedom of action is much more circumscribed than is generally admitted. The organizational influences which limit his leadership actions can be classified as structure, prescriptions, and proscriptions.

The organizational structure places each supervisor's position in context with other designated positions. It determines the relationships between his position and specific positions which impinge on his. The structure of the organization designates a certain position to which he looks for orders and information about his work. It gives a particular status to his position within a pattern of statuses from which he perceives that (1) certain positions are on a par, organizationally, with his, (2) other positions are subordinate, and (3) still others are superior.

The organizational structure determines those positions to which he should look for advice and assistance, and those positions to which he should give advice and assistance.

For instance, the organizational structure has predetermined that the supervisor of a clerical processing unit shall report to a supervisory position in a higher echelon. He shall have certain relationships with the supervisors of the work units which transmit work to and receive work from his unit. He shall discuss changes and clarification of procedures with certain staff units, such as organization and methods, cost accounting, and personnel. He shall consult supervisors of units which provide or receive special work assignments.

The organizational structure, however, establishes patterns other than those of the relationships of positions. These are the patterns of responsibility, authority, and expectations.

The supervisor is responsible for certain activities or results; he is presumably invested with the authority to achieve these. His set of authority and responsibility is interwoven with other sets to the end that all goals and functions of the organization are parceled out in small, manageable lots. This, of course, establishes a series of expectations: a single supervisor can perform his particular set of duties only upon the assumption that preceding or contiguous sets of duties have been, or are being carried out. At the same time, he is aware of the expectations of others that he will fulfill his functional role.

The structure of an organization establishes relationships between specified positions and specific expectations for these positions. The fact that these relationships and expectations are established is one thing; whether or not they are met is another.

PRESCRIPTIONS AND PROSCRIPTIONS

But let us return to the organizational influences which act to restrict the supervisor's exercise of leadership. These are the prescriptions and proscriptions generally in effect in all organizations, and those peculiar to a single organization. In brief these are the *thou shalt's* and the *thou shalt not's*.

Organizations not only prescribe certain duties for individual supervisory positions, they also prescribe specific methods and means of carrying out these duties and maintaining management-employee relations. These include rules, regulations, policy, and tradition. It does no good for the supervisor to say, *This seems to be the best way to handle such-and-such,* if the organization has established a routine for dealing with problems. For good or bad, there are rules that state that firings shall be executed in such a manner, accompanied by a certain notification; that training shall be conducted, and in this manner. Proscriptions are merely negative prescriptions; you may not discriminate against any employee because of politics or race; you shall not suspend any employee without following certain procedures and obtaining certain approvals.

Most of these prohibitions and rules apply to the area of interpersonal relations, precisely the area which is now arousing most interest on the part of administrators and managers. We have become concerned about the contrast between formally prescribed relationships and interpersonal relationships, and this brings us to the often discussed informal organization.

FORMAL AND INFORMAL ORGANIZATIONS

As we well know, the functions and activities of any organization are broken down into individual units of work called positions. Administrators must establish a pattern which will link these positions to each other and relate them to a system of authority and responsibility. Man-to-man are spelled out as plainly as possible for all to understand. Managers, then, build an official structure which we call the formal organization.

In these same organizations, employees react individually and in groups to institutionally determined roles. John, a worker, rides in the same carpool as Joe, a foreman. An unplanned communication develops. Harry, a machinist knows more about high-speed machining than his foreman or anyone else in his shop. An unofficial tool boss comes into being. Mary, who fought with Jane, is promoted over her. Jane now gives Mary's directions. A planned relationship fails to develop. The employees have built a structure which we call the informal organization.

Formal organization is a system of management-prescribed relations between positions in an organization.

Informal organization is a network of unofficial relations between people in an organization.

These definitions might lead us to the absurd conclusion that positions carry out formal activities and that employe4es spend their time in unofficial activities. We must recognize that organizational activities are in all cases carried out by people. The formal structure provides a needed framework within which interpersonal relations occur. What we call informal organization is the complex of normal, natural relations among employees. These personal relationships may be negative or positive. That is, they may impede or aid the achievement of organizational goals. For example, friendship between two supervisors greatly increases the probability of good cooperation and coordination between their sections. On the other hand, *buck passing* nullifies the formal structure by failure to meet a prescribed and expected responsibility.

It is improbable that an ideal organization exists where all activities are carried out in strict conformity to a formally prescribed pattern of functional roles. Informal organization arises because of the incompleteness and ambiguities in the network of formally prescribed relationships, or in response to the needs or inadequacies of supervisors or managers who hold prescribed functional roles in an organization. Many of these relationships are not prescribed by the organizational pattern; many cannot be prescribed; many should not be prescribed.

Management faces the problem of keeping the informal organization in harmony with the mission of the agency. One way to do this is to make sure that all employees have a clear understanding of and are sympathetic with that mission. The issuance of organizational charts, procedural manuals, and functional descriptions of the work to be done by divisions and sections helps communicate management's plans and goals. Issuances alone, of course, cannot do the whole job. They should be accompanied by oral discussion and explanation. Management must ensure that there is mutual understanding and acceptance of charts and procedures. More important is that management acquaint itself with the attitudes, activities, and peculiar brands of logic which govern the informal organization. Only through this type of knowledge can they and supervisors keep informal goals consistent with the agency mission.

SUPERVISION STATUS AND FUNCTIONAL ROLE

A well-established supervisor is respected by the employees who work with him. They defer to his wishes. It is clear that a superior-subordinate relationship has been established. That is, status of the supervisor has been established in relation to other employees of the same work group. This same supervisor gains the respect of employees when he behaves in as certain manner. He will be expected, generally, to follow the customs of the group in such matters as dress, recreation, and manner of speaking. The group has a set of expectations as to his behavior. His position is a functional role which carries with it a collection of rights and obligations.

The position of supervisor usually has a status distinct from the individual who occupies it: it is much like a position description which exists whether or not there is an incumbent. The status of a supervisory position is valued higher than that of an employee position both because of the functional role of leadership which is assigned to it and because of the status symbols of titles, rights, and privileges which go with it.

Social ranking, or status, is not simple because it involves both the position and the man. An individual may be ranked higher than others because of his education, social background, perceived leadership ability, or conformity to group customs and ideals. If such a man is ranked higher by the members of a work group than their supervisor, the supervisor's effectiveness may be seriously undermined.

If the organization does not build and reinforce a supervisor's status, his position can be undermined in a different way. This will happen when managers go around rather than through the supervisor or designate him as a straw boss, acting boss, or otherwise not a real boss.

Let us clarify this last point. A role, and corresponding status, establishes a set of expectations. Employees expect their supervisor to do certain things and to act in certain ways. They are prepared to respond to that expected behavior. When the supervisor's behavior does not conform to their expectations, they are surprised, confused, and ill-at-ease. It becomes necessary for them to resolve their confusion, if they can. They might do this by turning to one of their own members for leadership. If the confusion continues, or their attempted solutions are not satisfactory, they will probably become a poorly motivated, non-cohesive group which cannot function very well.

COMMUNICATION AND THE SUPERVISOR

In a recent survey, railroad workers reported that they rarely look to their supervisor for information about the company. This is startling, at least to us, because we ordinarily think of the supervisor as the link between management and worker. We expect the supervisor to be the prime source of information about the company. Actually, the railroad workers listed the supervisor next to last in the o5rder of their sources of information. Most surprising of all, the supervisors, themselves, stated that rumor and unofficial contacts were their principal sources of information. Here we see one of the reasons why supervisors may not be as effective as management desires.

The supervisor is not only being bypassed by his work group, he is being ignored, and his position weakened, by the very organization which is holding him responsible for the activities of his workers. If he is management's representative to the employee, then management has an obligation to keep him informed of its activities. This is necessary if he is to carry out his functions efficiently and maintain his leadership in the work group. The supervisor is expected to be a source of information; when he is not, his status is not clear, and employees are dissatisfied because he has not lived up to expectations.

By providing information to the supervisor to pass along to employees, we can strengthen his position as leader of the group, and increase satisfaction and cohesion within the group. Because he has more information than the other members, receives information sooner, and passes it along at the proper times, members turn to him as a source and also provide him with information in the hope of receiving some in return. From this, we can see an increase in group cohesiveness because:

- Employees are bound closer to their supervisor because he is *in the know*.
- There is less need to go outside the group for answers
- Employees will more quickly turn to the supervisor for enlightenment

The fact that he has the answers will also enhance the supervisor's standing in the eyes of his men. This increased status will serve to bolster his authority and control of the group and will probably result in improved morale and productivity.

The foregoing, of course, does not mean that all management information should be given out. There are obviously certain policy determinations and discussions which need not or cannot be transmitted to all supervisors. However, the supervisor must be kept as fully informed as possible so that he can answer questions when asked and can allay needless fears and anxieties. Further, the supervisor has the responsibility of encouraging employee questions and submissions of information. He must be able to present information to employees so that it is clearly understood and accepted. His attitude and manner should make it clear that he believes in what he is saying, that the information is necessary or desirable to the group, and that he is prepared to act on the basis of the information.

SUPERVISION AND JOB PERFORMANCE

The productivity of work groups is a product; employees' efforts are multiplied by the supervision they receive. Many investigators have analyzed this relationship and have discovered elements of supervision which differentiate high and low production groups. These researchers have identified certain types of supervisory practices which they classify as *employee-centered* and other types which they classify as *production centered*.

The difference between these two kinds of supervision lies not in specific practices but in the approach or orientation to supervision. The employee-centered supervisor directs most of his efforts toward increasing employee motivation. He is concerned more with realizing the potential energy of persons than with administrative and technological methods of increasing efficiency and productivity. He is the man who finds ways of causing employees to want to work harder with the same tools. These supervisors emphasize the personal relations between their employees and themselves.

Now, obviously, these pictures are overdrawn. No one supervisor has all the virtues of the ideal type of employee-centered supervisor. And, fortunately, no one supervisor has all the bad traits found in many production-centered supervisors. We should remember that the various practices that researchers have fond which distinguish these two kinds of supervision represent the many practices and methods of supervisors of all gradations between these extremes. We should be careful, too, of the implications of the labels attached to the two types. For instance, being production-centered is not necessarily bad, since the principal responsibility of any supervisor is maintaining the production level that is expected of his work group. Being employee-centered may not necessarily be good, if the only result is a happy, chuckling crew of loafers. To return to the researchers' findings, employee-centered supervisors:

- Recommend promotions, transfers, pay increases
- Inform men about what is happening in the company
- Keep men posted on how well they are doing
- Hear complaints and grievances sympathetically
- Speak up for subordinates

Production-centered supervisors, on the other hand, don't do those things. They check on employees more frequently, give more detailed and frequent instructions, don't give reasons for changes, and are more punitive when mistakes are made. Employee-centered supervisors were reported to contribute to high morale and high production, whereas production-centered supervision was associated with lower morale and less production.

More recent findings, however, show that the relationship between supervision and productivity is not this simple. Investigators now report that high production is more frequently associated with supervisory practices which combine employee-centered behavior with concern for production. (This concern is not the same, however, as anxiety about production, which is the hallmark of our production-centered supervisor.) Let us examine these apparently contradictory findings and the premises from which they are derived.

SUPERVISION AND MORALE

Why do supervisory activities cause high or low production? As the name implies, the activities of the employee-centered supervisor tend to relate him more closely and satisfactorily to his workers. The production-centered supervisor's practices tend to separate him from his group and to foster antagonism. An analysis of this difference may answer our question.

Earlier, we pointed out that the supervisor is a type of leader and that leadership is intimately related to the group in which it occurs We discover, now, that an employee-centered supervisor's primary activities are concerned with both his leadership and his group membership. Such a supervisor is a member of a group and occupies a leadership role in that group.

These facts are sometimes obscured when we speak of the supervisor as management's representative, or as the organizational link between management and the employee, or as the end of the chain of command. If we really want to understand what it is we expect of the supervisor, we must remember that he is the designated leader of a group of employees to whom he is bound by interaction and interdependence.

Most of his actions are aimed, consciously or unconsciously, at strengthening membership ties in the group. This includes both making members more conscious that he is a member of their group) and causing members to identify themselves more closely with the group. These ends are accomplished by:

- making the group more attractive to the worker: they find satisfaction of their needs for recognition, friendship, enjoyable work, etc.;
- maintaining open communication: employees can express their views and obtain information about the organization
- giving assistance: members can seek advice on personal problems as well as their work; and
- acting as a buffer between the group and management: he speaks up for his men and explains the reasons for management's decisions.

Such actions both strengthen group cohesiveness and solidarity and affirm the supervisor's leadership position in the group.

DEFINING MORALE

This brings us back to a point mentioned earlier. We had said that employee-centered supervisors contribute to high morale as well as to high production. But how can we explain units which have low morale and high productivity, or vice versa? Usually production and morale are considered separately, partly because they are measured against different criteria and partly because, in some instances, they seem to be independent of each other.

Some of this difficulty may stem from confusion over definitions of morale. Morale has been defined as, or measured by, absences from work, satisfaction with job or company, dissension among members of work groups, productivity, apathy or lack of interest, readiness to help others, and a general aura of happiness as rated by observers. Some of these criteria of morale are not subject to the influence of the supervisor, and some of them are not clearly related to productivity. Definitions like these invite findings of low morale coupled with high production.

Both productivity and morale can be influenced by environmental factors not under the control of group members or supervisors. Such things as plant layout, organizational structure and goals, lighting, ventilation, communications, and management planning may have an adverse or desirable effect.

We might resolve the dilemma by defining morale on the basis of our understanding of the supervisor as leader of a group; morale is the degree of satisfaction of group members with their leadership. In this light, the supervisor's employee-centered activities bear a clear relation to morale. His efforts to increase employee identification with the group and to strengthen his leadership lead to greater satisfaction with that leadership. By increasing group cohesiveness and by demonstrating that his influence and power can aid the group, he is able to enhance his leadership status and afford satisfaction to the group.

SUPERVISION, PRODUCTION, AND MORALE

There are factors within the organization itself which determine whether increased production is possible:

- Are production goals expressed in terms understandable to employees and are they realistic?
- Do supervisors responsible for production respect the agency mission and production goals?
- If employees do not know how to do the job well, does management provide a trainer—often the supervisor—who can teach efficient work methods?

There are other factors within the work group which determine whether increased production will be attained:

- Is leadership present which can bring about the desired level of production?
- Are production goals accepted by employees as reasonable and attainable?
- If group effort is involved, are members able to coordinate their efforts?

Research findings confirm the view that an employee-centered supervisor can achieve higher morale than a production-centered supervisor. Managers may well ask what is the relationship between this and production.

Supervision is production-oriented to the extent that it focuses attention on achieving organizational goals, and plans and devises methods for attaining them; it is employee-centered to the extent that it focuses attention on employee attitudes toward those goals, and plans and works toward maintenance of employee satisfaction.

High productivity and low morale result when a supervisor plans and organizes work efficiently but cannot achieve high membership satisfaction. Low production and high morale result when a supervisor, though keeping members satisfied with his leadership, either has not gained acceptance of organizational goals or does not have the technical competence to achieve them.

The relationship between supervision, morale, and productivity is an interdependent one, with the supervisor playing an integral role due to his ability to influence productivity and morale independently of each other.

A supervisor who can plan his work well has good technical knowledge, and who can install better production methods can raise production without necessarily increasing group satisfaction. On the other hand, a supervisor who can motivate his employees and keep them satisfied with his leadership can gain high production in spite of technical difficulties and environmental obstacles.

CLIMATE AND SUPERVISION

Climate, the intangible environment of an organization made up of attitudes, beliefs, and traditions, plays a large part in morale, productivity, and supervision. Usually when we speak of climate and its relationship to morale and productivity, we talk about the merits of *democratic* versus *authoritarian* climate. Employees seem to produce more and have higher morale in a democratic climate, whereas in an authoritarian climate, the reverse seems to be true or so the researchers tell us. We would do well to determine what these terms mean to supervision.

Perhaps most of our difficulty in understanding and applying these concepts comes from our emotional reactions to the words themselves. For example, authoritarian climate is usually painted as the very blackest kind of dictatorship. This is not surprising, because we are usually expected to believe that it is invariably bad. Conversely, democratic climate is drawn to make the driven snow look impure by comparison.

Now these descriptions are most probably true when we talk about our political processes, or town meetings, or freedom of speech. However, the same labels have been used by social scientists in other contexts and have also been applied to government and business organizations, without it, it seems, any recognition that the meanings and their social values may have changed somewhat

For example, these labels were used in experiments conducted in an informal classroom setting using 11-year-old boys as subjects. The descriptive labels applied to the climate of the setting as well as the type of leadership practiced. When these labels were transferred to a management setting, it seems that many presumed that they principally meant the king of leadership rather than climate. We can see that there is a great difference between the experimental and management settings and that leadership practices for one might be inappropriate for the other.

It is doubtful that formal work organizations can be anything but authoritarian, in that goals are set by management and a hierarchy exists through which decisions and orders from the top are transmitted downward. Organizations are authoritarian by structure and need; direction and control are placed in the hands of a few in order to gain fast and efficient decision making. Now this does not mean to describe a dictatorship. It is merely the recognition of the fact that direction of organizational affairs comes from above. It should be noted that leadership in some natural groups is, in this sense, authoritarian.

Granting that formal organizations have this kind of authoritarian leadership, can there be a democratic climate? Certainly there can be, but we would want to define and delimit this term. A more realistic meaning of democratic climate in organizations is the use of permissive and participatory methods in management-employee relations. That is, a mutual exchange of information and explanation with the granting of individual freedom within certain restricted and defined limits. However, it is not our purpose to debate the merits of authoritarianism versus democracy. We recognize that within the small work group there is a need for freedom from constraint and an increase in participation in order to achieve organizational goals within the framework of the organizational movement.

Another aspect of climate is best expressed by this familiar, and true, saying: actions speak louder than words. Of particular concern to us is this effect of management climate on the behavior of supervisors, particularly in employee-centered activities.

There have been reports of disappointment with efforts to make supervisors ore employee-centered. Managers state that, since research has shown ways of improving human relations, supervisors should begin to practice these methods. Usually a training course in human relations is established; and supervisors are given this training. Managers then sit back and wait for the expected improvements, only to find that there are none.

If we wish to produce changes in the supervisor's behavior, the climate must be made appropriate and rewarding to the changed behavior. This means that top-level attitudes and behavior cannot deny or contradict the change we are attempting to effect. Basic changes in organizational behavior cannot be made with any permanence, unless we provide an environment that is receptive to the changes and rewards those persons who do change.

IMPROVING SUPERVISION

Anyone who has read this far might expect to find *A Dozen Rules for Dealing With Employees* or *29 Steps to Supervisory Success*. We will not provide such a list.

Simple rules suffer from their simplicity. They ignore the complexities of human behavior. Reliance upon rules may cause supervisors to concentrate on superficial aspects of their relations with employees. It may preclude genuine understanding.

The supervisor who relies on a list of rules tends to think of people in mechanistic terms. In a certain situation, he uses *Rule No. 3*. Employees are not treated as thinking and feeling persons, but rather as figures in a formula: Rule 3 applied to employee X = Production.

Employees usually recognize mechanical manipulation and become dissatisfied and resentful. They lose faith in, and respect for, their supervisor, and this may be reflected in lower morale and productivity.

We do not mean that supervisors must become social science experts if they wish to improve. Reports of current research indicate that there are two major parts of their job which can be strengthened through self-improvement: (1) Work planning, including technical skills, and (2) motivation of employees.

The most effective supervisors combine excellence in the administrative and technical aspects of their work with friendly and considerate personal relations with their employees.

CRITICAL PERSONAL RELATIONS

Later in this chapter we shall talk about administrative aspects of supervision, but first let us comment on *friendly and considerate personal relations*. We have discussed this subject throughout the preceding chapters, but we want to review some of the critical supervisory influences on personal relations.

Closeness of Supervision: The closeness of supervision has an important effect on productivity and morale. Mann and Dent found that supervisors of low-producing units supervise very closely, while high-producing supervisors exercise only general supervision. It was found that the low-producing supervisors:

- check on employees more frequently
- give more detailed and frequent instructions
- limit employee's freedom to do job in own way

Workers who felt less closely supervised reported that they were better satisfied with their jobs and the company. We should note that the manner or attitude of the supervisor has an important bearing on whether employees perceive supervision as being close or general.

These findings are another way of saying that supervision does not mean standing over the employee and telling him what to do and when and how to do it. The more effective supervisor tells his employees what is required, giving general instructions.

COMMUNICATION

Supervisors of high-production units consider communication as one of the most important aspects of their job. Effective communication is used by these supervisors to achieve better interpersonal relations and improved employee motivation. Low-production supervisors do not rate communications as highly important.

High-producing supervisors find that an important aid to more effective communication is listening. They are ready to listen to both personal problems or interests and questions about the work. This does not mean that they are *nosey* or meddle in their employees' personal lives, but rather that they show a willingness to listen, and do listen, if their employees wish to discuss problems.

These supervisors inform employees about forthcoming changes in work; they discuss agency policy with employees; and they make sure that each employee knows how well he is doing. What these supervisors do is use two-way communication effectively. Unless the supervisor freely imparts information, he will not receive information in return.

Attitudes and perception are frequently affected by communication or the lack of it. Research surveys reveal that many supervisors are not aware of their employees' attitudes, nor do they know what personal reactions their supervision arouses. Through frank discussion with employees, they have been surprised to discover employee beliefs about which they were ignorant. Discussion sometimes reveals that the supervisor and his employees have totally different impressions about the same event. The supervisor should be constantly on the alert for misconceptions about his words and deeds. He must remember that, although his actions are perfectly clear to himself, they may be, and frequently are, viewed differently by employees.

Failure to communicate information results in misconceptions and false assumptions. What you say and how you say it will strongly affect your employees' attitudes and perceptions. By giving them available information, you can prevent misconceptions; by discussion, you may be able to change attitudes; by questioning, you can discover what the perceptions and assumptions really are. And it need hardly be added that actions should conform very closely to words.

If we were to attempt to reduce the above discussion on communication to rules, we would have a long list which would be based on one cardinal principle: Don't make assumptions!

- Don't assume that your employees know; tell them.
- Don't assume that you know how they feel; find out.
- Don't assume that they understand; clarify.

20 SUPERVISORY HINTS

1. Avoid inconsistency.
2. Always give employees a chance to explain their action before taking disciplinary action. Don't allow too much time for a "cooling off" period before disciplining an employee.
3. Be specific in your criticisms.
4. Delegate responsibility wisely.
5. Do not argue or lose your temper, and avoid being impatient.
6. Promote mutual respect and be fair, impartial, and open-minded.
7. Keep in mind that asking for employees' advice and input can be helpful in decision making.
8. If you make promises, keep them.
9. Always keep the feelings, abilities, dignity and motives of your staff in mind.
10. Remain loyal to your employees' interests.
11. Never criticize employees in front of others, or treat employees like children.
12. Admit mistakes. Don't place blame on your employees, or make excuses.
13. Be reasonable in your expectations, give complete instructions, and establish well-planned goals.
14. Be knowledgeable about office details and procedures, but avoid becoming bogged down in details.
15. Avoid supervising too closely or too loosely. Employees should also view you as an approachable supervisor.
16. Remember that employees' personal problems may affect job performance, but become involved only when appropriate.
17. Work to develop workers, and to instill a feeling of cooperation while working toward mutual goals.
18. Do not overpraise or underpraise, be properly appreciative.
19. Never ask an employee to discipline someone for you.
20. A complaint, even if unjustified, should be taken seriously.

NOTES

FRAME CONSTRUCTION

Section I. FLOOR FRAMES AND FLOOR COVERINGS

1. Framing

After the foundation is built and the batterboards placed, the carpenter builds the framework. The framework includes the beams, trusses, foundation walls, outside walls, flooring, partitions, roofing, and ceiling.

a. Light Framing. Light framing is used in barracks, bathhouses, administration buildings, light shop buildings, hospitals, and similar buildings. Figure 1 shows some details for a 20-foot-wide building; the ground level; window openings, braces, and splices; and names the framing parts.

b. Light Frame Construction. Much of the framing can be done while staking out and squaring is being completed. When the skeleton is far enough along, boards can be nailed on without need for cutting if they are standard 8-, 10-, 12-, 16-, or 18-foot lengths. The better skilled men should construct the frame. With good organization, a large force of men can be kept busy during framing.

c. Expedient Framing. Expedient framing depends on the conditions. The ideas below may suggest other expedients.

(1) *Light siding.* Chicken wire and water resistant bituminous paper can be sandwiched to provide adequate temporary framing in temperate climates.

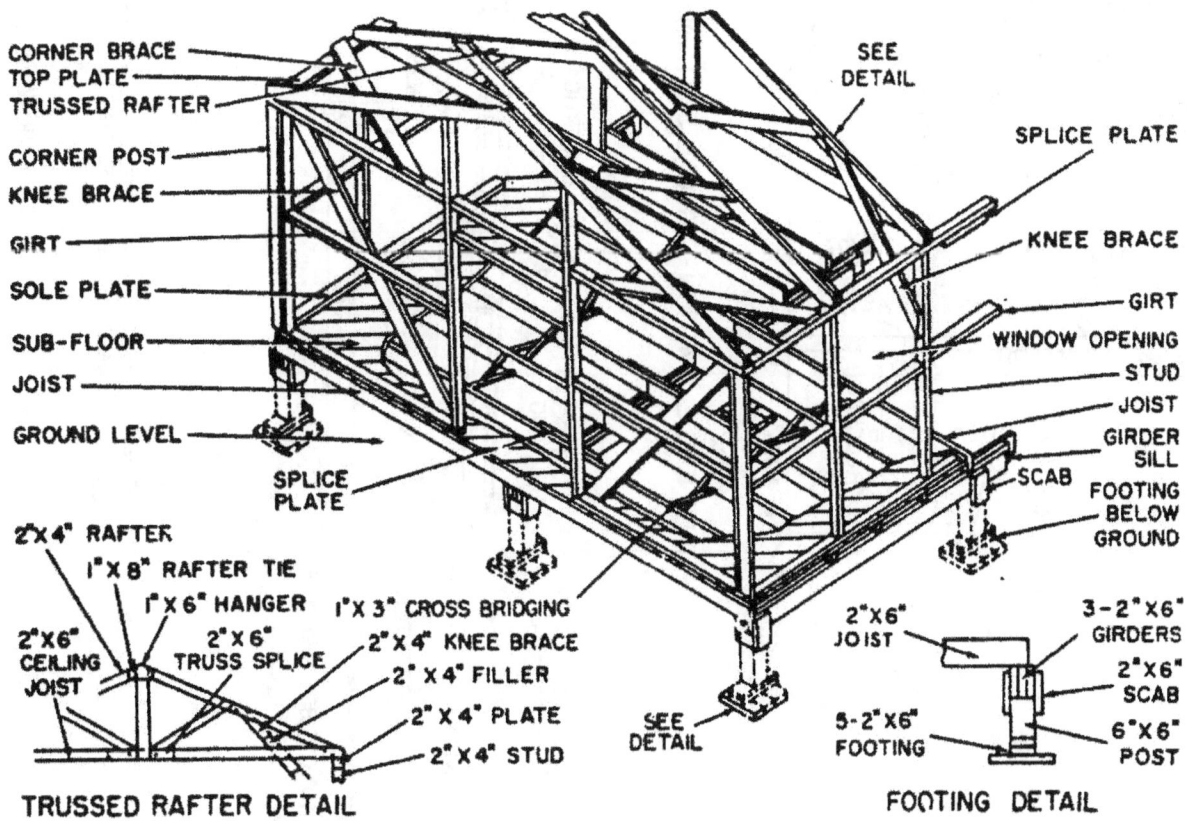

Figure 1. View of a light frame building substructure.

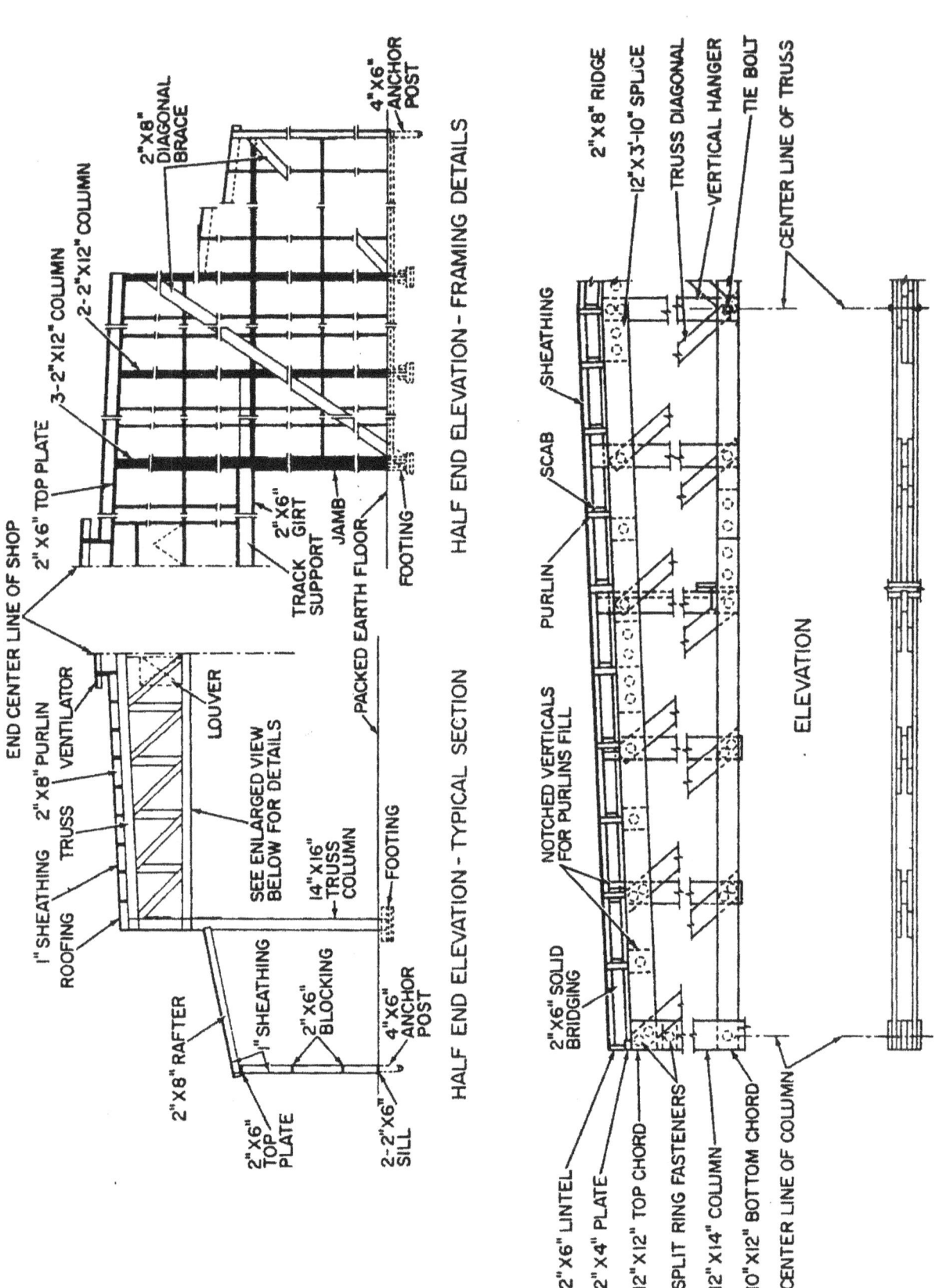

Figure 2. Sectional view of a heavy frame building.

(2) *Salvaged framing.* Salvaged sheet metal such as corrugated material or gasoline cans can be used as siding in the construction of emergency housing.

(3) *Local timber.* Poles trimmed from saplings or bamboo can be constructed into reasonably sound framing. Such materials may be secured with native vines as a further expedient.

(4) *Wood substitute framing.* Adobe soil, straw, and water puddled to proper consistency can be used for form walls, floors, and foundations. A similar mixture may be used to form sun-dried bricks for construction use.

(5) *Excavations.* Proper excavation and simple log cribbing may be covered with sod and carefully drained to provide adequate shelter.

d. *Heavy Framing.* Heavy frame buildings are more permanent, generally warehouses, depots, and shops. Figure 2 shows the details of heavy frame construction.

2. Sills

a. *Types.* The sill (fig. 1) is the foundation that supports all the building above it. It is the first part of the building to be set in place. It rests directly on the foundation piers or on the ground; it is joined at the corners and spliced when necessary. Figure 3 shows the most common sills. The type used depends on the type of construction used in the frame.

(1) *Box sills.* Box sills are used often with the very common style of platform framing, either with or without the sill plate. In this type of sill (1 and 2, fig. 3), the part that lies on the foundation wall or ground is called the sill plate. The sill is laid edgewise on the outside edge of the sill plate.

(2) *T-sills.* There are two types of T-sill construction; one commonly used in dry, warm climates (3, fig. 3), and one commonly used in less warm climates (4, fig. 3). Their construction is similar except that in the latter case the joists are nailed directly to the studs, as well as to the sills, and headers are used between the floor joists.

(3) *Braced framing sill.* The sill shown in 5, figure 3, is generally used in braced-framing construction. The floor joists are notched out and nailed directly to the sill and studs.

(4) *Built-up sills.* Where built-up sills are used, the joints are staggered (1, fig. 4). The corner joints are made as shown in 2, figure 4.

b. *Sill Requirement for Piers.* If piers are used in the foundation, heavier sills are used. They

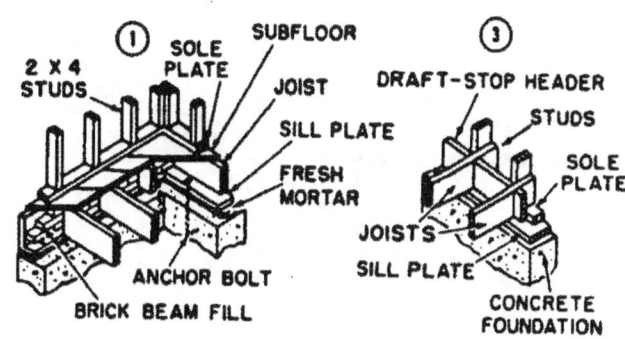

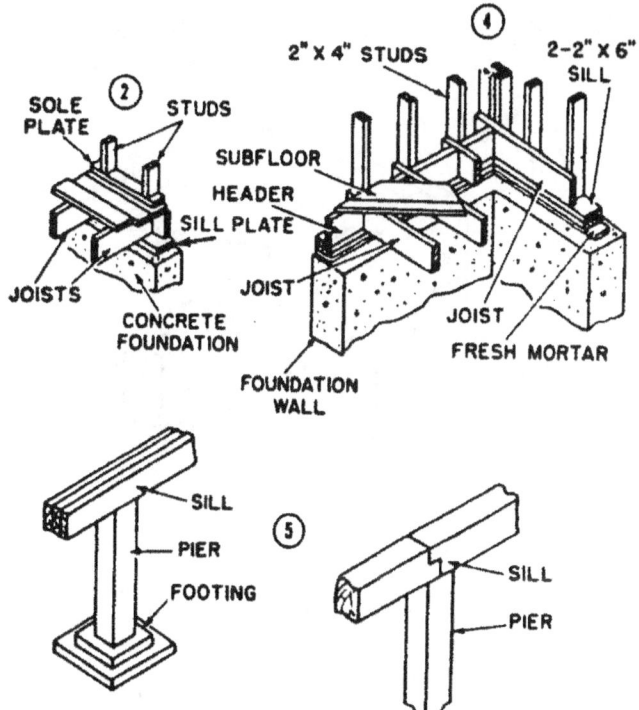

Figure 3. Types of sills.

are single heavy timbers or built up of two or more pieces of timber. Where heavy timber or built-up sills are used, the joints should occur over piers. The size of the sill depends upon the load to be carried and upon the spacing of the piers. The sill plates are laid directly on graded earth or on piers. Where earth floors are used, the studs are nailed directly to the sill plate.

3. Girders

The distance between two outside walls is often too great to be spanned by a single joist. When two or more joists are needed to cover the span, intermediate support for inboard joist-ends is provided by one or more girders. A girder is a large beam that supports other smaller beams or joists.

a. *Construction.* A girder may be made up of

PLAN VIEW OF GIRDER SHOWING METHOD OF STAGGERING JOINTS

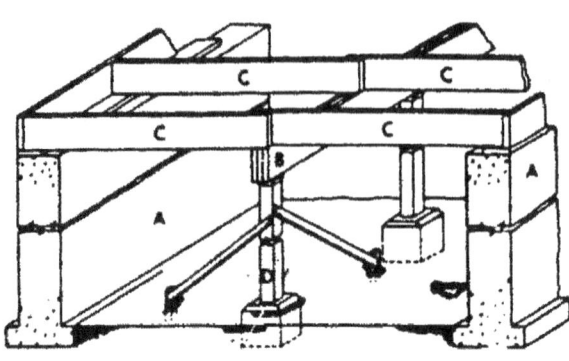

Figure 5. Built-up girder.

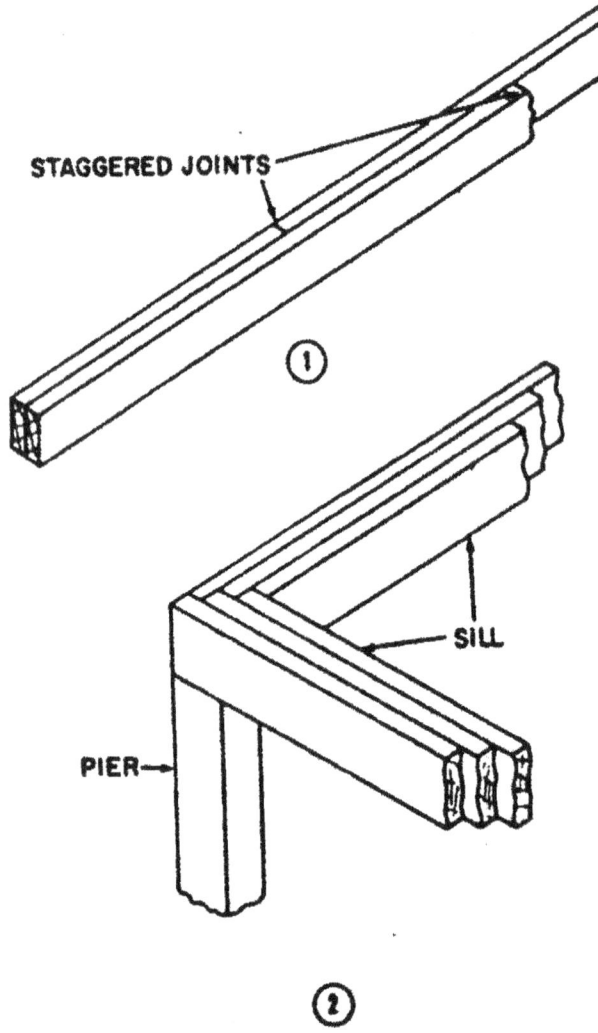

Figure 4. Sill fabrication.

d. Use of Ledger Board. A girder with a ledge board upon which the joists rest is used where vertical space is limited. This arrangement is useful in providing more headroom in basements.

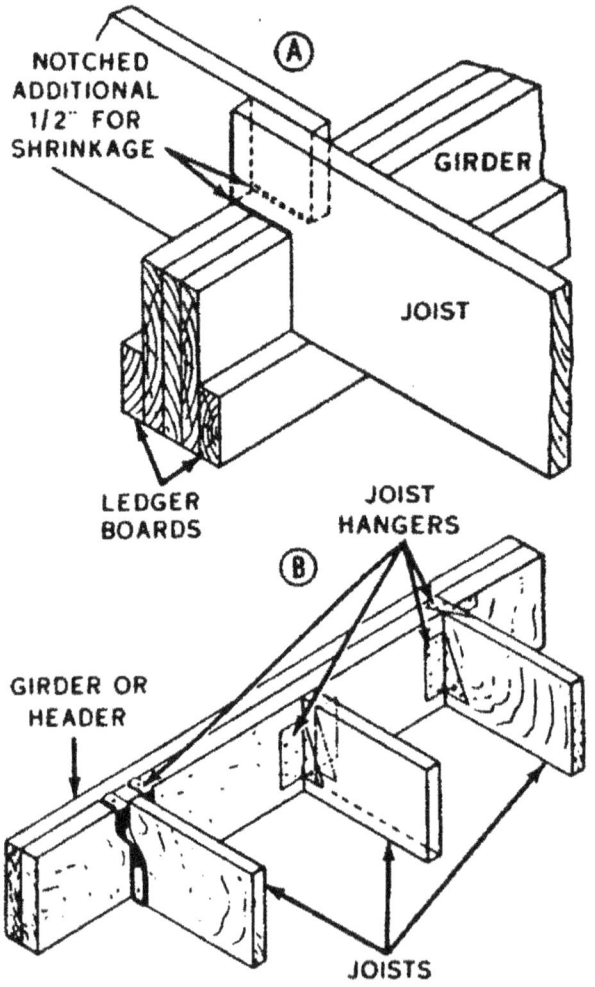

Figure 6. Joist-to-girder attachment.

several beams nailed together with 16d common nails; or it may be solid wood, steel, reinforced concrete, or a combination of these materials.

b. Design Requirements. Girders carry a very large proportion of the weight of a building. They must be well designed, rigid, and properly supported at the foundation walls and on the columns. Precautions must be taken to avoid or counteract any future settling or shrinking that might cause distortion of the building. The girders must also be installed so that they will properly support joists.

c. Illustration. Figure 5 shows a built-up girder. A shows the two outside masonry walls, B the built-up girder, C the joists, and D the support columns which support the girder B. Notice that the joists rest on top of the girder. This type of girder is commonly used in house construction. It is generally made of three planks spiked together (fig. 5) with 16d common nails.

e. Joist Hangers. A girder over which joist hangers have been placed to carry the joists is also used where there is little headroom or where the joists carry an extremely heavy load and nailing cannot be relied on. These girders are illustrated in figure 6.

f. Size Requirements. The principles which govern the size of a girder are—
   (1) The distance between girder posts.
   (2) The girder load area.
   (3) The total floor load per square foot on the girder.
   (4) The load per linear foot on the girder.
   (5) The total load on the girder.
   (6) The material to be used.

g. Size Determination. A girder should be large enough to support any ordinary load placed upon it; any size larger than that is wasted material. The carpenter should understand the effect of length, width, and depth on the strength of a wood girder before attempting to determine its size.

h. Depth. When the depth of a girder is doubled, the safe load is increased four times. In other words, a girder that is 3 inches wide and 12 inches deep will carry four times as much wight as a girder 3 inches wide and 6 inches deep. In order to obtain greater carrying capacity through the efficient use of material, it is better to increase the depth within limits than it is to increase the width of the girder. The sizes of built-up wood girders for various loads and spans may be determined by using table 1. (LOCATED IN BACK OF CHAPTER)

i. Load Area. The load area of a building is carried by both foundation walls and the girder. Because the ends of each joist rest on the girder, there is more weight on the girder than there is on either of the walls. Before considering the load on the girder, it may be well to consider a single joist. Suppose that a 10-foot plank weighing 5 pounds per foot is lifted by two men. If the men were at opposite ends of the plank, they would each be supporting 25 pounds.

   (1) Now assume that one of these men lifts the end of another 10-foot plank with the same weight as the first one, and a third man lifts the opposite end. The two men on the outside are each supporting one-half of the weight of one plank, or 25 pounds apiece, but the man in the center is supporting one-half of each of the two planks, or a total of 50 pounds.

   (2) The two men on the outside represent the foundation walls, and the center man represents the girder; therefore, the girder carries one-half of the weight, while the other half is equally divided between the outside walls. However, the girder may not always be located halfway between the outer walls. To explain this, the same three men will lift two planks which weigh 5 pounds per foot. One of the planks is 8 feet long and the other is 12 feet long. Since the total length of these two planks is the same as before and the weight per foot is the same, the total weight in both cases is 100 pounds.

   (3) One of the outside men is supporting one-half of the 8-foot plank, or 20 pounds. The man on the opposite outside end is supporting one-half of the 12-foot plank, or 30 pounds. The man in the center is supporting one-half of each plank, or a total of 50 pounds. This is the same total weight he was lifting before. A general rule that can be applied when determining the girder load area is that a girder will carry the weight of the floor on each side to the midpoint of joists which rest upon it.

j. Floor Load. After the girder load area is known, the total floor load per square foot must be determined in order to select a safe girder size. Both dead and live loads must be considered in finding the total floor load.

   (1) The first type of load consists of all weight of the building structure. This is called the dead load. The dead load per square foot of floor area, which is carried to the girder either directly or indirectly by way of bearing partitions, will vary according to the method of construction and building height. The structural parts included in the dead load are—

   Floor joists for all floor levels.
   Flooring materials, including attic if it is floored.
   Bearing partitions.
   Attic partitions.
   Attic joists for top floor.
   Ceiling lath and plaster, including basement ceiling if it is plastered.

   (2) For a building of light-frame construction similar to an ordinary frame house, the dead load allowance per square foot of all the structural parts must be added together to determine the total dead load. The allowance for average subfloor, finish floor, and joists without basement plaster should be 10 pounds per square foot. If the basement ceiling is plastered, an additional 10 pounds should be allowed. When girders (or bearing partitions) support the first floor partition, a load allowance of 20 pounds must be

allowed for ceiling plaster and joists when the attic is unfloored. If the attic is floored and used for storage, an additional 10 pounds (per sq ft) should be allowed.

(3) The second type of load to be considered is the weight of furniture, persons, and other movable loads which are not actually a part of the building but are still carried by the girder. This is called the live load. Snow on the roof is considered a part of the live load. The live load per square foot will vary according to the use of the building and local weather conditions. The allowance for the live load on floors used for living purposes is usually 30 pounds per square foot. If the attic is floored and used for light storage, an additional 20 pounds per square foot should be allowed. The allowance per square foot for live loads is usually governed by specifications and regulations.

(4) When the total load per square foot of floor area is known, the load per linear foot on the girder is easily figured. Assume that the girder load area of the building shown in figure 7 is sliced into 1-foot lengths across the girder. Each slice represents the weight supported by 1 foot of the girder. If the slice is divided into 1-foot units, each unit will represent 1 square foot of the total floor area. The load per linear foot of girder is determined by multiplying the number of units by the total load per square foot. Note in figure 7 that the girder is off center. Therefore, the joist length on one side of the girder is 7 feet (one-half of 14 feet) and the other side is 5 feet (one-half of 10 feet), for a total distance of 12 feet across the load area. Since each slice is 1 foot wide, it has a total floor area of 12 square feet. Now, if we assume that the total floor load for each square foot is 70 pounds, multiply the length times the width (7' x 12') to get the total square feet supported by the girder (7' x 12' = 84 sq ft).

```
     84 sq ft
  x  70 lb per sq ft (live and dead load)
   5,880 lb total load on girder
```

k. Material. Wooden girders are more common than steel in small frame-type buildings. Solid timber may be used or they may be built up by using two or more 2-inch planks. Built-up girders have the advantage of not warping as easily as solid wooden girders and are less likely to have decayed wood in the center.

(1) When built-up girders are used, the pieces should be securely spiked together to prevent them from buckling individually. A two-

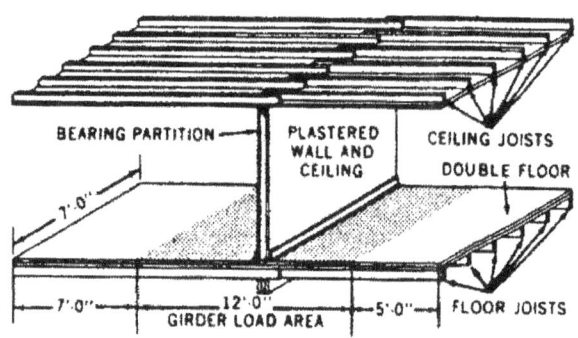

Figure 7. Girder load area.

piece girder of 2-inch planks should be spiked on both sides with 16d common nails. The nails should be located near the bottom, spaced approximately 2 feet apart near the ends and 1 foot apart in the center. A three-piece girder should be nailed in the same way as a two-piece girder.

(2) Regardless of whether the girder is built-up or solid, it should be of well-seasoned material. For a specific total girder load and span, the size of the girder will vary according to the kinds of wood used. The reason for this variation is that some kinds are stronger than others.

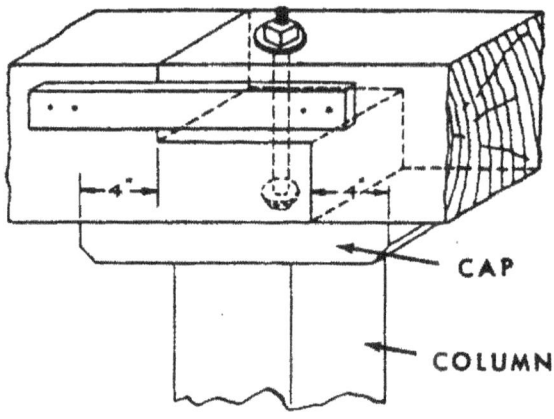

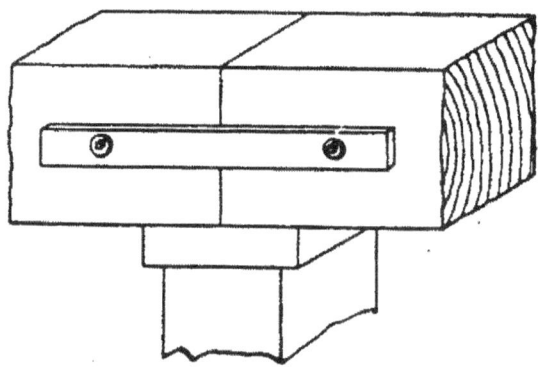

Figure 8. Half-lap and butt joints.

l. Splicing. To make a built-up girder, select straight lumber free from knots and other defects. The stock should be long enough so that no more than one joint will occur over the span between footings. The joints in the beam should be staggered, with care taken to insure that the planks are squared at each joint and butted tightly together. Sometimes a half-lap joint is used to join solid beams. In order to do this correctly, the beam should be placed on one edge so that the annual rings run from top to bottom. The lines for the half-lap joint are then laid out as illustrated in figure 8, and the cuts are made along these lines. The cuts are then checked with a steel square to assure a matching joint. To make the matching joint on the other beam, proceed in the same way and repeat the process.

(1) The next step is to tack a temporary strap across the joint to hold it tightly together. Now drill a hole through the joist with a bit about 1/16 inch larger than the bolt to be used. Fasten together with a bolt, washer, and nut.

(2) Another type of joint is called the strapped butt joint. The ends of the beam should be cut square, and the straps, which generally are 18 inches long, are bolted to each side of the beams.

m. Supports. When building small houses where the services of an architect are not available, it is important that the carpenter have some knowledge of the principles that determine the proper size of girder supports.

(1) A column or post is a vertical member designed to carry the live and dead loads imposed upon it. It may be made of wood, metal, or masonry. The wooden columns may be solid timbers or may be made up of several wooden members spiked together with 16d or 20d common nails. Metal columns are made of heavy pipe, large steel angles, or I-beams.

(2) Regardless of the material used in a column, it must have some form of bearing plate at the top and bottom. These plates distribute the load evenly over the cross sectional area of the column. Basement posts that support girders should be set on masonry footings. Columns should be securely fastened to the load-bearing member at the top and to the footing on which they rest at the bottom. Figure 9 shows a solid wooden column with a metal bearing cap drilled to provide a means of fastening it to the column and to the girder. The bottom of this type of column may be fastened to the masonry footing by a metal dowel inserted in a hole drilled in the bottom of the column and in the masonry footing. The base at this point is coated with asphalt to prevent rust or rot.

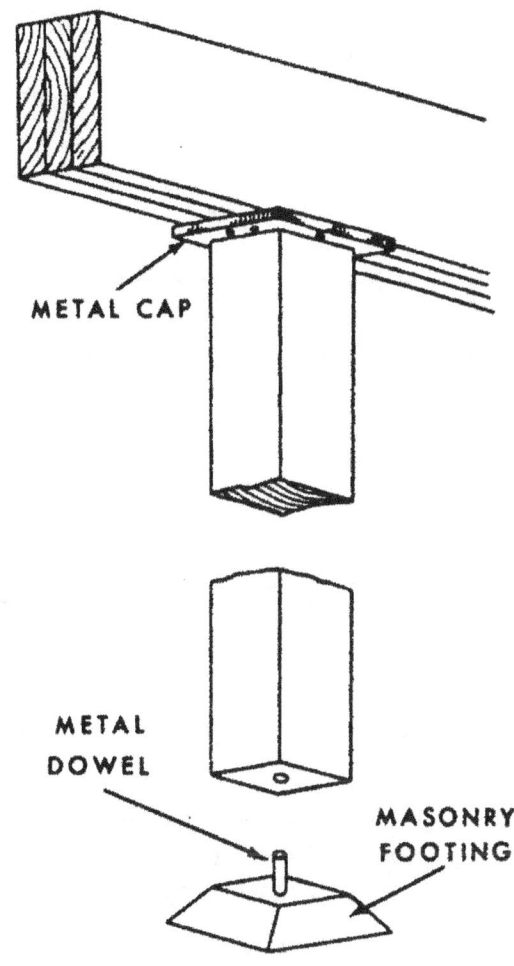

Figure 9. Solid wood column with metal bearing cap.

(3) When locating columns, it is well to avoid spans of more than 10 feet between columns that are to support the girders. The farther apart the columns are spaced, the heavier the girder must be to carry the joists over the span between the columns.

(4) A good arrangement of the girder and supporting columns for a 24- x 40-foot building is shown in figure 10. Column B will support one-half of the girder load existing in the half of the building lying between the wall A and column C. Column C will support one-half of the girder load between columns B and D. Likewise, column D will share equally the girder loads with column C and the wall E.

n. Girder Forms. Girder forms for making concrete girders and beams are constructed from 2-inch-thick material (fig. 11) dressed on all sides. The bottom piece of material should be constructed in one piece to avoid the necessity of cleats. The bottom piece of the form should never

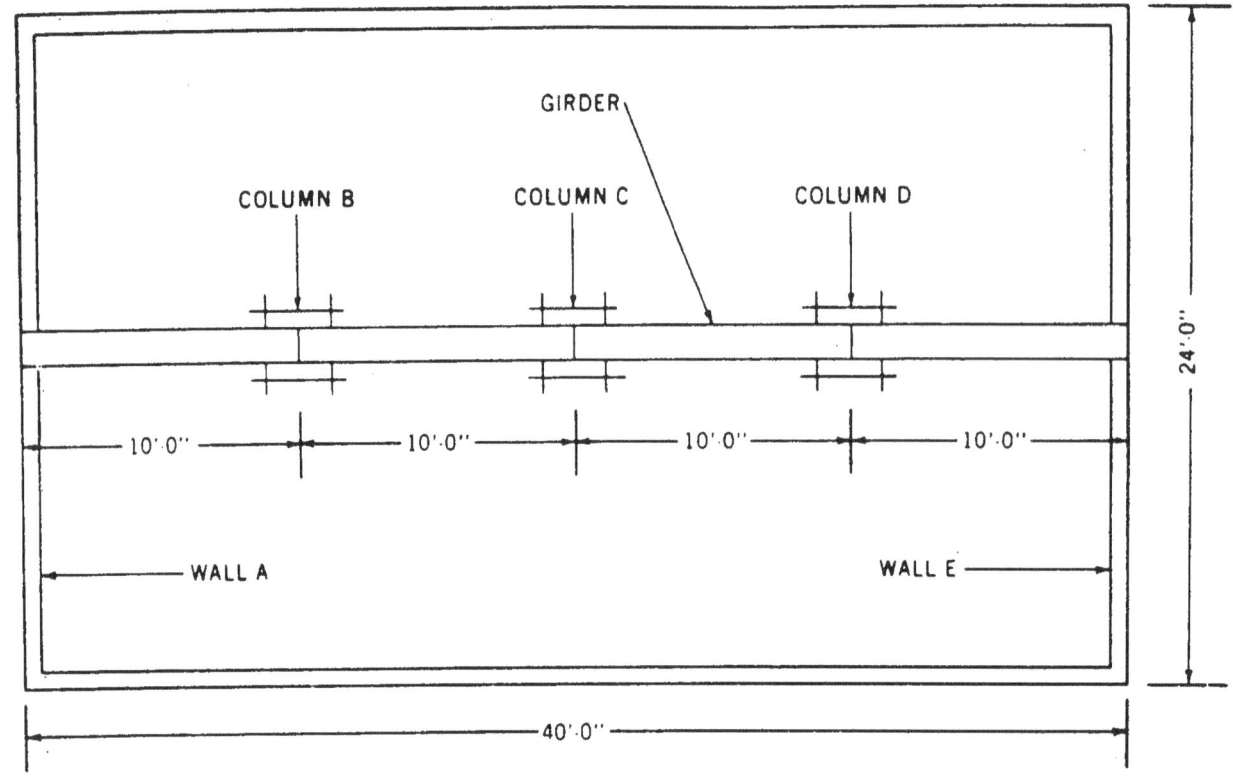

Figure 10. Column spacing.

overlap the side pieces. The side pieces must always overlap the bottom. The temporary cleats shown in figure 11 are tacked on to prevent the form from collapsing when handled.

4. Floor Joists

Joists are the wooden members that make up the body of the floor frame. The flooring or subflooring is nailed to them. They are usually 2 or 3 inches thick. Joists as small as 2 by 6 inches are sometimes used in light buildings. These are too small for floors with spans over 10 feet but are frequently used for ceiling joists. Joists usually carry a uniform load of materials and personnel. The latter loads carry a uniform

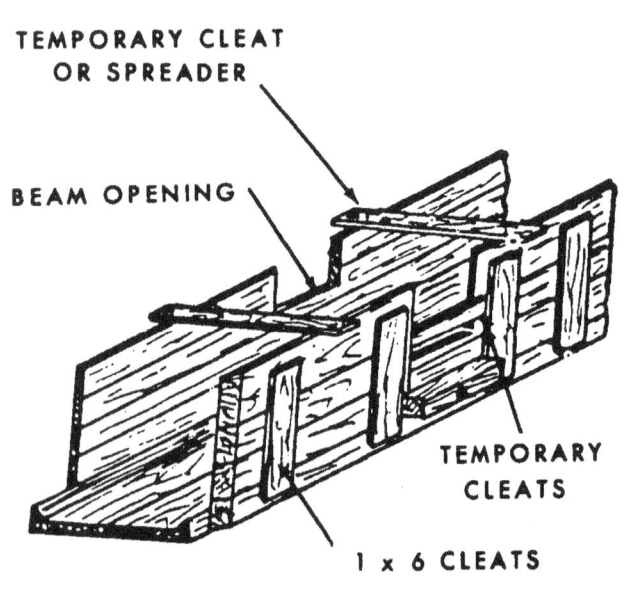

Figure 11. Girder and beam form.

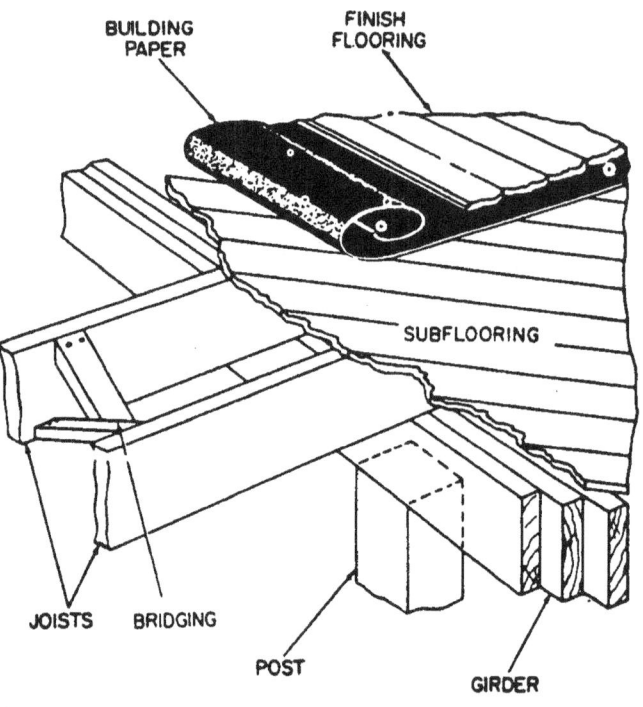

Figure 12. Floor joists.

load of materials and personnel. The latter loads are "live loads"; the weight of joists and floors is a "dead load". The joists carry the flooring directly on their upper surface and they are supported at their ends by sills, girders, bearing partitions, or bearing walls (fig. 12). They are spaced 16 or 24 inches apart, center to center; sometimes the spacing is 12 inches, but where such spacing is necessary, heavier joists should be used. Two-inch material should not be used for joists more than 12 inches apart.

5. Connecting Joists to Sills, Girders, and I-Beams

a. Joining to Sills. In joining joists to sills, be sure that the connection is able to hold the load that the joists will carry. A joist resting upon the sill is shown in 1, figure 13. This method (of several methods) is most commonly used because it provides the strongest possible joint. The methods shown in 2 and 3, figure 13, are used where it is not desirable to use joists on top of the sill. The ledger plate (*e* below) should be securely nailed and the joist should not be notched over one-third of its depth to prevent splitting (4, fig. 13).

b. Joining to Girders. In the framing of the joists to the girders, the joists must be level. Therefore, if the girder is not the same height as the sill, the joist must be notched as shown in 3, figure 13. If the girder and sill are of the same height, the joist must be connected to the sill and girder to keep the joist level. In placing joists, always have the crown up since this counteracts the weight on the joist; in most cases there will be no sag below a straight line. Overhead joists are joined to plates as shown in 1 and 2, figure 14. The inner end of the joist rests on the plates of the partition walls. When a joist is to rest on plates or girders, either the joist is cut long enough to extend the full width of the plate or girder, or it is cut so as to meet in the center of the plate or girder and is connected with a scab. Where two joist ends lie side by side on a plate, they should be nailed together. Joists may also be joined to girders by using ledger strips (3 and 4, fig. 14).

c. Iron Stirrups. One of the strongest supports for the joists is straps or hangers (iron stirrups) as shown in 5 of figure 13.

d. I-Beams. The simplest and probably the best way to carry joists on steel girders is to rest them on top, as shown in 6, figure 13, provided headroom is not too much restricted. If there is a lack of headroom, use the method shown in 5, figure 13.

e. Use of Ledger Plates (fig. 14). In connecting joists to girders and sills where piers are used, a 2 by 4 is nailed to the face of the sill or girder, flush with the bottom edge; this is called a "ledger plate" (1, fig. 14). These pieces should be nailed securely with 20-penny nails about 12 inches apart. Where 2 by 4 or 2

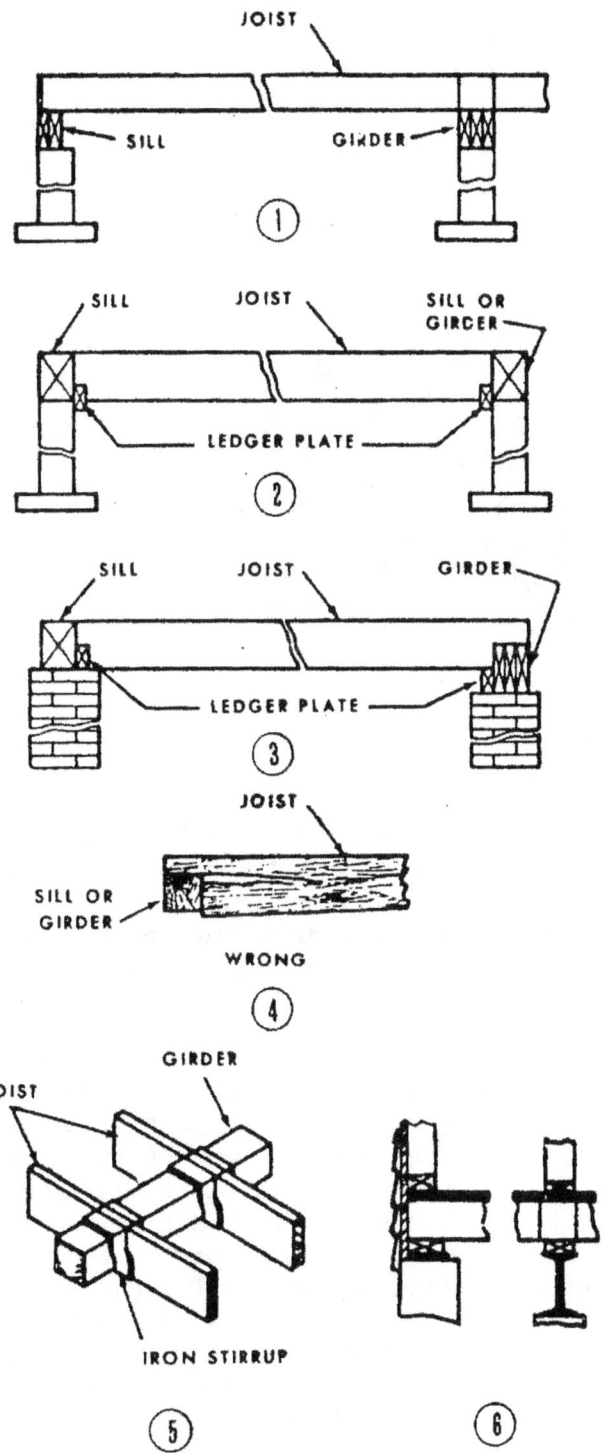

Figure 13. Sill and joist connections.

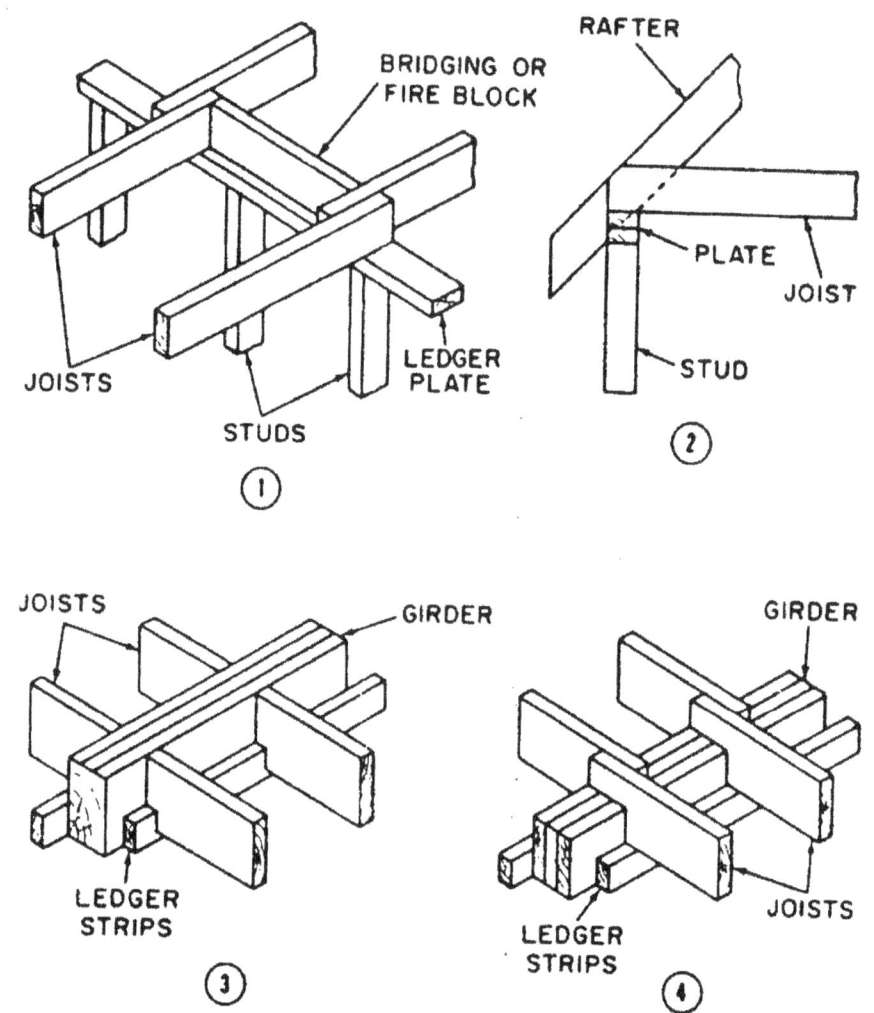

Figure 14. Ledger plates.

by 8 joists are used, it is better to use 2 by 2's to prevent the joists from splitting at the notch. When joists are 10 inches deep and deeper, 2 by 4's may be used without reducing the strength of the joists. If a notch is used, joist ties may be used to overcome this loss of strength. These ties are short 1 by 4 boards nailed across the joist; the ends of the boards are flush with the top and bottom edge of the joists.

6. Bridging

a. General. When joists are used over a long span, they have a tendency to sway from side to side. Floor frames are bridged in order to stiffen the floor frame, to prevent unequal deflection of the joists, and to enable an overload joist to receive some help from the joists on either side of it. A pattern for the bridging stock is obtained by placing a piece of material between the joists as shown in figure 15, then marking and sawing it. When sawed, the cut will form the correct angle. Always nail the top of the bridging with 8- or 10-penny nails. Do not nail the bottom of the bridging until the rough floor has been laid, in order to keep the bridging from pushing up any joist which might cause an unevenness in the floor.

b. Construction. Bridging is of two kinds: solid (or horizontal) bridging (1, fig. 15) and cross bridging (2, fig. 15). Cross bridging is the one most generally used; it is very effective and requires less material than horizontal bridging. Cross bridging looks like a cross and consists of pieces of lumber, usually 1 by 3 or 2 by 3 inches in size, cut in diagonally between the floor joists. Each piece is nailed to the top of each joist and forms a cross (x) between the joists. These pieces between joists should be placed as near to each other as possible. Bridging should be nailed and the bottoms left until the subfloor is laid. This permits the joists to adjust themselves to their final positions. The bottom ends of bridging

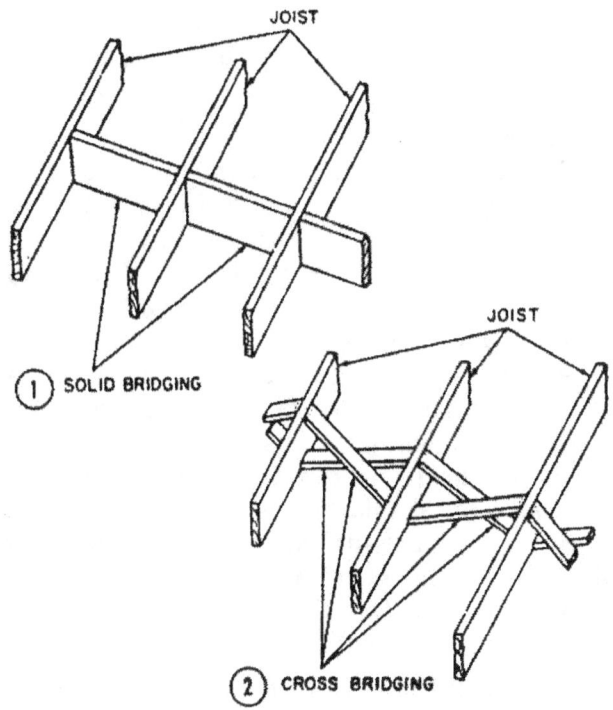

Figure 15. Types of bridging.

may then be nailed, forming a continuous truss across the whole length of the floor and preventing any overloaded joist from sagging below the others. Cutting and fitting the bridging by hand is a slow process; a power saw should be used if it is available. After joists have once been placed, a pattern may be made and used to speed up the process of cutting. On joists over 8 feet long, one line of bridging should be placed and on joists over 16 feet long, two lines.

7. Floor Openings

a. General. Floor openings for stairwells, ventilators, and chimneys are framed by a combination of headers and trimmers (fig. 16). Headers run at right angles to the direction of the joists and are doubled. Trimmers run parallel to the joists and are actually doubled joists. The joists are framed to the headers where the headers form the opening frame at right angles to the joists. These shorter joists, framed to the headers, are called tail beams, tail joists, or header joists. The number of headers and trimmers needed at any opening depends upon the shape of the opening, whether it is a simple rectangle or contains additional angles; upon the direction in which the opening runs in relation to the direction in which the joists run; and upon the position of the opening in relation to partitions or walls. Figure 16 gives examples of openings, one of which runs parallel to the

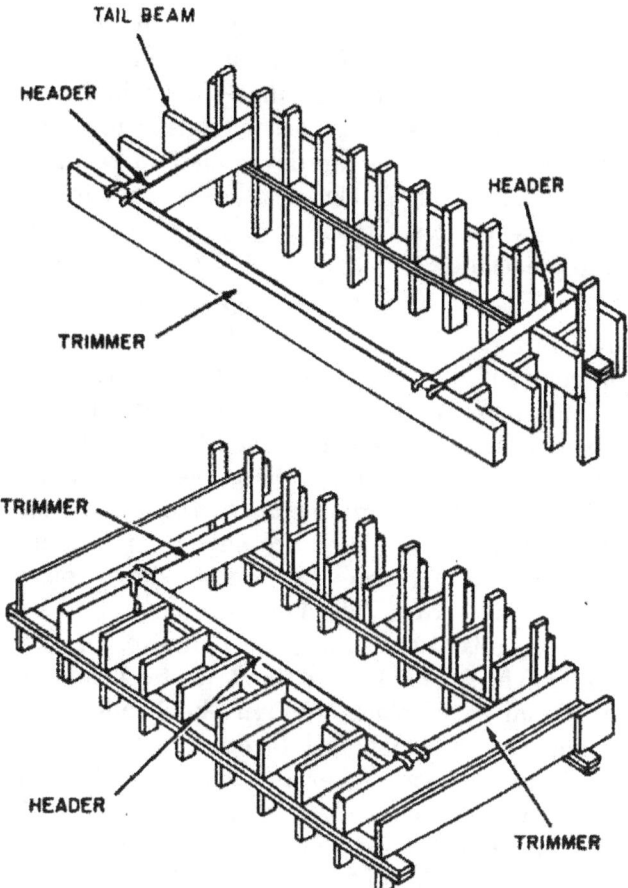

Figure 16. Floor openings.

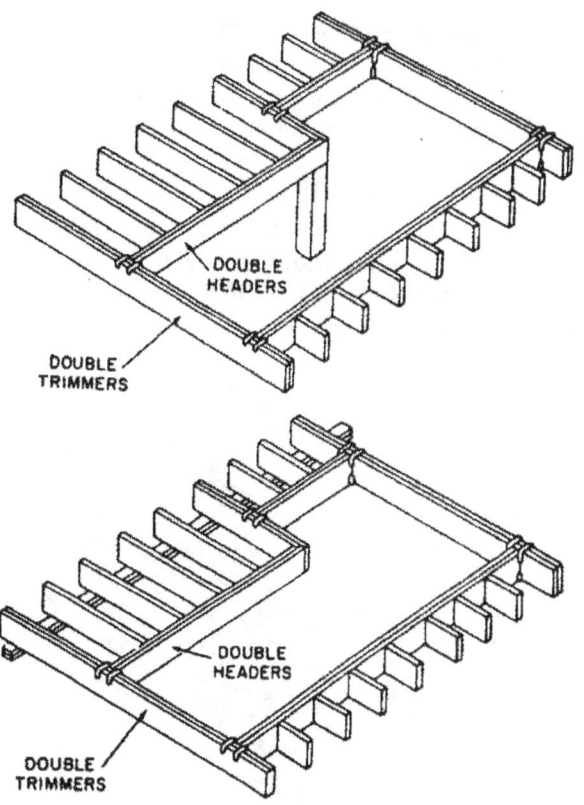

Figure 17. Double headers and double trimmers.

169

joist and requires two headers and one trimmer, while the other runs at right angles to the run of the joists and, therefore, requires one header and two trimmers. The openings shown in figure 17 are constructed with corner angles supported in different ways. The cantilever method requires that the angle be fairly close to a supporting partition with joists from an adjacent span that run to the header.

b. Construction. To frame openings of the type shown in figure 18, first install joists A and C, then cut four pieces of timber that are the same size as the joists with their length corresponding to the distance between the joists A and C at the outside wall. Nail two of these pieces between the joists at the desired distances from the ends of the joists; these pieces are shown as headers Nos. 1 and 2, figure 18. Install short joists X and Y, as shown. The nails should be 16- or 20-penny nails. By omitting headers Nos. 3 and 4 and joists B and D, the short joists X and Y can be nailed in place through the header and the headers can be nailed through the joists A and B into its end. After the header and short joists have been securely nailed, headers Nos. 3 and 4 are nailed beside Nos. 1 and 2. Then joist B is placed beside joists A and joist D beside C, and all are nailed securely.

8. Subfloors and Finish Floors

a. Subfloors. After the foundation and basic framework of a building are completed, the floor is constructed. The subfloor, if included in the plans, is laid diagonally on the joists and nailed with 8- to 10-penny nails. The floor joists form a framework for the subfloor. Subflooring boards 8 inches wide or over should have three or more nails per joist. Where the subfloor is over 1 inch thick, larger nails should be used. Figure 12 shows the method of laying a subfloor. Preferably it is laid before the walls are framed so that it can be used as a floor to work on while framing the walls.

b. Finish Floors.

(1) *General.* A finish floor in the theater of operations, in most cases, is of 3/4-inch material, square edged (fig. 19) or tongued and grooved (fig. 20), and varying from 3 1/4 to 7 1/4 inches wide. It is laid directly on floor joists or on a subfloor and nailed with 8-penny common nails in every joist. When laid on a subfloor, it is best to use building paper between the two floors to keep out dampness and insects. In warehouses, where heavy loads are to be carried on the floor, 2-inch material should be used. The flooring, in this case, also is face-nailed with 16- or 20-penny nails. It is not tongued and grooved and ranges in width from 4 to 12 inches. The joints are made on the center of the joist.

(2) *Wood floors.* Wood floors must be strong enough to carry the load. The type of building and the use for which it is intended determines the general arrangement of the floor system,

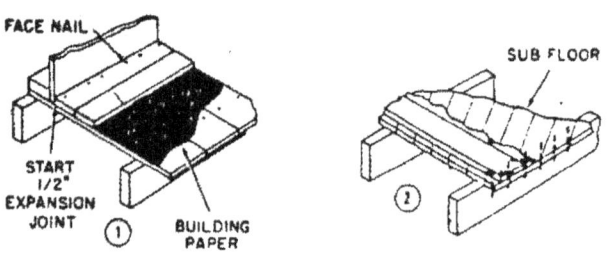

Figure 19. Methods for nailing square-edged flooring.

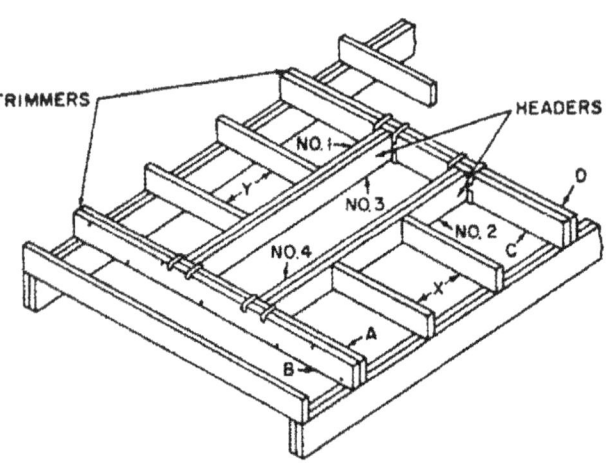

Figure 18. Floor opening construction.

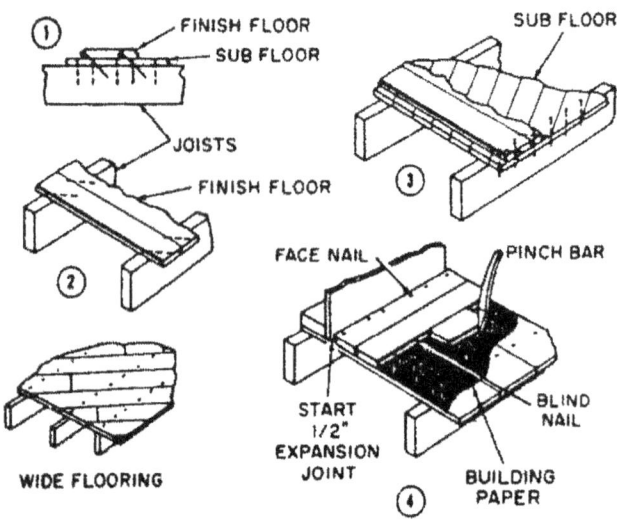

Figure 20. Methods for nailing tongued-and-grooved flooring.

thickness of the sheathing, and approximate spacing of the joists.

(3) *Concrete floors.* Concrete floors may be constructed for shops where earthen or wood floors are not suitable such as in repair and assembly shops for airplanes and heavy equipment and in certain kinds of warehouses. These floors are made by pouring concrete on the ground after the earth has been graded and tamped. This type of floor is likely to be damp unless protected. Drainage is provided, both for the floor area and for the area near the floor, to prevent flooding after heavy rains. The floor should be reinforced with steel or wire mesh. Where concrete floors are to be poured, a foundation wall may be poured first and the floor poured after the building is completed. This gives protection to the concrete floor while it sets.

(4) *Miscellaneous types of floors.* Miscellaneous floors may include earth, adobe brick, duckboard, or rushes. Use of miscellaneous flooring is usually determined by a shortage of conventional materials, the need to save time or labor, the extremely temporary nature of the facilities, or the special nature of the structure. The selection of material is usually determined by availability. Duckboard is widely used for shower flooring; earthen floors are common and conserve both materials and labor if the ground site is even without extensive grading. Rush or thatch floors are primarily an insulating measure and must be replaced frequently.

(5) *Supports.* In certain parts of the floor frame, in order to support some very heavily concentrated load or a partition wall, it may be necessary to double the joist or to place two joists together (fig. 21).

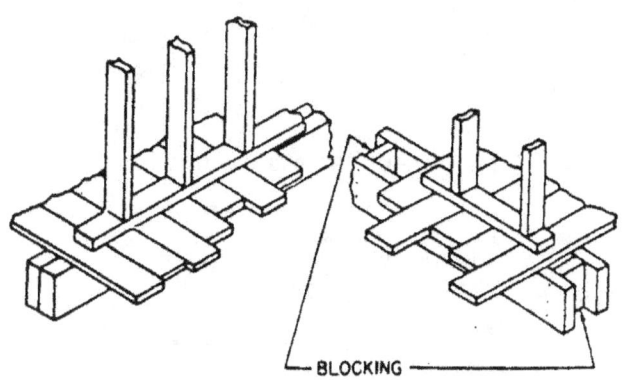

Figure 21. Reinforced joists.

Section II. WALLS AND WALL COVERINGS

9. General

Wall framing (fig. 22) is composed of regular studs, diagonal bracing, cripples, trimmers, headers, and fire blocks and is supported by the floor sole plate. The vertical members of the wall framing are the studs, which support the top plates and all of the weight of the upper part of the building or everything above the top plate line. They provide the framework to which the wall sheathing is anlled on the outside and which supports the lath, plaster, and insulation on the inside.

10. Wall Components

Walls and partitions which are classed as framed constructions (fig. 23) are composed of structural elements which are usually closely spaced, slender, vertical members called studs. These are arranged in a row with their ends bearing on a long horizontal member called a bottom plate or sole plate, and their tops capped with another plate, called a top plate. Double top plates are used in bearing walls and partitions. The bearing strength of stud walls is determined by the strength of the studs.

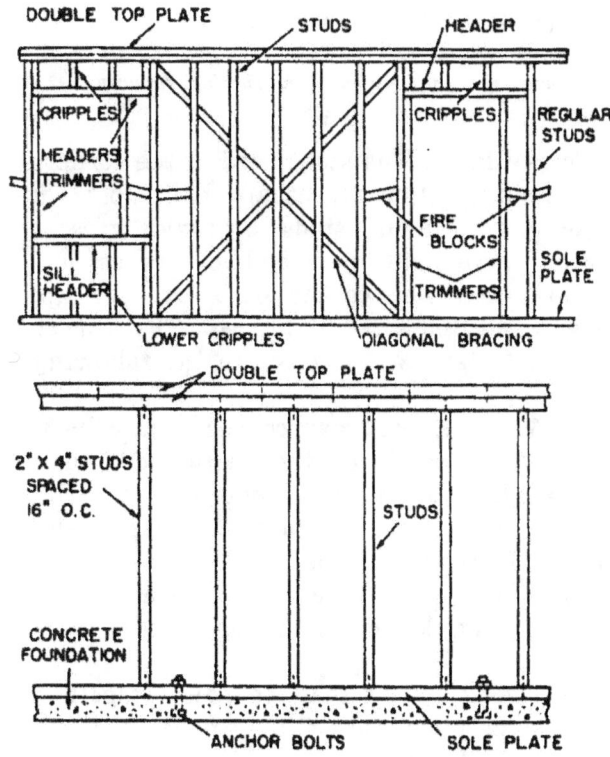

Figure 22. Typical wall frame details.

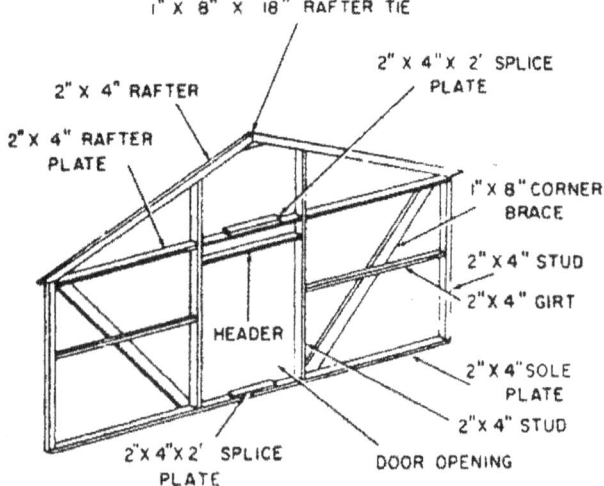

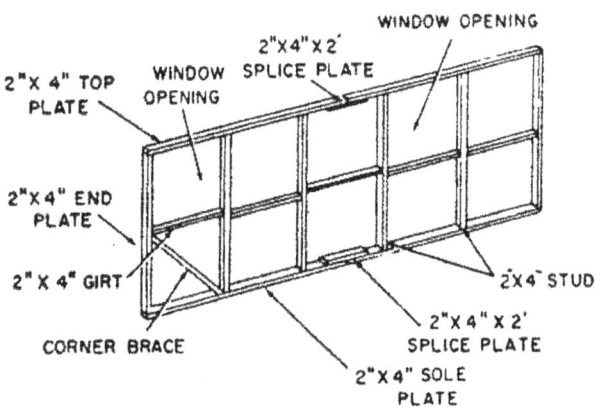

Figure 23. Typical wall construction showing openings.

a. *Corner Posts.* The studs used at the corners of frame construction are usually built up from three or more ordinary studs to provide greater strength. These built-up assemblies are corner-partition posts. The corner posts are set up, plumbed, and temporarily braced. The corner posts (fig. 24) may be made in the following ways:

(1) A corner post may consist of a 4 by 6 with a 2 by 4 nailed on the board side, flush with one edge, as shown in figure 24. This type of corner is for a 4-inch wall. Where walls are thicker, heavier timber is used.

(2) A 4 by 4 may be used with a 2 by 4 nailed to two of the adjoining sides, shown in 2, figure 24.

(3) Two 2 by 4's may be nailed together with blocks between and a 2 by 4 flush with one edge, shown in 3, figure 24.

(4) A 2 by 4 may be nailed to the edge of another 2 by 4, the edge of one flush with the side of the other (4, fig. 24). This type is used extensively in the theater of operations where no inside finish is needed.

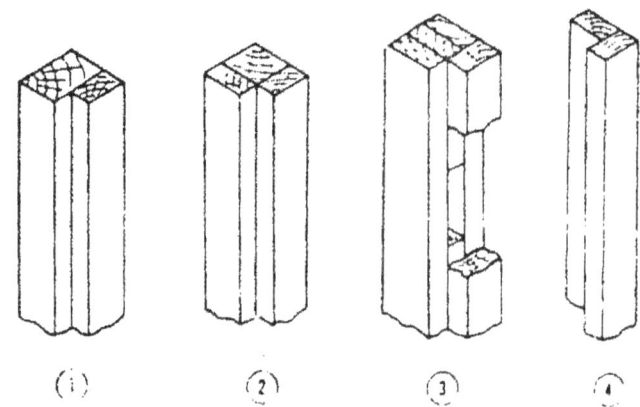

Figure 24. Corner post construction.

b. *T-Posts.* Whenever a partition meets an outside wall, a stud wide enough to extend beyond the partition on both sides is used; this provides a solid nailing base for the inside wall finish. This type of stud is called a T-post (fig. 25) and is made in the following different ways:

(1) A 2 by 4 may be nailed and centered on the face side of a 4 by 6 (1, fig. 25).

(2) A 2 by 4 may be nailed and centered on two 4 by 4's nailed together (2, fig. 25).

(3) Two 2 by 4's may be nailed together with a block between them and a 2 by 4 centered on the wide side (3, fig. 25).

(4) A 2 by 4 may be nailed and centered on the face side of a 2 by 6, with a horizontal bridging nailed behind them to give support and stiffness (4, fig. 25).

c. *Partition and Double T-Posts.* Where a partition is finished on one side only, the partition post used consists of a simple stud, set in the outside wall, in line with the side of the partition

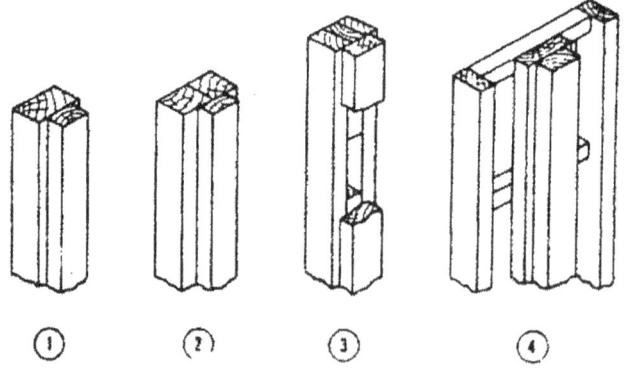

Figure 25. T-post construction.

wall, and finished as stud A in 1, figure 26. These posts are nailed in place along with the corner post. The exact position of the partition walls must be determined before the posts are placed. Where the walls are more than 4 inches thick, wider timber is used. In special cases, for example where partition walls cross, a double T-post is used. This is made by using methods in *b*(1), (2), or (3) above, and nailing another 2 by 4 to the opposite wide side, as shown in 2, 3, and 4, figure 26.

d. Studs.

(1) After the sills, plates, and braces are in place, and the window and door openings are laid out, the studs are placed and nailed with two 16- or 20-penny nails through the top plate. Then the remaining or intermediate studs are laid out on the sills or soles by measuring from one corner the distances the studs are to be set apart. Studs are normally spaced 12, 16, and 24 inches on centers, depending upon the type of outside and inside finish. Where vertical siding is used, studs are set wider apart since the horizontal girts between them provide nailing surface.

(2) When it is desirable to double the post of the door opening, first place the outside studs into position and nail them securely. Then cut short studs, or *filler studs*, the size of the opening, and nail these to the inside face of the outside studs as shown in figure 27. In making a window opening, a bottom header must be framed; this header is either single or double. When it is doubled, the bottom piece is nailed to the opening studs at the proper height and the top piece of the bottom header is nailed into place flush with the bottom section. The door header is framed as shown in figure 27. The filler stud rests on the sole at the bottom.

e. Girts. Girts are always the same width as the studs and are flush with the face of the stud, both outside and inside. Girts are used in hasty construction where the outside walls are covered with vertical siding. Studs are placed from 2 to 10 feet apart, with girts, spaced about 4 feet apart, running horizontally between them (fig. 27). The vertical siding acts in the same way as to studs and helps to carry the weight of the roof. This type of construction is used extensively in the theater of operations.

f. Top Plate and Sole Plate.

(1) *Top plate.* The top plate ties the studding together at the top and forms a finish for the walls; it furnishes a support for the lower ends of the rafters (fig. 22). The top plate serves as a connecting link between the wall and the roof, just as the sills and girders are connecting links between the floors and the walls.

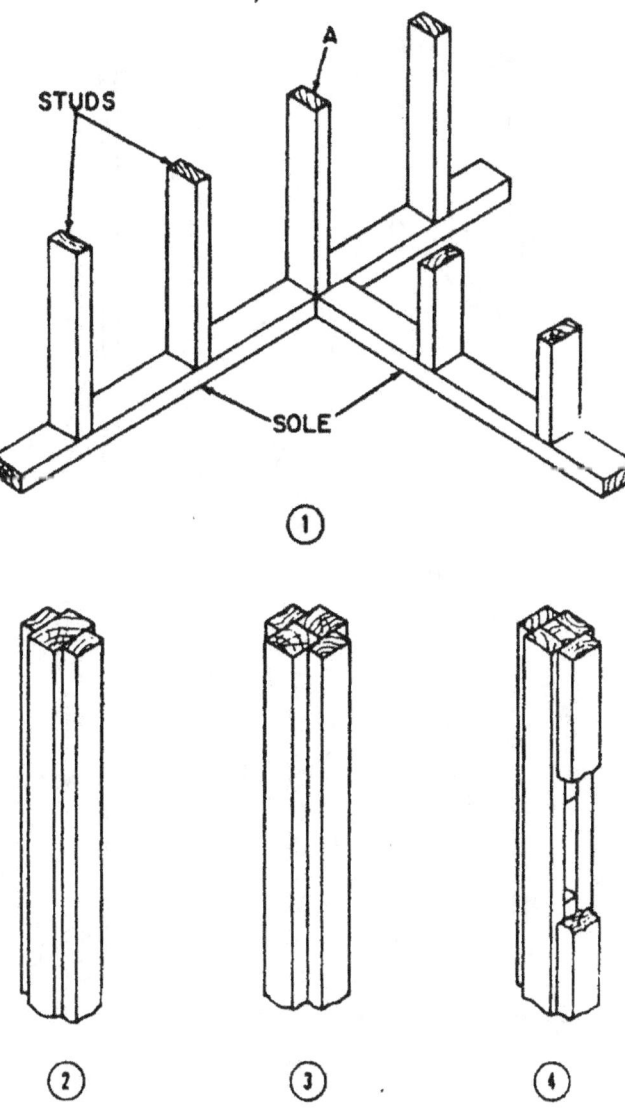

Figure 26. Partition posts.

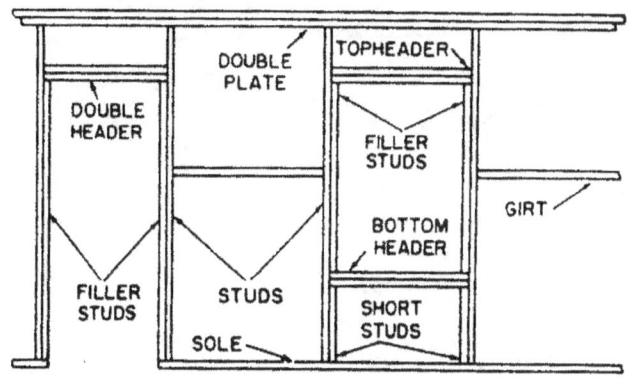

Figure 27. Door and window framing.

The plate is made up of one or two pieces of timber of the same size as the studs. In cases where the studs at the end of the building extend to the rafters, no plate is used at the end of the building. When it is used on top of partition walls, it is sometimes called the cap. Where the plate is doubled, the first plate or bottom section is nailed with 16- or 20-penny nails to the top of the corner posts and to the studs. The connection at the corner is made as shown in 1, figure 28. After the single plate is nailed securely and the corner braces are nailed into place, the top part of the plate is then nailed to the bottom section with 16- or 20-penny nails either over each stud, or spaced with two nails every 2 feet. The edges of the top section should be flush with the bottom section and the corner joints lapped as shown in 1 and 2, figure 28.

(2) *Sole plate.* All partition walls and outside walls are finished either with a 2 by 4 or with a piece of timber corresponding to the thickness of the wall; this timber is laid horizontally on the floor or joists. It carries the bottom end of the studs (fig. 22). This timber is called the "sole" or "sole plate". The sole should be nailed with two 16- or 20-penny nails at each joist that it crosses. If it is laid lengthwise on top of a girder or joist, it should be nailed with two nails every 2 feet.

g. Bridging. Frame walls are bridged, in most cases, to make them more sturdy. There are two methods of bridging:

(1) *Diagonal bridging.* Diagonal bridging is nailed between the studs at an angle (1, fig. 29). It is more effective than the horizontal type since it forms a continuous truss and tends to keep the walls from sagging. Whenever possible, both interior partitions and exterior walls should be bridged alike.

(2) *Horizontal bridging.* Horizontal bridging is nailed between the studs horizontally and halfway between the sole and the plate (2, fig. 29). This bridging is cut to lengths which correspond to the distance between the studs at the bottom. Such bridging not only stiffens the wall but also will help straighten studs.

11. Partitions

Partition walls divide the inside space of a building. These walls in most cases are framed as part of the building. Where floors are to be installed after the outside of the building is completed, the partition walls are left unframed. There are two types of partition walls: the bearing, and the non-bearing types. The bearing type supports ceiling joists. The nonbearing type supports only itself. This type may be put in at any time after

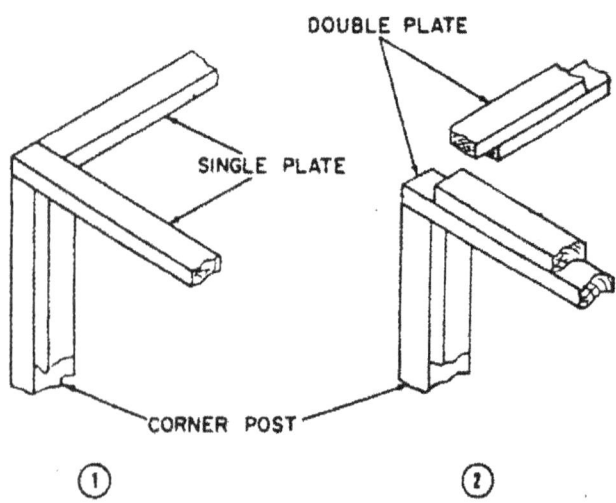

Figure 28. Plate construction.

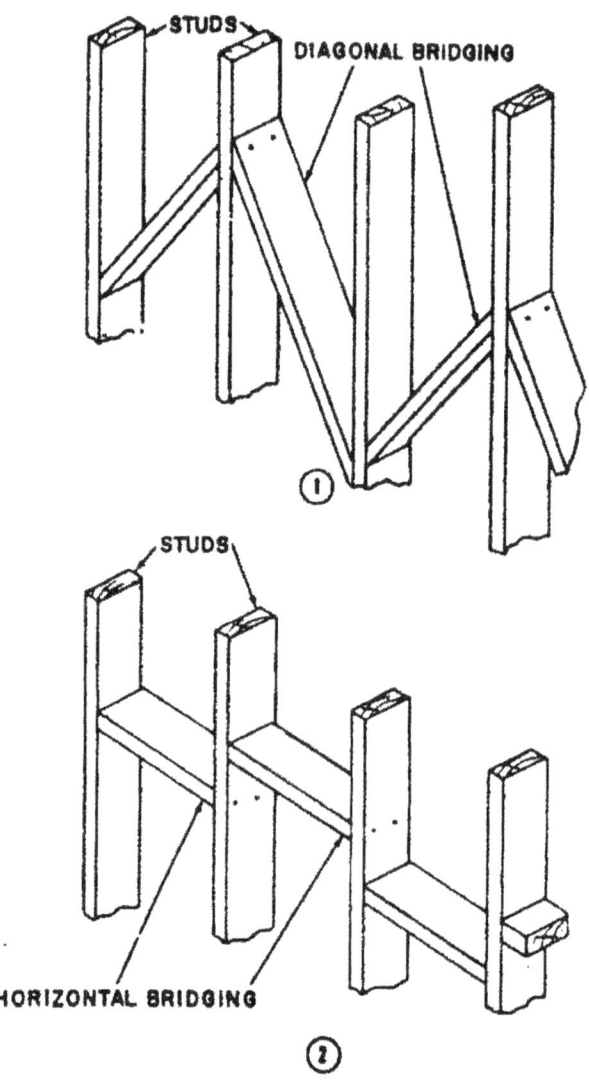

Figure 29. Types of wall bridging.

the other framework is installed. Only one cap or plate is used. A sole plate should be used in every case, as it helps to distribute the load over a larger area. Partition walls are framed the same as outside walls, and door openings are framed as outside openings. Where there are corners or where one partition wall joins another, corner posts or T-posts are used as in the outside walls; these posts provide nailing surfaces for the inside wall finish. Partition walls in the theater of operations one-story building may or may not extend to the roof. The top of the studs has a plate when the wall does not extend to the roof; but when the wall extends to the roof, the studs are joined to the rafters.

12. Methods of Plumbing Posts and Straightening Walls

a. General. After the corner post, T-post, and intermediate wall studs have been nailed to the plates or girts, the walls must be plumbed and straightened so that the permanent braces and rafters may be installed. This is done by using a level or plumb bob and a chalkline.

b. Plumbing Posts.

(1) To plumb a corner with a plumb bob, first attach to the bob a string long enough to extend to or below the bottom of the post. Lay a rule on top of the post so that 2 inches of the rule extends over the post on the side to be plumbed; then hang the bob-line over the rule so that the line is 2 inches from the post and extends to the bottom of it, as shown in 1, figure 30. With another rule, measure the distance from the post to the center of the line at the bottom of the post; if it does not measure 2 inches, the post is not plumb. Move the post inward or outward until the distance from the post to the center of the line is exactly 2 inches. Then nail the temporary brace in place. Repeat this procedure from the other outside face of the post. The post is then plumb. This process is carried out for the remaining corner posts of the building. If a plumb bob or level is not available, a rock, a half-brick, or some small piece of metal may be used instead.

(2) An alternate method of plumbing a post is illustrated in 2, figure 30. Attach the plumb bob string securely to the top of the post to be plumbed, making sure that the string is long enough to allow the plumb bob to hang near the bottom of the post. Use two blocks of wood identical in thickness as gage blocks. Tack one block near the top of the post between the plumb bob string and the post (gage block No. 1), in-

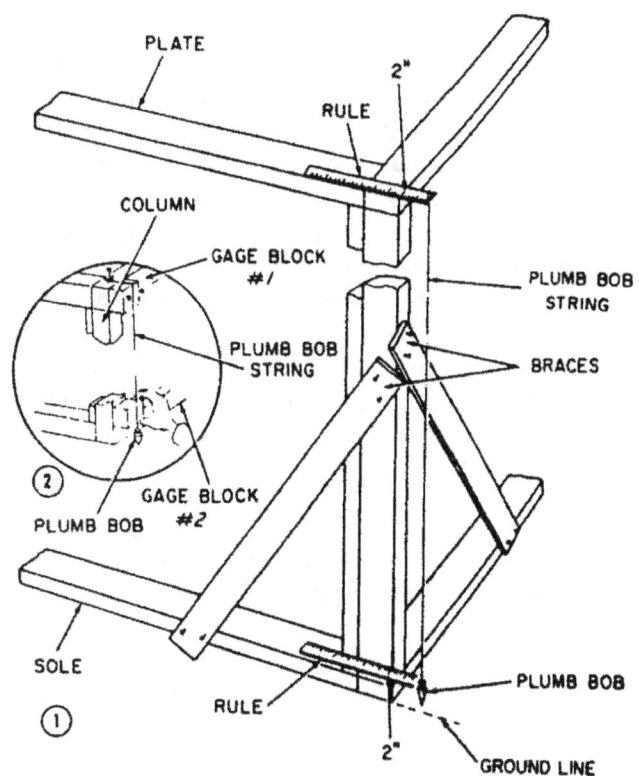

Figure 30. Plumbing a post.

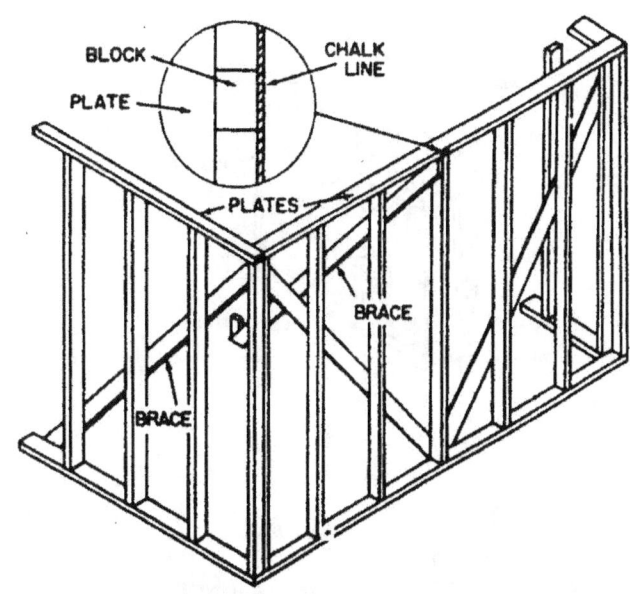

Figure 31. Straightening a wall.

serting the second block between the plumb bob string and the bottom of the post (gage block No. 2). If the entire face of the second block makes contact with the string, the post is plumb.

c. Straightening Walls (fig. 31). Plumb one corner post with the level or plumb bob and nail temporary braces to hold the post in place (*b* above). Repeat this procedure for all corner posts. Fasten a chalkline to the outside of one post at the top and stretch the line to the post the same as for the first post. Place a small 3/4-inch block under each end of the line as shown in figure 31 to give clearance. Place temporary braces at intervals small enough to hold the wall straight. When the wall is far enough away from the line to permit a 3/4-inch block to slide between the line and the plate, the brace is nailed. This procedure is carried out for the entire perimeter of the building. Inside partition walls should be straightened the same way.

13. Braces

Bracing is used to stiffen framed construction and make it rigid. The purpose of bracing may be to resist winds, storm, twist, or strain stemming from any cause. Good bracing keeps corners square and plumb and prevents warping, sagging, and shifts resulting from lateral forces that would otherwise tend to distort the frame and cause badly fitting doors and windows and the cracking of plaster. There are three commonly used methods of bracing frame structures:

a. Let-In Bracing (1, fig. 32). Let-in bracing is set into the edges of studs so as to be flush with the surface. The studs are always cut to let in the braces; the braces are never cut. Usually 1 by 4's or 1 by 6's are used, set diagonally from top plates to sole plates.

b. Cut-In Bracing (2, fig. 32). Cut-in bracing is toenailed between studs. It usually consists of 2 by 4's cut at an angle to permit toenailing, inserted in diagonal progression between studs running up and down from corner posts to sill or plates.

c. Diagonal Sheathing (3, fig. 32). The strongest type of bracing is sheathing applied diagonally. Each board acts as a brace of the wall. If plywood sheathing 5/8-inch thick or more is used, other methods of bracing may be omitted.

14. Exterior Walls

The exterior surfaces of a building usually consist of vertical, horizontal, or diagonal sheathing and composition, sheet-metal, or corrugated roofing. However, in theaters of operation the materials are not always available and substitutes must be provided. Concrete block, brick, rubble stone, metal, or earth may be substituted for wood in treeless regions. In the tropics, improvised siding and roofs can be made from bamboo and grasses. Roofing felt, sandwiched between two layers of light wire mesh, may serve for wall and roof materials where climate is suitable.

a. Sheathing. Sheathing is nailed directly onto the framework of the building. Its purpose is to strengthen the building, to provide a base wall onto which the finish siding can be nailed,

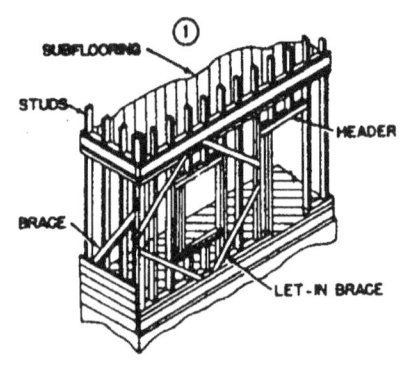

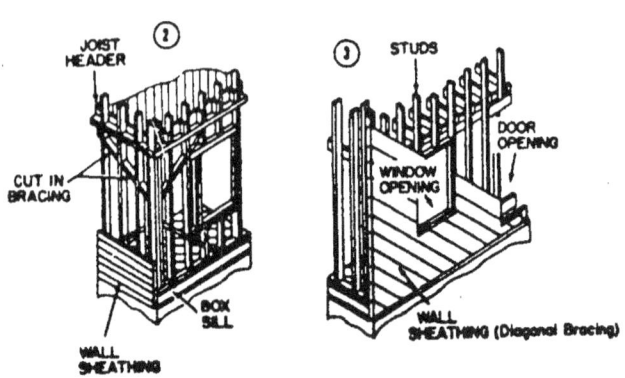

Figure 32. Common types of bracing.

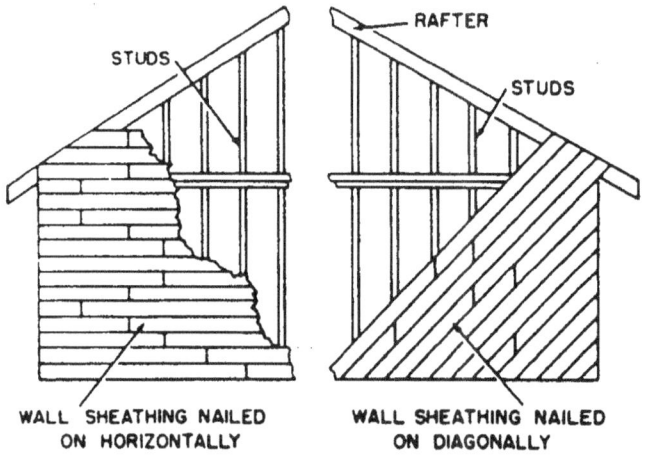

Figure 33. Diagonal and horizontal wooden sheathing.

to act as insulation, and in some cases to be a base for further insulation. Some of the common types of sheathing include—

(1) Wood, 11/16-inch thick by 6, 8, 10, or 12 inch wide of No. 1 common square or matched-edge material. It may be nailed on horizontally or diagonally (fig. 33).

(2) Gypsum board wall-sheathing, 1/2 inch thick by 24 inches wide and 8 feet long.

(3) Fiberboard, 25/32 inch thick by 24 by 48 inches wide and 8, 9, 10, and 12 feet long.

(4) Plywood, 5/16, 3/8, 1/2, 5/8 inches thick by 48 inches wide and 8, 9, 10, and 12 feet long.

  b. *Application.*

(1) Wood wall sheathing comes in almost all widths, lengths, and grades. Generally, widths are from 6 to 12 inches, with lengths selected for economical use. Almost all solid wood wall sheathing used is 13/16 inches thick and either square or matched edge. This material may be nailed on horizontally or diagonally (fig. 33). Diagonal application adds much greater strength to the structure. Sheathing should be nailed on with three 8-penny common nails to each bearing if the pieces are over 6 inches wide. Wooden sheathing is laid on tight, with all joints made over the studs. If the sheathing is to be put on horizontally, it should be started at the foundation and worked toward the top. If it is to be put on diagonally, it should be started at the corners of the building and worked toward the center or middle of the building.

(2) Gypsum board sheathing (fig. 34) is made by casting a gypsum core within a heavy water-resistant fibrous envelope. The long edges of the 4- by 8-foot boards are tongued and grooved. Each board is a full 1/2 inch thick. Its use is mostly with wood siding that can be nailed directly through the sheathing and into the studs. Gypsum sheathing is fireproof, water resistant, and windproof; does not warp nor absorb water; and does not require the use of building papers.

(3) Plywood as a wall sheathing (fig. 34) is highly recommended by its size, weight, stability, and structural properties, plus the ease and speed of application. It adds consider-

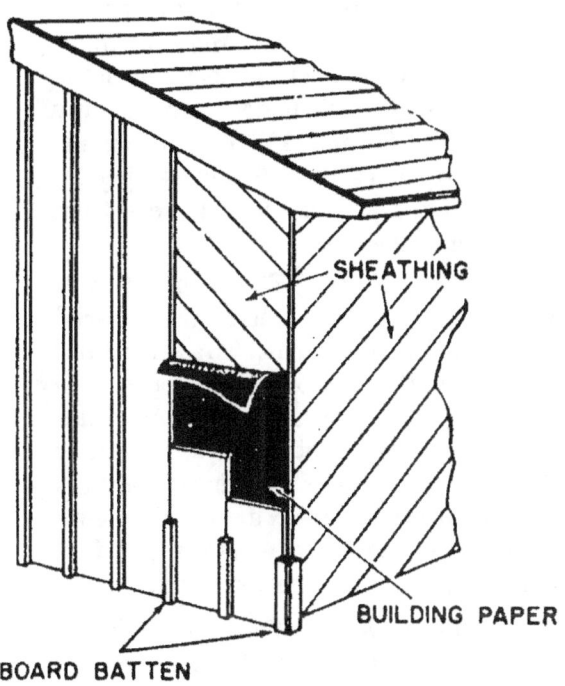

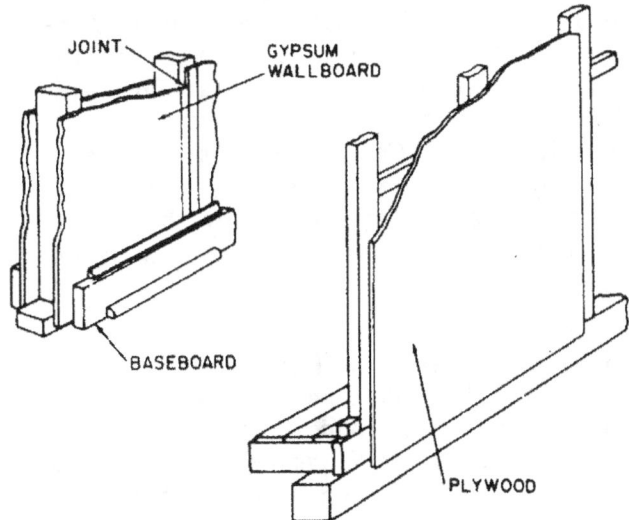

Figure 34. Gypsum and plywood sheathing.

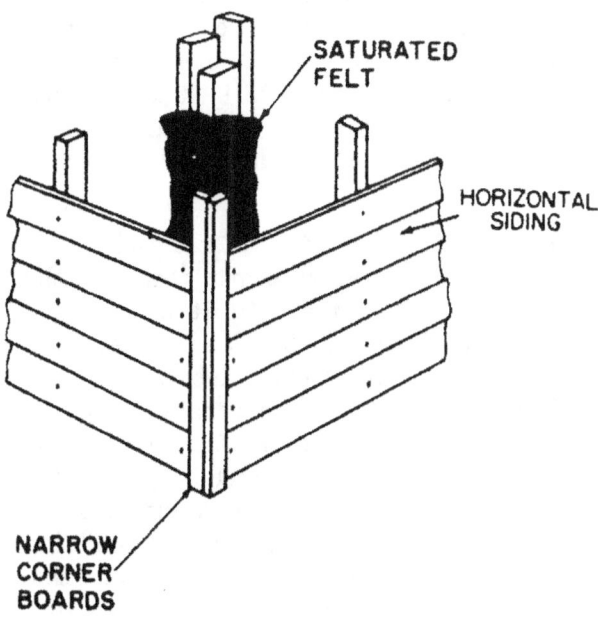

Figure 35. Vertical and horizontal wooden siding.

ably more strength to the frame than does diagonally applied wood boards. When plywood sheathing is used, corner bracing can be omitted. Large size panels save the time required for application and still provide a tight, draft-free installation of high insulation value. Minimum thicknesses of plywood wall sheathing is 5/16 inch for 16-inch stud spacing and 3/8 inch for 24-inch stud spacing. The panels should be installed with the face grain parallel to the studs. A little more stiffness can be gained by installing them across the studs, but this requires more cutting and fitting. Use 6-penny common nails for 5/16-, 3/8-, and 1/2-inch panels and 8-penny common nails for 5/8- and 13/16-inch panels. Space the nails not more than 6 inches on center at the edges of the panels and not more than 12 inches on center elsewhere.

c. Vertical Wooden Siding. This type of coverage is nailed to girts. The cracks are covered with wood strips called battens. The sheathing is nailed securely with 8- or 10-penny nails. The vertical sheathing requires less framing than siding since the sheathing acts as a support for the plate. To make this type of wall more weatherproof, some type of tar paper or light roll roofing may be applied over the entire surface and fastened with roofing nails and battens (fig. 35).

d. Horizontal Wood Siding. Wood siding is cut to various patterns and sizes to be used as the finished outside surface of a structure. The siding for outside wall coverings should be of a decay-resisting species that will hold tight at the joints and take and hold paint well. It should by all means be well seasoned lumber. Siding is made in sizes ranging from 1/2 inch to 3/4 inch by 12 inches. There are two principal types of siding (fig. 3): beveled siding and drop siding.

(1) *Beveled siding* (fig. 3). Beveled siding is made with beveled boards thin at the top edge and thick at the butt. It is the most common form of wood siding and comes in 1 inch for narrow widths, and 2 inches and over for the wide types. They are usually nailed at the butt edge and through the tip edge of the board below. Very narrow siding is quite often nailed near its thin edge like shingles. It is nailed to solid sheathing over which building paper has been attached. Window and door casings are first framed. The siding butts are put against the edges of these frames. Corners may be mitered, or the corner boards may be first nailed to the sheathing and then the siding is fitted against the edges.

(2) *Drop siding* (fig. 3). Drop siding is designed to be used as a combination of sheathing and siding, or with separate sheathing. It comes in a wide variety of face profiles and is either shiplapped or tongued and grooved. If used as a combined sheathing and siding material, tongue and grooved lumber is nailed directly to the studs with the tongue up. When sheathing is not used, the door and window casings are set after the siding is up. If sheathing is first used and then building paper is added, drop siding is applied like beveled siding, after the window and door casings are in place.

(3) *Corrugated metal sheets.* Corrugated metal is used extensively as a wall cover since little framing, time, and labor are required to install it. It is applied vertically and nailed to girts with the nails placed in the ridges. Sheathing can be used behind the iron with or without building paper. Since tar paper used behind metal will cause the metal to rust, a resin-sized paper should be used.

(4) *Building paper.*

(a) Building paper is of several types, the most common of which is the resin-sized. It is generally red or buff in color (sometimes black) and comes in rolls, usually 36 inches wide. Each roll contains 500 square feet and weighs from 18 to 50 pounds. Ordinarily, it is not waterproof. Another type is heavy paper saturated with a coaltar product, sometimes called sheathing paper. It is waterproof and protects against heat and cold.

(b) In wood-frame buildings to be covered with either siding, shingles, or iron, building paper is used to protect against heat, cold, or dampness. Building paper is applied horizontally along a wall from the bottom of the structure upward and nailed with roofing nails at the laps. Thus the overlapping of the paper helps water runoff. Care must be taken not to tear the paper. The waterproof type paper is used also in the built-up roof where the roof is nearly flat. Several layers are used with tar between each layer.

15. Interior Walls and Partitions

a. Wall and Partition Coverings. Wall and partition coverings are divided into two general types—wet wall material, generally plaster; and dry wall material including wood, plaster board, plywood, and fiberboard. Only dry wall material will be covered in this manual.

b. Dry Wall Materials. Dry wall material—

gypsumboard, fiberboard, or plywood, usually comes in sheets 1/2 inch thick and 4 x 8 feet in size, but may be obtained in other sizes. It is normally applied in either single or double thickness with panels placed as shown in figure 36. When covering both walls and ceilings, always start with the ceiling (para 17). Annular ringed nails should be used for applying finished-joint drywall to reduce nail popping.

(1) Apply dry wall as follows:

(*a*) Start in one corner and work around the room. Make sure that joints break at the centerline of a stud.

(*b*) Use 1/2-inch thick recessed-edge wallboard and span the entire height of the wall if possible.

(*c*) Use 13-gage nails, 1 5/8 inches long. Start nailing at the center of the board and work outward. Space the nails 3/8 inch in from the edge of the board and about 8 inches apart. Dimple nails below surface of panel with a ball-peen hammer. Be careful not to break the surface of the board by the blow of the hammer.

(*d*) Procedures for cutting and sealing wallboard are covered in (3) below.

(2) Fit dry wall materials to rough or uneven walls as follows:

(*a*) Place a piece of scrap material in the angle (fig. 37) and scribe (mark) it to indicate the surface peculiarities.

(*b*) Saw the scrap material along the scribed line.

(*c*) Place the scribed strip on the wallboard to be used. Keep the straight edge of the scrap material parallel with the edge of the wallboard. Scribe the good piece of wallboard.

(*d*) Saw the wallboard along the scribed line.

(3) Cut panels by sawing, or by scoring with an awl and snapping over a straight edge (fig. 38). *Cut with finish side up to avoid damaging surface.* Cut openings for pipe and electrical receptacles with a keyhole saw. Nail panels to wall studs with 13-gage nails, 8 inches on centers. *All panel end joints must center on studs.* Cover nails with cement. Joints may be left open, beveled, lapped, filled, covered with battens or moldings, or treated with cement and tape. The treatment of joints varies slightly with different materials. Generally, all cracks over 1/8 inch must be filled with special crack filler before joint cement is applied. The cement is spread over joints with a plasterer's trowel. Apply the cement evenly and thin (feather) edges on surface of wall panel. Fill channels in recessed edges with cement, carrying it 1 inch past channel edges. At corners, apply cement in a channel-wide band and feather edges. Press perforated tape into wet cement and smooth tape down with trowel. Clean off excess cement. At corners, fold tape down center before applying, and smooth each side of corner separately when applied. When cement is dry, apply a second coat of thinned cement to hide tape.

Figure 36. Placing wallboard.

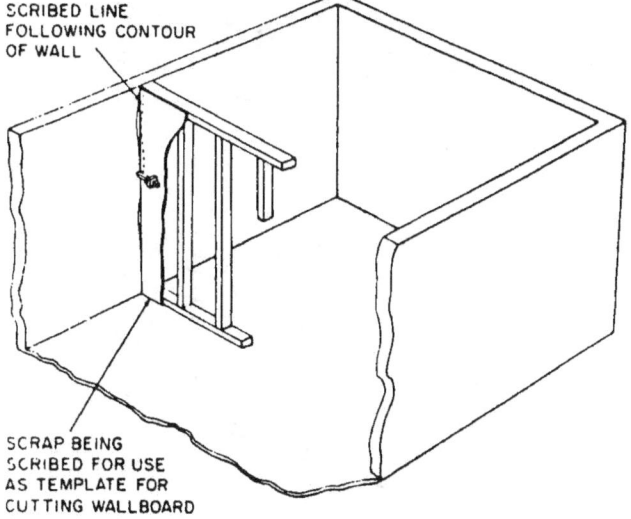

Figure 37. Fitting single-piece wallboard to uneven walls.

Feather the edges carefully to preserve flat appearance of wall. When the final coat is dry, smooth the joint with sandpaper.

c. Sheetrock. Sheetrock sheets are very brittle and require careful handling to prevent breakage. Approximately 1 1/4 inches of a sheet's edge is made 1/16 inch thinner than the body of the sheet. When two sheets are placed side by side, their edges form a recess to receive perforated paper tape and gypsum cement which conceals the joints between the sheets. A 1/8-inch space between the edges of the sheets helps to hold the filler cement in place. The sheets are usually fastened in place with blued nails which have an oversize head and are 1 1/2 inches long. The nails along the edges are covered with perforated tape and cement. Nails are spaced about 5 inches apart and 3/8 inch from the edge. Those in the middle of the sheets are spaced 8 or 9 inches apart and are set below the surface to receive the filler cement. It is common practice to strike the nailheads one extra blow for setting. This makes a slight depression (hammer mark) which holds the cement around the nailhead.

d. Wood Paneling. Plywood panels are used extensively as interior wall covering and can be obtained on the market in sizes from 1/4 to 3/4 inch thick; 36 to 48 inches wide; and 60, 72, 84, or 96 inches long. Plywood gives a wall a wood finish surface. If desired, the less expensive plywoods can be used and covered with paint or wallpaper or can be decorated in the same way as plastered surfaces. These panels are usually applied vertically from floor to ceiling and fastened with 4d finishing nails. Special strips or battens of either wood or metal may be used to conceal the joints when flush joints are used. Joints can also be treated with moldings, either in the form of battens fastened over the joints or applied as splines between the panels.

16. Moldings

The various interior trims of a building should have a definite architectural relationship in the design to that of the doors, windows, and the general architecture of the building.

a. Base Molding. Base molding serves as a finish between the finished wall and floor. It is available in several widths and forms. Two-piece base consists of a baseboard topped with a small base cap (A, fig. 39). When plaster is not straight and true, the small base molding will conform more closely to the variations than will the wider base alone. A common size for this type of baseboard is 5/8 by 3 1/4 inches or wider. One-piece baseboard is 5/8 by 3 1/4 inches or wider. One-piece base varies in size from 7/16 by 2 1/4 inches to 1/2 by 3 1/4 inches and wider (Band C, fig. 39). Although a wood member is desirable at the junction of the wall and carpeting to serve as a protective "bumper", wood trim is sometimes eliminated entirely. Most baseboards are finished with a base shoe, 1/2 by 3/4 inch in size (A, B, and C, fig. 39). A single-base molding without the shoe is sometimes placed at the wall-floor junction, especially where carpeting might be used.

b. Installation of Base Molding. Square-edged baseboard should be installed with a butt joint at inside corners and a mitered joint at outside corners (D, fig. 39). It should be nailed to each stud with two eightpenny finishing nails. Molded single-piece base, base moldings, and base shoe should have a coped joint at inside corners and

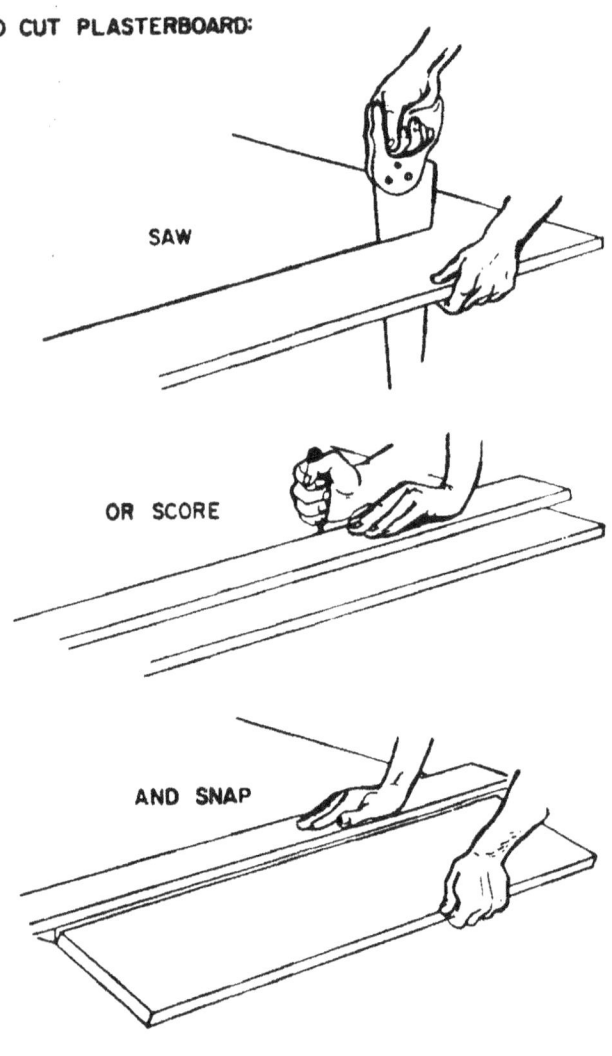

Figure 38. Cutting wallboard.

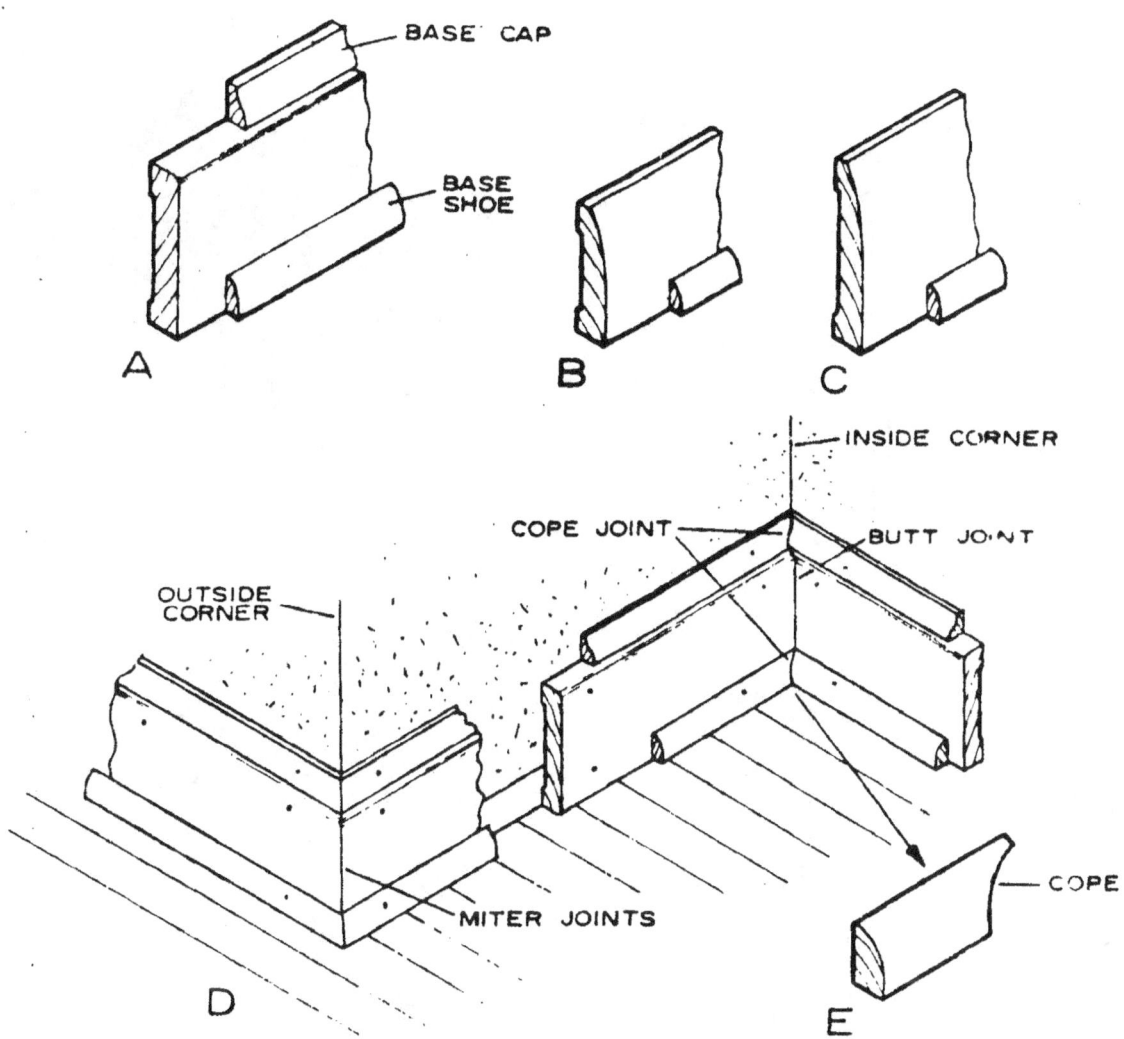

A, Square-edge base; B, narrow ranch base; C, wide ranch base; D, installation; E, cope.

Figure 39. Base molding.

a mitered joint at outside corners. A coped joint is one in which the first piece is square-cut against the plaster or base and the second molding coped. This is done by sawing a 45° miter cut and with a coping saw trimming the molding along the inner line of the miter (E, fig. 39). The base shoe should be nailed into the subfloor with long slender nails and not into the baseboard itself. Thus, if there is a small amount of shrinkage of the joists, no opening will occur under the shoe.

17. Ceiling Covering

In present-day construction, dry, rigid wallboards are used instead of laths and plaster to cover ceilings, as well as walls (para 15). The most common drywall finishes are gypsumboard, fiberboard, and plywood. Sheets of gypsumboard and fiberboard are attached directly to the joists. Smaller pieces of fiberboard (tiles) require furring strips (wooden strips nailed across joints) to which they are attached.

a. Gypsumboard.

(1) *Nailing to ceiling.* The 4-foot by 8-foot boards are nailed to the ceiling with 5-penny-nails through 1/2-inch thick gypsum or 4-penny nails through 3/8-inch gypsum. The nails are spaced 5 to 7 inches apart, off center, and driven about 1/16 inch below the surface of the board.

(2) *Cutting panels and treatment of joints.* The cutting of the panels and the treatment of joints are the same as those of walls and partitions (para 15b(3).

(3) *Brace for paneling ceiling.* A brace is constructed and used (fig. 40) to raise and hold a panel in place to aid in fitting and nailing

181

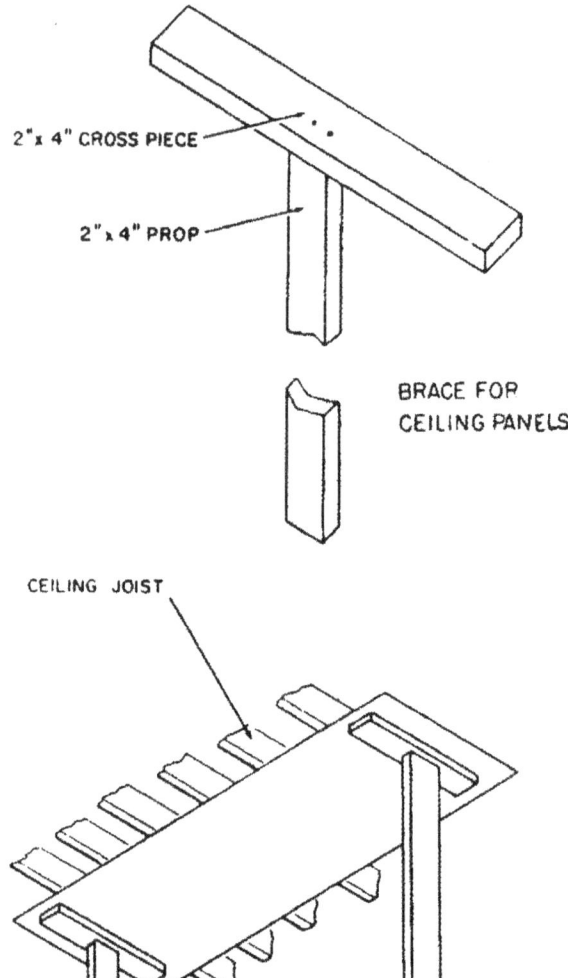

Figure 40. Brace for raising and holding ceiling panels.

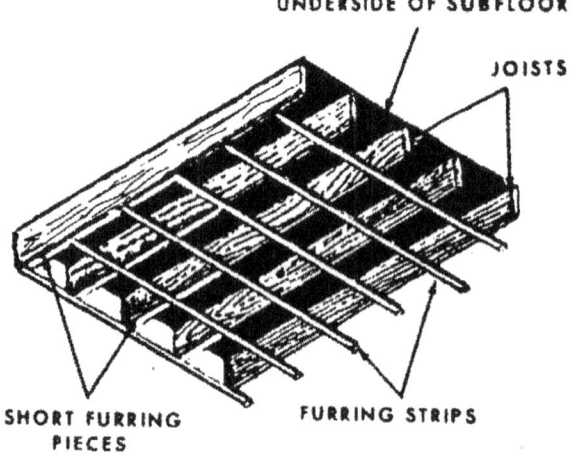

Figure 41. Furring strips on ceiling joists.

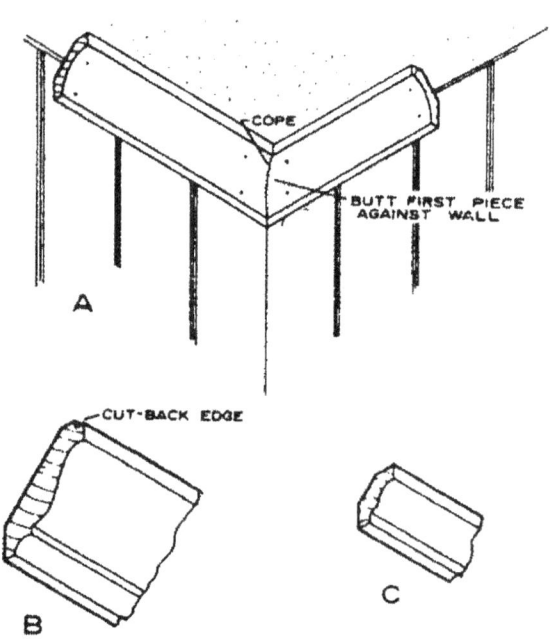

Ceiling moldings; A, Installation (inside corner); B, crown molding; C, small crown molding.

Figure 42. Ceiling molding.

the wallboard to the ceiling. Eight inch nail spacing is used in nailing the panels to the joists.

b. Fiberboard. Fiberboard sheets are obtained in thicknesses from 1/2 to 2 inches. The joints between the sheets may be covered with batten strips of either wood or fiberboard to further improve its appearance. When fiberboard sheets must be cut, a special fiberboard knife is recommended to obtain a smooth cut.

(1) *Tiles.* Fiberboard sheets are also made in small pieces called tiles which are often used for covering ceilings. These tiles may be square or rectangular to fit standard joist spacing. They may be made with a lap joint which permits blind nailing or stapling through the edge. They may also be of tongue-and-groove construction fastened in place with 2-penny box nails driven through special metal clips.

(2) *Furring strips.* For fiberboard tiles that need solid backing, furring strips are placed at right angles across the bottom of the joists and short furring pieces are placed along the joists between the furring strips, as shown in figure 41.

(3) *Tile installed in metal channels.* Metal channels are nailed to furring strips and the tiles are slid into them horizontally. In lowering ceilings, usually in older buildings, metal channels are suspended on wire to "drop" a ceiling below the original ceiling. Some large (2 x 4-ft) panels are installed in individual frames.

18. Ceiling Molding

Ceiling moldings are sometimes used at the junction of wall and ceiling for an architectural effect or to terminate dry-wall paneling of gypsumboard or wood (A, fig. 42). As in the base moldings, inside corners should also be copejointed. This insures a tight joint and retains a good fit if there are minor moisture changes. A cutback edge at the outside of the molding will partially conceal any unevenness of the plaster and make painting easier where there are color changes (B, fig. 42). For gypsum dry-wall construction, a small simple molding might be desirable (C, fig. 42). Finish nails should be driven into the upper wallplates and also into the ceiling joists for large moldings when possible.

Section III. DOOR FRAMES, WINDOW FRAMES, AND OTHER WALL OPENINGS

19. Doors

Door and window openings in exterior walls generally require headers. Regular studs are normally placed 16 inches on center apart. Extra studs are added at the sides of all such openings. Openings should allow 1/2 inch between the back at jambs and framing member for the plumbing and leveling of jambs.

a. Door Frames.

(1) Before the exterior covering is placed on the outside walls, the door openings are prepared for the frames. To prepare the openings, square off any uneven pieces of sheathing and wrap heavy building paper around the sides and top. Since the sill must be worked into a portion of the rough flooring, no paper is put on the floor. Position the paper from a point even with the inside portion of the stud to a point about 6 inches on the sheathed walls and tack it down with small nails.

(2) Outside door frames are constructed in several ways. In most hasty construction, the frames will be as shown in figure 43. This type requires no construction of frame because the studs on each side of the opening act as a frame. The outside finish is applied to the wall before the door is hung. The casing is then nailed to the sides of the opening which is set back the width of the stud. A 3/4- by 3/4-inch piece is nailed over the door to act as a support for the drip cap and is also set back the width of the stud. Hinge blocks are nailed to the casing where the hinges are to be placed. The door frame is now complete and ready for the door to be hung. Figure 43 shows the elevation of a single outside door.

(3) Inside door frames, like outside frames, are constructed in several ways. In most hasty construction, the type shown in figure 44 is used. The interior type is constructed like the outside type, except that no casing is used on inside door frames. Hinge blocks are nailed to the inside wall finish, where the hinges are to be placed, to provide a nailing surface for the hinge flush with the door. Figure 44 shows the elevation of a single inside door. Both the outside and inside door frames may be modified to suit climatic conditions.

b. Door Jambs. Door jambs (fig. 45) are the linings of the framing of door openings.

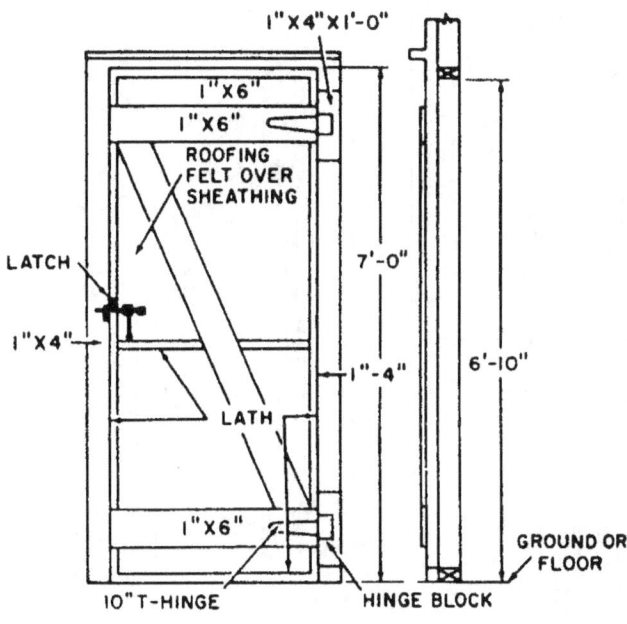

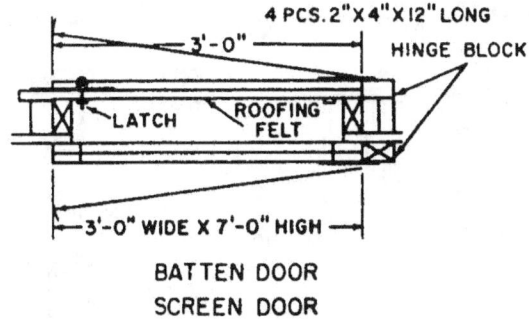

Figure 43. Single outside door.

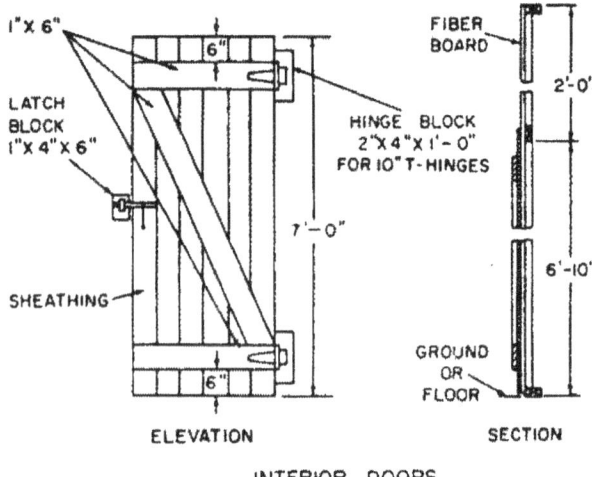

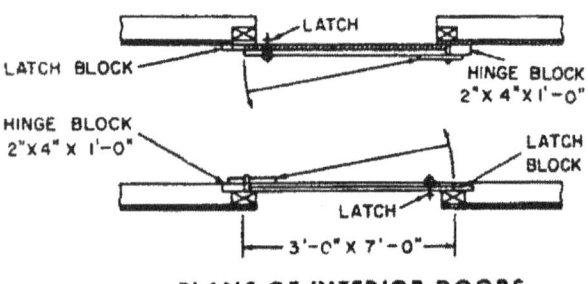

Figure 44. Single inside door.

Casings and stops are nailed to the door jambs and the door is hung from them. Inside jambs are made of 3/4-inch stock and outside jambs of 1 3/8-inch stock. The width of the stock will vary with the thickness to the walls. Inside jambs are built up with 3/8- by 1 3/8-inch stops nailed to the jamb, while outside jambs are usually rabbeted out to receive the door. Jambs are made and set as follows:

(1) Regardless of how carefully rough openings are made, be sure to plumb the jambs and level the heads, when jambs are set.

(2) Rough openings are usually made 2 1/2 inches larger each way than the size of the door to be hung. For example, a 2-foot 8-inch by 6-foot 8-inch door would need a rough opening of 2 feet 10 1/2 inches by 6 feet 10 1/2 inches. This extra space allows for the jambs, the wedging, and the clearance space for the door to swing.

(3) Level the floor across the opening to determine any variation in floor heights at the point where the jambs rest on the floor.

(4) Now cut the head jamb with both ends square, having allowed width of the door plus the depth of both dadoes and a full 3/16 inch for door clearance.

(5) From the lower edge of the dado, measure a distance equal to the height of the door plus the clearance wanted under it. Mark and cut square.

(6) On the opposite jamb do the same, only make additions or subtractions for the variation in the floor, if any.

(7) Now nail the jambs and jamb heads together with 8-penny common nails through the dado into the head jamb.

(8) Set the jambs into the opening and place small blocks under each jamb on the subfloor just as thick as the finish floor will be. This is to allow the finish floor to go under.

(9) Plumb the jambs and level the jamb head.

(10) Wedge the sides with shingles between the jambs and the studs, to aline, and then nail securely in place.

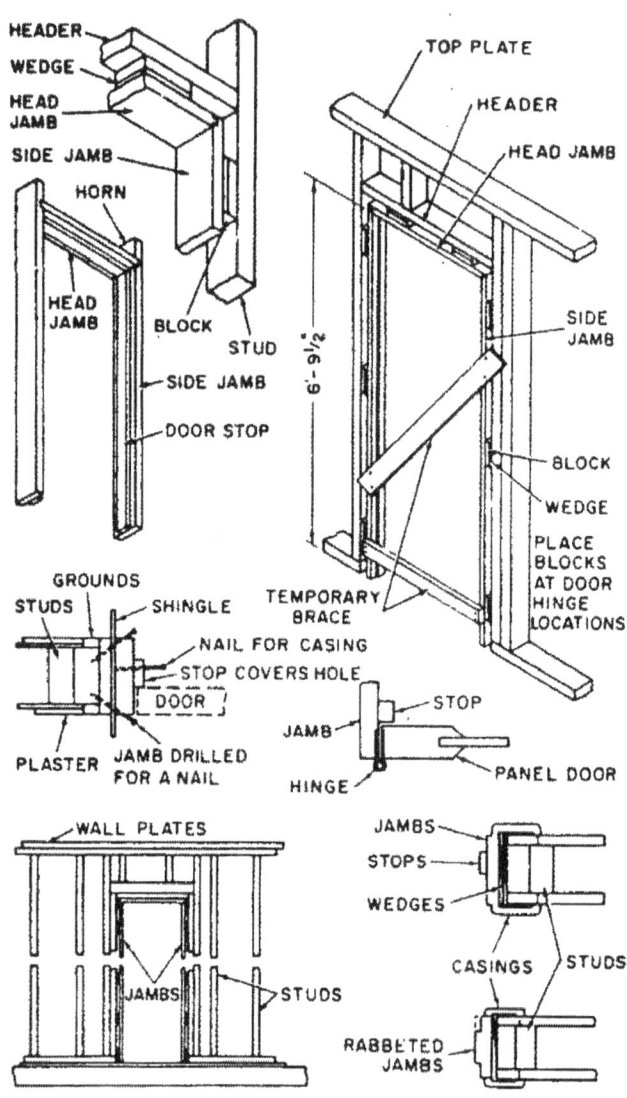

Figure 45. Door jamb and door trim.

(11) Take care not to wedge the jamb unevenly.

(12) Use a straightedge 5 or 6 feet long inside the jambs to help prevent uneven wedging.

(13) Check jambs and head carefully, because jambs placed out of plumb will have a tendency to swing the door open or shut, depending on the direction in which the jamb is out of plumb.

c. Door Trim. Door trim material is nailed onto the jambs to provide a finish between the jambs and the wall. It is frequently called "casing" (fig. 45). Sizes vary from 1/2 to 3/4 inch in thickness, and from 2 1/2 to 6 inches in width. Most trim has a concave back, to fit over uneven plaster. In mitered work, care must be taken to make all joints clean, square, neat, and well fitted. (If the trim is to be mitered at the top corners, a miter box, miter square, hammer nail set, and block plane will be needed.) Door openings are cased up as follows:

(1) Leave a margin of 1/4-inch from the edge of the jamb to the casing all around.

(2) Cut one of the side casings square and even at the bottom, with the bottom of the jamb.

(3) Cut the top or mitered end next, allowing 1/4-inch extra length for the margin at the top.

(4) Nail the casing onto the jamb and even with the 1/4-inch margin line, starting at the top and working toward the bottom.

(5) Use 4-penny finishing nails along the jamb side and 6-penny or 8-penny case nails along the outer edge of the casings.

(6) The nails along the outer edge will need to be long enough to go through the casing and into the studs.

(7) Set all nailheads about 1/8 inch below the surface of the wood with a nail set.

(8) Now apply the casing for the other side and then the head casing.

20. Windows

Windows are generally classified as sliding, double hung, and casement (fig. 46). All windows, whatever the type, consist essentially of two parts, the frame and the sash. The frame is made up of four basic parts: the head, the jambs (two), and the sill. The sash is the framework which holds the glass in the window. Where the openings are provided, studding must be cut away and its equivalent strength replaced by doubling the studs on each side of the opening to form trimmers and inserting a header at the top. If the opening is wide, the header should be doubled and trussed. At the bottom of the opening, the bottom header or rough sill is inserted.

a. Window Frames. These are the frames into which the window sashes are fitted and hung. They are set into the rough opening in the wall framing and are intended to hold the sashes in place. The rough window opening is made at least 10 inches larger each way (width and height) than the window glass (pane) size to be used. If the sash to be used is, for instance, a two-light window, 24 by 26 inches, add 10 inches to the width (24 inches) to obtain the total width of 34 inches for the rough opening. Add the upper and lower glasses (26 inches each) and an additional 10 inches for the total height of the rough opening, 62 inches. These allowances are standard and provide for weights, springs, balances, room for plumbing and squaring, and for regular adjustments.

b. Double-Hung Window. The double-hung window (fig. 47) is made up of two parts: an upper and a lower sash, which slide vertically past one another. Screens can be located on the outside of a double-hung window without interfering with its operation, and ventilators and window air conditioners can be placed with the window mostly closed. However, for full ventilation of a room, only one-half of the area of the window can be used, and any current of air

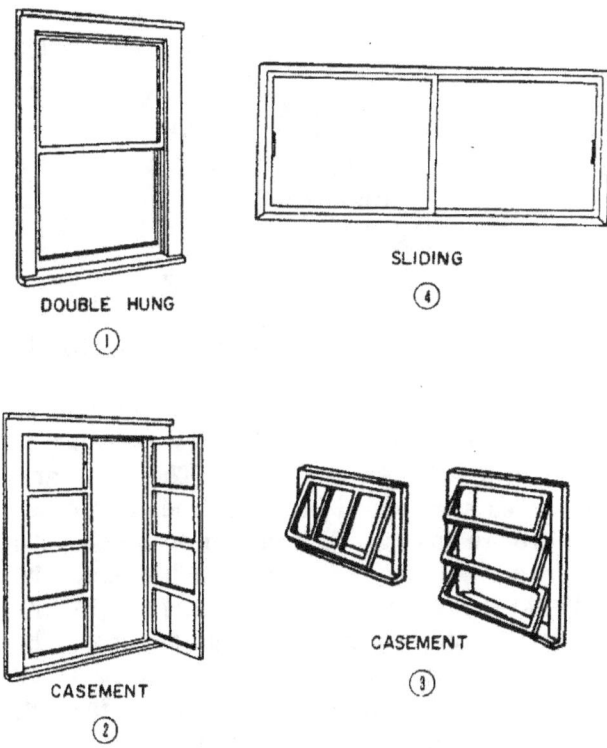

Figure 46. Types of windows.

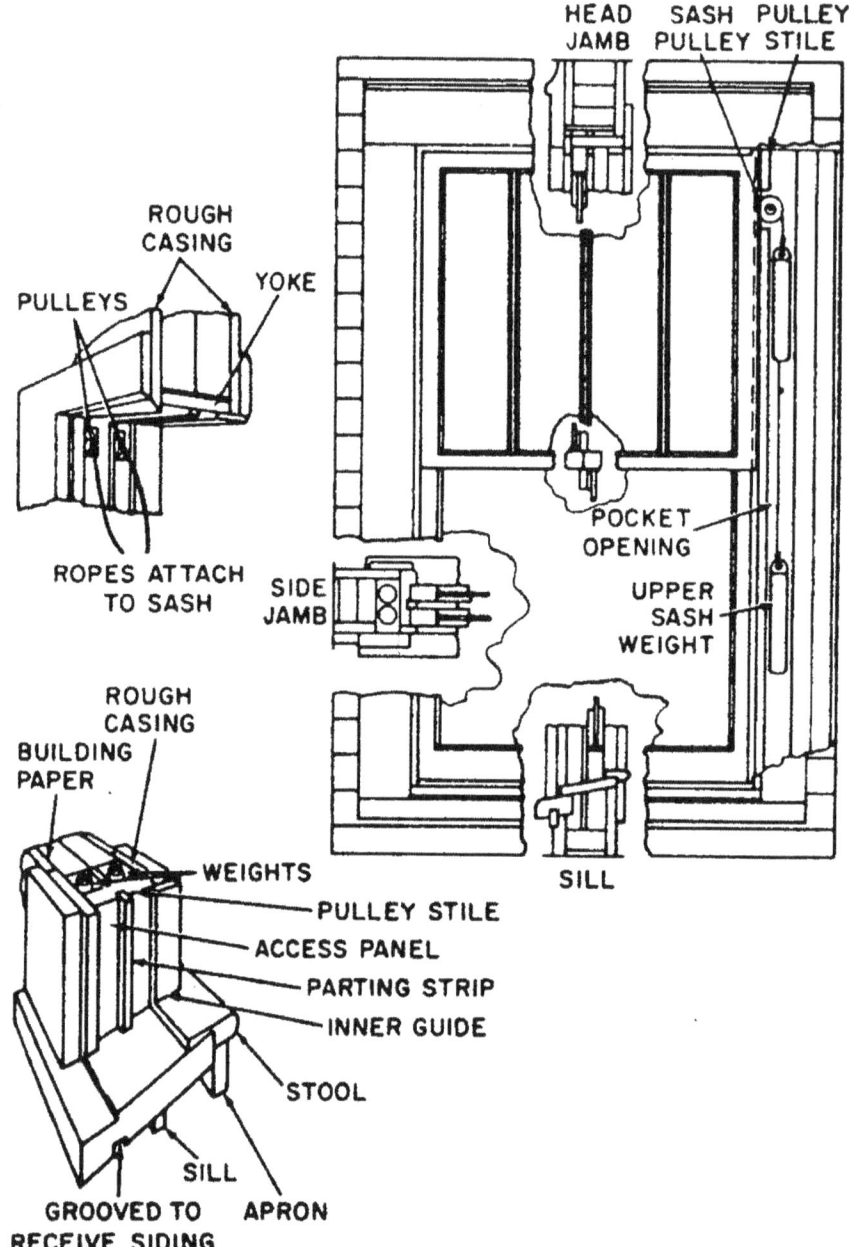

Figure 47. Double-hung window.

passing across its face is to some extent lost to the room.

(1) The box frame (fig. 47) consists of a top piece or yoke, two side pieces or jambs called pulley stiles, and the sill. The yoke and pulley stiles are dadoed into the inner and outer pieces (rough casing), forming an open box with the opening toward the studs and headers. The rough casing provides nailing surface to the studs and headers forming the plaster stop. The outside rough casing is also a blind stop for sheathing which should fit snugly against it, with building paper lapping the joint.

(2) The 2-inch space between the framing studs and the pulley stile forms the box for counterweights which balance the window sash. The weight box is divided by a thin strip known as the pendulum, which separates the weights for the two sash units. In the stiles near the sill is an opening for easy access to the weights. This opening has a removable strip which is part of the stile and channel for the lower sash (fig. 47).

(3) Yoke and stile faces are divided by a parting strip which is dadoed into them, but removable so that the upper sash can be taken out. The strip forms the center guide for the upper and lower sash, while the outerrough casing,

projecting slightly beyond the stiles and yoke, forms the outer guide. The inner guide for the sash is formed by a strip or stop, usually with a molding form on the inner edge. This stop is removable to permit the removal of the lower sash.

(4) At the upper parts of the stiles, two pulleys on each side (one for each sash) are mortised flush with the stile faces for the weight cord or chain.

(5) The sill is part of the box frame and slants downward and outward. It usually has one or two 1/4-inch brakes, one occurring at the point where the lower sash rests on the sill, and another near the outer edge to form a seat for window screens or storm sash. These brakes prevent water, dripping on the sill, from being blown under the sash. The underside of the sill, near its outer edge, is grooved to receive the edge of siding material to form a watertight seal.

(6) On the room side of the sill is another piece, the stool, which has a rabbet on its underside into which the sill fits. The stool edge projects from the will, forming a horizontal stop for the lower sash. The stool is part of the interior trim of the window, made up of side and top casings and an apron under the stool. The framed finished side and top casings are on the weather face. A drip cap rests on top of the outside head casing and is covered with metal flashing to form a watertight juncture with the siding material.

c. *Hinged or Casement Windows.* There are basically two types of casement windows, the outswinging and the inswinging types, and these may be hinged at the sides, top, or bottom. The casement window which opens out requires the window screen to be located on the inside with some device cut into its frame to operate the casement. Inswinging casements, like double-hung windows, are clear of screens, but they are extremely difficult to make watertight, particularly against a driving rainstorm. Casements have the advantage of their entire area being opened to air currents, with the added advantage of catching a parallel breeze and slanting it into a room.

(1) Casement windows are considerably less complicated in their construction, being simple frames and sash. The frames are usually made of planks 1 3/4 inch thick with rabbets cut in them to receive the sash. Usually there is an additional rabbet for screens or storm sash. The frames are rabbeted 1/2 inch deep and 1 1/2 or 1 7/8 inches wide for sash 1 3/8 or 1 3/4 inches thick. The additional rabbet is usually 15/16 or 1 3/16 inches wide, depending on whether the screen or storm sash is 7/8 or 1 1/8-inch thick.

(2) Outswinging casement windows have the rabbet for the sash on the outer edges of the frame, the inner edge being rabbeted for the screen. Sill construction is like that for a double-hung window, with the stool much wider and forming a stop for the bottom rail. Casement-window frames are of a width to extend to the sheathing face on the weather side and to the plaster face on the room side (fig. 48).

(3) When there are two casement windows in a row in one frame, they may be separated by a vertical double jamb called a mullion, or the stiles may come together in pairs like a french door. The edges of the stiles may be a reverse rabbet; a beveled reverse rabbet with battens, one attached to each stile; or beveled astragals (T-shaped molding), one attached to each stile. The battens and astragals insure better weather-tightness. The latter are more resistant to loosening through use. Two pairs of casement sash in one frame are hinged to a mullion in the center (fig. 48).

(4) Inswinging casement-window frames are like the outswinging type with the sash rabbet cut in the inner edge of the frame (fig. 48). The sill construction is slightly different, being of one piece (similar to that of a door sill) with

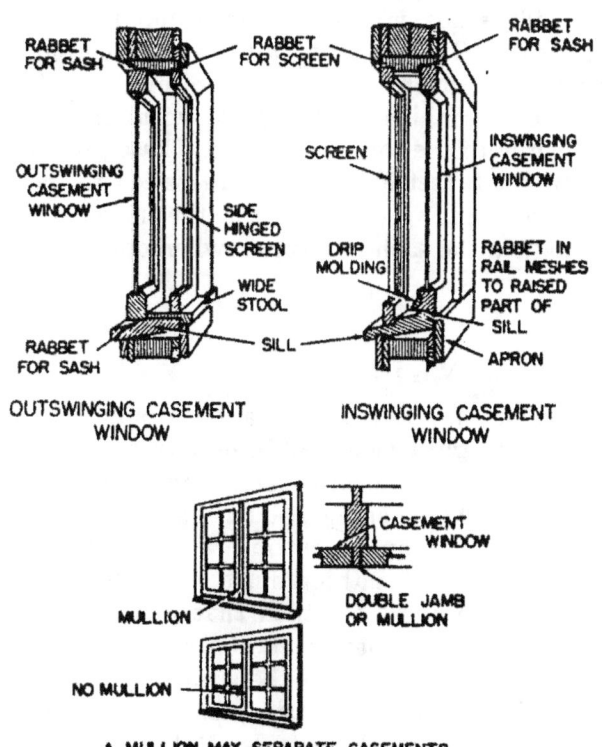

Figure 48. Casement windows.

a rabbet cut for a screen or storm sash toward the front edge, and the back raised where the sash rail seats. This surface is rabbeted at its back edge to form a stop for the rail which is also rabbeted to mesh.

(5) Sills in general have a usual slope of about 1 in 5 inches so that they shed water quickly. They are wider than the frames, extending usually about 1½ inches beyond the sheathing. They also form a base for the outside finished casing.

(6) The bottom sash rail of an inswinging casement window is constructed differently from the outswinging type. The bottom edge is rabbeted to mesh with the rabbet on the sill, and a drip molding is set in the weather face to prevent rain from being blown under the sash.

d. Window Frames In hasty construction, millwork window frames are seldom used. The window frames are mere openings left in the walls with the stops all nailed to the stud. The sash may be hinged to the inside or the outside of the wall or constructed so as to slide. The latter type of sash is most common in Army construction because it requires little time to install. Figure 49 shows the section and plan of a window and window frame of the type used in the field. After the outside walls have been finished, a 1 by 3 is nailed on top of the girt at the bottom of the window opening to form a sill. A 1 by 2 is nailed to the bottom of the plate and on the side studs which acts as a top for the window sash. One guide is nailed at the bottom of the opening flush with the bottom of the girt, and another is nailed to the plate with the top edge flush with the top of the plate. These guides are 1 by 3's, 8 feet long. Stops are nailed to the bottom girt and plate, between the next two studs, to hold the sash in position when open (fig. 49).

21. Other Wall Openings

a. Stovepipes. Stovepipes carried outside a building through a side wall eliminate the need for flashing and waterproofing around the pipe (fig. 50). The opening should be cut in an area selected to avoid cutting studs, braces, plates, and so on. Sheathing must be cut back in a radius 6 inches greater than that of the pipe. Safety thimbles or other insulation must be used on the inside and outside of the sheathing. Sheet metal insulation may be constructed and used as a single insulator on the outside. Make openings as follows:

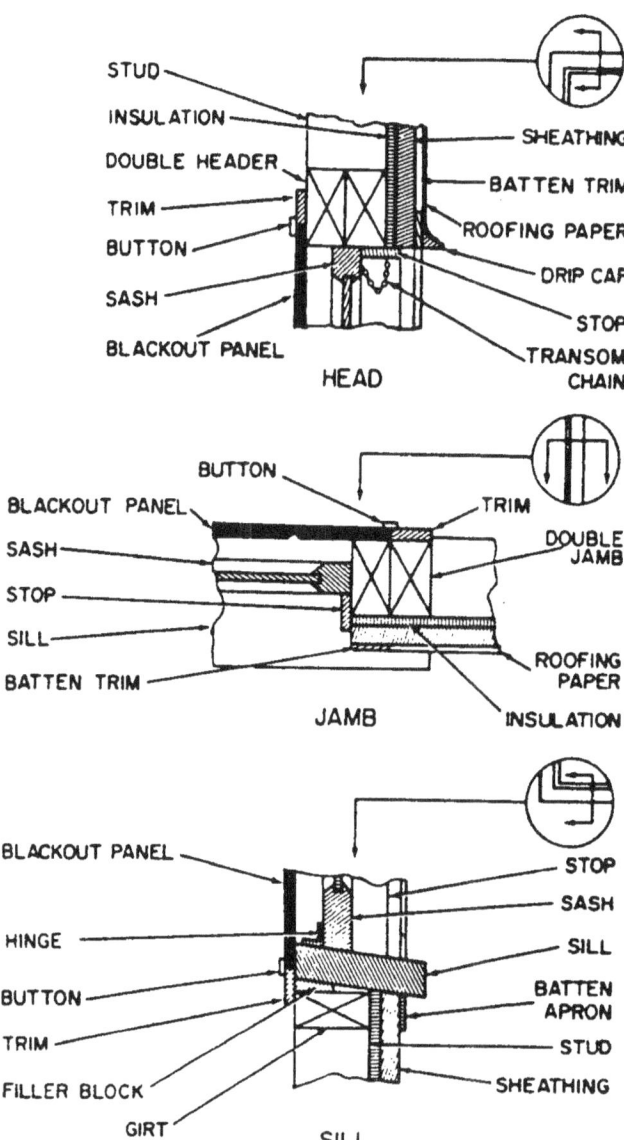

Figure 49. Detail of wall section with window frame and sash.

(1) Cut a hole through the sheet metal where the stovepipe is to penetrate.

(2) Mark a circle on the metal 1/2-inch larger in diameter than the pipe and then make another circle within this circle with a diameter 2 inches less than the diameter of the first.

(3) With a straightedge, draw lines through the center of the circle from the circumference. These marks should be from 1/2 to 3/4 inch apart along the outer circumference.

(4) Cut out the center circle, then cut to the outside of the circle along the lines drawn. After the lines have been cut, bend the metal strips outward at a 45° angle and force the pipe through the hole to the desired position. Very little water will leak around this joint.

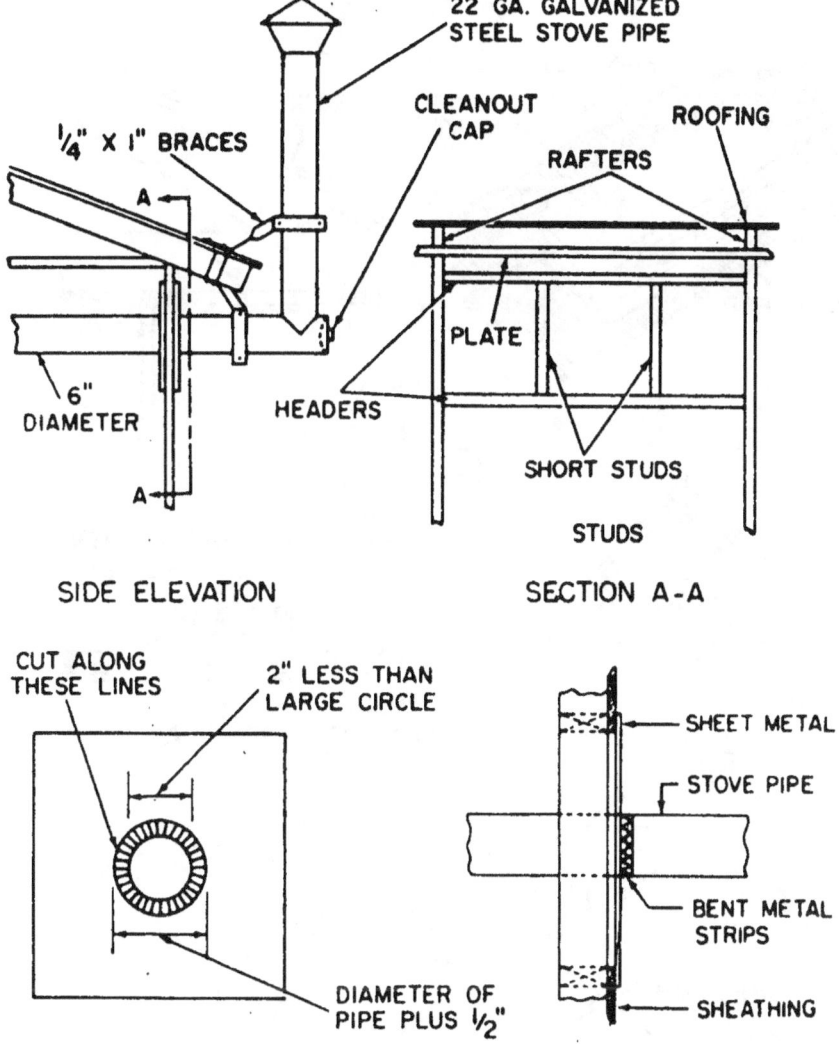

Figure 50. Preparation of wall opening for stovepipe.

b. Ventilators. Adequate ventilation is necessary to prevent condensation in buildings. Condensation may occur in the walls, in the crawl space under the structure, in basements, on windows, and so on. Condensation is most likely to occur in structures during the first 6 to 8 months after a building is built and in extreme cold weather when interior humidity is high. Proper ventilation under the roof allows moisture-laden air to escape during the winter heating season and also allows the hot dry air of the summer season to escape. The upper areas of a structure are usually ventilated by the use of louvers or ventilators.

(1) *Types of ventilators* (fig. 51). Types of ventilators used are as follows:

(a) Roof louvers (1).

(b) Cornice ventilators (2).

(c) Gable louvers (3).

(d) Flat-roof ventilators (4).

(e) Crawl-space ventilation (5).

(f) Ridge ventilators (6).

(2) *Upper structure ventilation.* One of the most common methods of ventilating is by the use of wood or metal louver frames. There are many types, sizes, and shapes of louvers. The following are facts to consider when building or installing the various kinds of ventilation:

(a) The size and number of ventilators are determined by the size of the area to be ventilated.

(b) The minimum net open area should be 1/4 square inch per square foot of ceiling area.

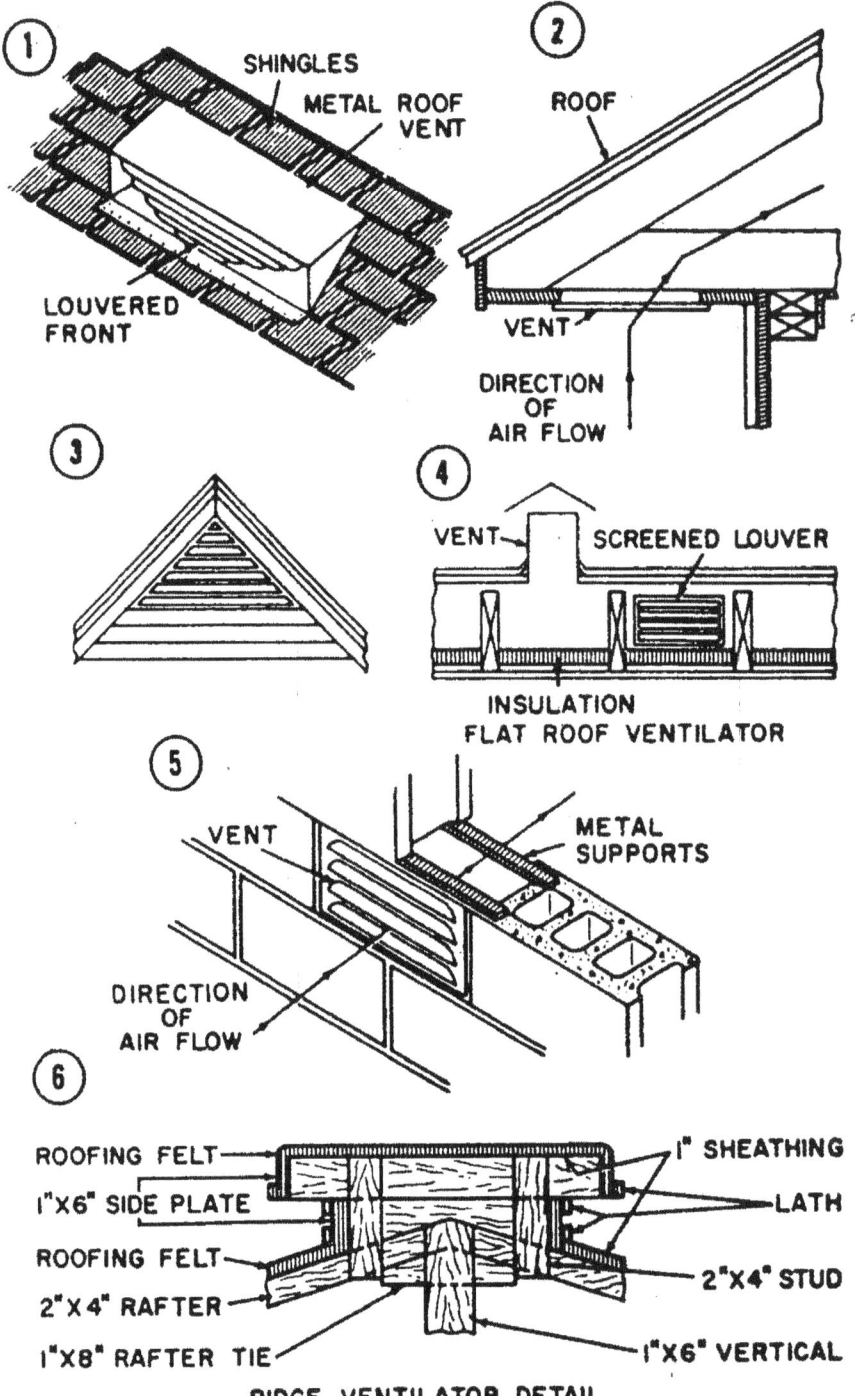

Figure 51. Types of ventilators.

(c) Most louver frames are usually 5 inches wide.

(d) Back edge should be rabbeted out for a screen or door, or both.

(e) Three-quarter-inch slats are used and spaced about 1 3/4 inches apart.

(f) Sufficient slant or slope to the slats should be provided to prevent rain from driving in.

(g) For best results, upper structure louvers should be placed as near the top of the gable as possible.

(3) *Crawl-space ventilation.* Crawl spaces under foundations of basementless structures should be well ventilated. Air circulation under the floors prevents excessive condensation that causes warping, swelling, twisting, and rotting of the lumber. These crawl-space ventilators are usually called "foundation louvers" (5, fig. 51). They are set into the foundation at the time it is

being built. A good foundation vent should be equipped with a copper or bronze screen and adjustable shutters for opening and closing the louver. The sizes for the louvers should be figured on the same basis as that used for upper structure louvers—1/4-inch for each square foot of underfloor space.

Section IV. STAIRWAYS

22. Steps and Stairs

Stairwork is made up of the framing on the sides, known as stringers or carriages, and the steps, known as treads. Sometimes pieces are framed into the stairs at the back of the treads; these pieces are known as risers. The stringers or carriages may consist of materials 2 or 3 inches thick and 4 or more inches wide which are cut to form the step of the stairs. Blocks (fig. 52) may also be nailed on to form the steps. There are usually three stringers to a stair, one at each of the two outer edges and one at the center. The floor joists must be properly framed around the stair well, or wellhole, in order to have enough space for the erection of the stair framing and the finished trim of the entire staircase.

a. The step or stair stringer may be made of 2 by 4's, with triangular blocks nailed to one edge to form the stringer. The blocks are cut from 2 by 6's and nailed to the 2 by 4, as shown in 1, figure 52. The step stringers are fastened at the top and bottom as shown in 2, figure 52. Figures 52 and 53 show the foundation and give the details of the sizes of the step treads, handrails, the methods of installing them, and the post construction. This type of step is most common in field construction.

b. When timbers heavier than 2 by 4's are used for stringers, they are laid out and cut as shown in figure 54.

23. Stairway Framing

a. To frame simple, straight string stairs, take a narrow piece of straight stock, called a story pole, and mark on it the distance from the lower

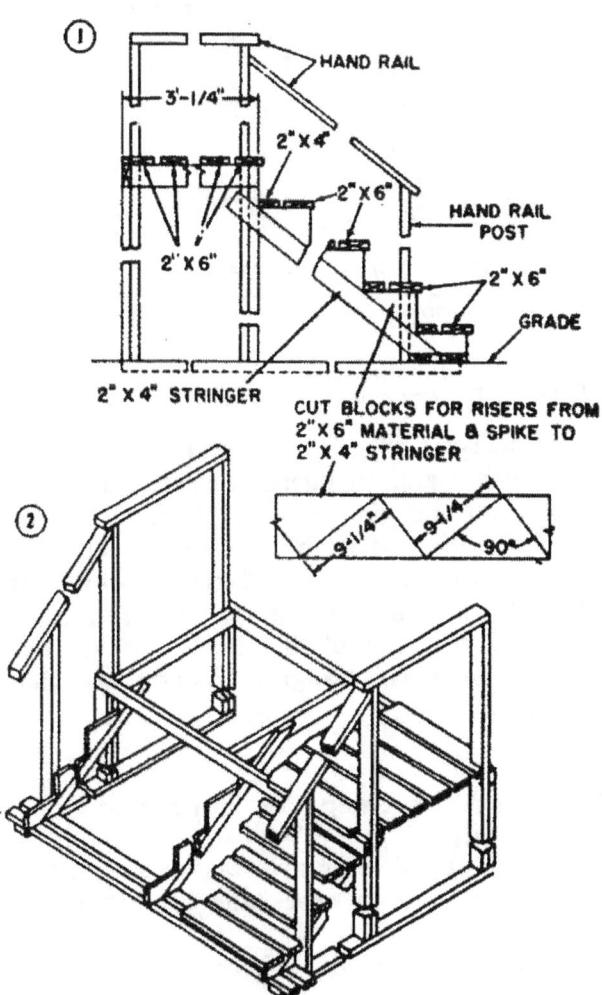

Figure 52. Step construction.

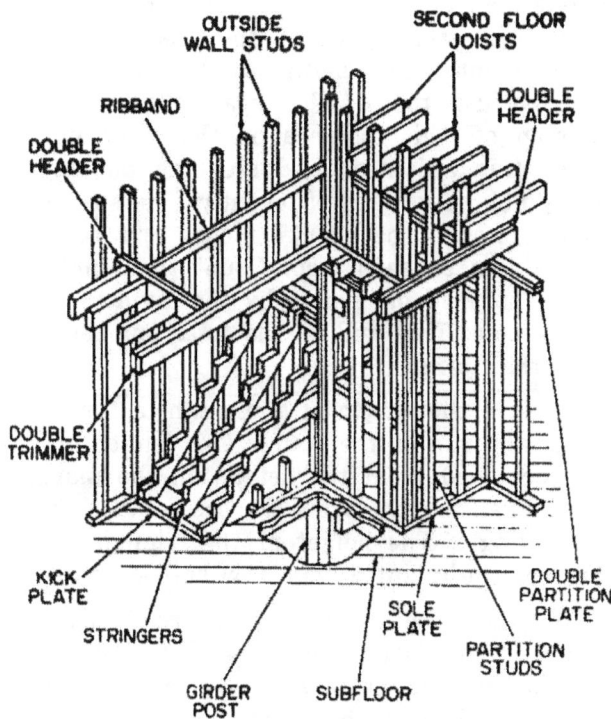

Figure 53. Details of complete stair construction.

191

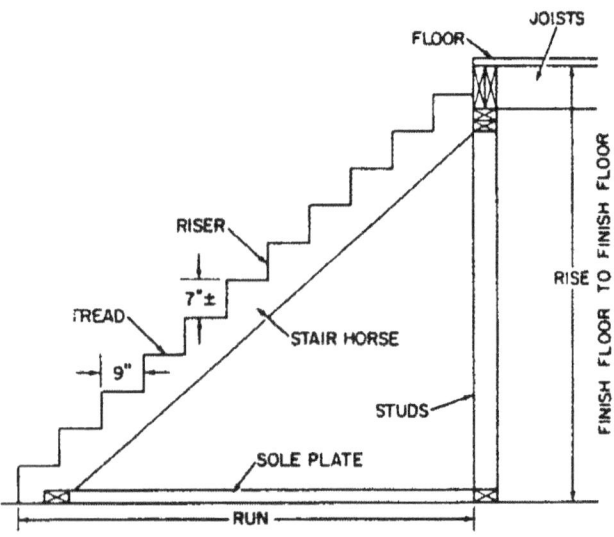

Figure 54. Method of laying out stair stringers.

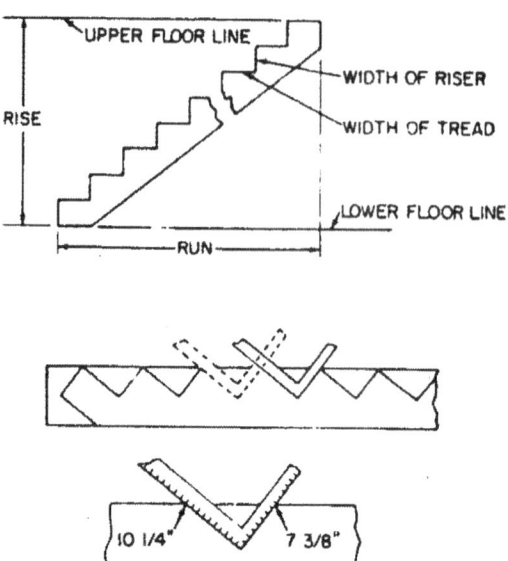

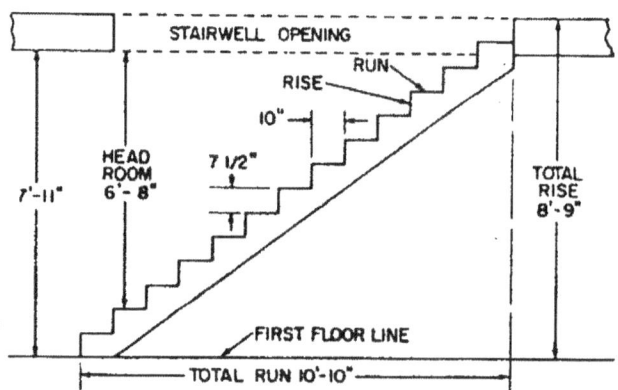

Figure 55. Principal parts of stair construction.

floor to the upper floor level. This is the lower room height, plus the thickness of the floor joists, and the rough and finished flooring. It is also the total rise of the stairs. If it is kept in mind that a flight of stairs forms a right angled triangle (fig. 55), with the rise being the height of the triangle, the run being the base of the triangle, and the length of the stringers being the hypotenuse of the triangle, it will help in laying out the stair distances. Set dividers at 7 inches, the average distance from one step to another, and step off this distance on the story pole. If this distance will not divide into the length of the story pole evenly, adjust the divider span slightly and again step off this distance on the story pole. Continue this adjusting and stepping off until the story pole is marked off evenly. The span of the dividers must be near 7 inches and represents the rise of each step. Count the number of spaces stepped off evenly by the dividers, on the story pole. This will be the total number of risers in the stairs.

b. Measure the length of the wellhole for the length of the run of the stairs. This length may also be obtained from the details on the plans. The stair well length forms the base of a right-angled triangle. The height of the triangle and the base of the triangle have now been obtained.

c. To obtain the width of each tread, divide the number of risers, less one—since there is always one more riser than tread—into the run of the stairs. The numbers thus obtained are to be used on the steel square in laying off the run and rise of each tread and riser on the stringer stock (fig. 54). These figures will be about 7 inches and 10 inches, respectively, since the ideal run and rise totals 17 inches. Lay off the run and rise of each step on the stringer stock equal to the number of risers previously obtained by dividing the story pole into equal spaces. The distance of the height, base, and hypotenuse of a right-angled triangle are thus obtained.

24. Check on Design of Risers and Treads

a. Rules. The following are two rules of thumb that may be used to check the dimensions of risers and treads:

(1) Riser + tread = between 17 and 19 inches.

(2) Riser x tread = between 70 and 75 inches.

b. Check. If the sum of the height of the riser and the width of the tread ((1) above) falls between 17 and 19 inches, and the product of the height of the riser and the width of the tread equals between 70 and 75 inches, the design is satisfactory.

TABLE 1

SIZES OF BUILT-UP WOOD GIRDERS FOR VARIOUS LOADS AND SPANS

Based on Douglas Fir 4-SQUARE Guide-Line FRAMINIG

Deflection Not Over 1/360 Of Span—Allowable Fiber Stress 1600 lbs. per sq. in.

LOAD PER LINEAR FOOT OF GIRDER	LENGTH OF SPAN				
	6'-0"	7'-0"	8'-0"	9'-0"	10'-0"
	NOMINAL SIZE OF GIRDER REQUIRED				
750	6x8 in.	6x8 in.	6x8 in.	6x10 in.	6x10 in.
900	6x8	6x8	6x10	6x10	8x10
1050	6x8	6x10	8x10	8x10	8x12
1200	6x10	8x10	8x10	8x10	8x12
1350	6x10	8x10	8x10	8x12	10x12
1500	8x10	8x10	8x12	10x12	10x12
1650	8x10	8x12	10x12	10x12	10x14
1800	8x10	8x12	10x12	10x12	10x14
1950	8x12	10x12	10x12	10x14	12x14
2100	8x12	10x12	10x14	12x14	12x14
2250	10x12	10x12	10x14	12x14	12x14
2400	10x12	10x14	10x14	12x14	
2550	10x12	10x14	12x14	12x14	
2700	10x12	10x14	12x14		
2850	10x14	12x14	12x14		
3000	10x14	12x14			
3150	10x14	12x14			
3300	12x14	12x14			

The 6-in. girder is figured as being made with three pieces 2 in. dressed to 1-5/8 in. thickness

The 8-in. girder is figured as being made with four pieces 2 in. dressed to 1-5/8 in. thickness.

The 10-in. girder is figured as being made with five pieces 2-in. dressed to 1-5/8 in. thickness.

The 12-in. girder is figured as being made with six pieces 2 in. dressed to 1-5/8 in. thickness.

Note—For solid girders multiply above loads by 1.130 when 6-inch girder is used; 1.150 when 8-in. girder is used; 1.170 when 10-in. girder is used and 1.180 when 12-in. girder is used.

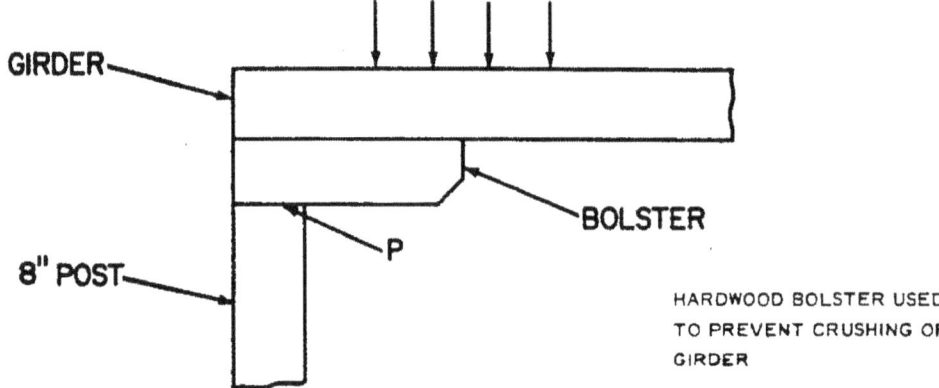

HARDWOOD BOLSTER USED TO PREVENT CRUSHING OF GIRDER

MANPOWER ESTIMATES—CARPENTRY

This appendix contains tables which may be used in preparing manpower estimates for carpentry work. The tables do not include provision for loading and hauling materials to the jobsite.
All tables presume average working conditions in terms of weather, skill, crew size, accessibility, and the availability of equipment.

Table D-1. Rough Framing [1]

Description	Unit	Man-hr/unit		
Beams (3-2" x 8")	MFBM [2]	40		
Blocking	MFBM	32		
Bridging	100 pairs	5		
Ceiling joists	MFBM	32		
Door bucks	ea.	3		
Floor joists, sills	MFBM	32		
Furring including plugging	1000 linft	32		
Grounds for plaster	1000 linft	48		
Rafters	MFBM	48		
Trusses	ea.	Man-hr assembly	Man-hr placement	Hours hoist time
Span ft				
20		2.5	4	8
30		5	8	12
40		12	8	16
50		20	6 [3]	8 [3]
60		24	6 [3]	9 [3]
80		32	6 [3]	11 [3]
Wall frames, plates	MFBM	56		

[1] Typical crew: 1 leader, 8 men.
Minimal crew: 1 leader, 2 men.
[2] Thousand board feet measure.
[3] Assumes use of organizational crane.

Table D-2. Sheathing and Siding [1]

Description	Unit	Man-hr/unit
Roof decking	1000 sq ft	
plywood		24
tongue & groove		32
Siding	1000 sq ft	
corrugated asbestos		32
drop siding		32
narrow bevel		48
plywood		24
shingles		40
Wall sheathing	1000 sq ft	
Bldg paper		16
fiber board		24
tongue & groove		24
plywood		16

[1] Typical crew: 1 leader, 4 men.

Table D-3. Flooring [1]

Description	Unit	Man-hr/unit
Linoleum	1000 sq ft	32
Soft tile	1000 sq ft	
cemented		24
nailed		32
Wood floors	1000 sq ft	
Finish floor		
hardwood		32
softwood		24
Subfloor		
plywood		16
tongue & groove		24

[1] Typical crew: 1 leader, 4 men.

Table D-4. Insulation [1]

Description	Unit	Man-hr/unit
Acoustic	1000 sq ft	
Quilt		8
Strip		24
Thermal	1000 sq ft	
Board		
ceiling		24
floor		8
roof		16
wall		32
Foil alone		16
Rigid foam		32
Rock wool		
batts		24
loose		16

[1] Typical crew: 1 leader, 8 men.

Table D-5. Finish Carpentry [1]

Description	Unit	Man-hr/unit
Baseboard (2 member)	1000 linft	72
Ceilings	1000 sq ft	
cemented tile		32
panel w/suspension		72
plasterboard (including tape)[2]		64
wood		48
Door frame, trim	ea.	2.5
Installing prefab. closets	ea.	16
Molding (chair)	1000 linft	48
Plasterboard (complete)	1000 sq ft	110
Setting kitchen cabinets	ea.	1.5
Sliding door w/pocket	ea.	8
Shelving	1000 sq ft	64
Stairs		
closed stringer, built on job	story	16
closed stringer, prefab.	story	8
open stringer	story	24
Walls	1000 sq ft	
plasterboard (including tape)		48
plywood		80
Wood frame, trim	ea.	3

[1] Typical crew: 1 leader, 8 men.
[2] Includes installation of furring strips when necessary.

Table D-6. Wood Door Installation [1]

Description	Unit	Man-hr/unit
Caulking (w/gun)	1000 linft	16
Doors w/hardware	ea.	
exterior [2]		2
interior [2]		1.5
manual sliding (including tracks)		8
motorized sliding [3]		56
overhead (including machinery)		16
screendoors		1.5
Weatherstripping	ea. opening	1.5

[1] Typical crew: 1 leader, 4 men.
[2] For double doors add 50% to labor estimates.
[3] Includes tracks and all necessary machinery, with control equipment.

Table D-7. Wood Window Installation [1]

Description	Unit	Man-hr/unit
Caulking (w/gun)	1000 linft	16
Screens	ea.	1.5
Weatherstripping	ea. opening	1.5
Windows (avg 20 sq ft) casement double hung jalousie louvers skylight sliding	ea.	 1.5 2.5 2.5 4 8 2.5
Venetian blinds	ea.	1

[1] Typical crew: 1 leader, 4 men.

Table D-8. Built-Up Roofing, Insulation and Flashing [1]
(pitch 1/2"—3"/ft)

Description	Unit	Man-hr/unit
Flashing	1000 linft	60
Insulation	1000 sq ft	25
Roofing 2 ply 3 ply 4 ply 5 ply	1000 sq ft	 12 20 25 30

[1] Typical crew: 1 leader, 6 men.
Table includes melting asphalt, laying felt, mopping, and laying gravel.

Table D-9. Roll Roofing [1]
(pitch at least 2"/ft)

Description	Unit	Man-hr/unit
Asphaltic aluminum (including primer)	1000 sq ft	18
Canvas (including 2 coats paint)	1000 sq ft	25
Paper (plain) & felt	1000 sq ft	7

[1] Typical crew: 1 leader, 6 men.
Table includes cleaning deck, applying prime coat, and laying rolls.

Table D-10. Shingle Roofing [1]
(pitch at least 3"/ft)

Description	Unit	Man-hr/unit
Asbestos	1000 sq ft	45
Asphalt	1000 sq ft	30
Metal	1000 sq ft	50
Slate	1000 sq ft	55
Wood	1000 sq ft	35

[1] Typical crew: 1 leader, 4 men.
Table includes placing and nailing.

Table D-11. Metal, Asbestos-Cement and Tile Roofing [1]
(pitch at least 3"/ft)

Description	Unit	Man-hr/unit
Asbestos-cement metal purlins wood purlins	1000 sq ft	 45 35
Metal — corrugated & V-crimp metal purlins wood purlins	1000 sq ft	 36 18
Tile clay metal	1000 sq ft	 55 60

[1] Typical crew: 1 leader, 5 men.
Table includes placing, caulking, drilling, and fastening materials.

Table D-12. Pile Bracing and Capping [1]

Description	Unit	Man-hr/unit
Bracing [2] diagonal horizontal	ea.	 0.8 1
Capping wood	1000 linft	 100

[1] Typical crew: 1 leader, 6 men.
[2] Table based on 4 in x 10 in x 4 ft bracing members.
Pile bracing includes cutting, drilling, handling, and fastening materials.

Table D-13. Pier Framing [1]

Description	Unit	Man-hr/unit
Bridging	1000 linft	40
Bull rail	1000 linft	60
Bumper	1000 linft	36
4" deck	1000 sq ft	20
Stringers	MFBM [2]	200
2" wearing surface	1000 sq ft	16

[1] Typical crew: 1 leader, 10 men.
[2] 1000 board-foot measure.
Installation of pier framing includes the cutting, drilling, handling, and fastening of stringers, bridging, all decking, rails, and bumpers.

Table D-14. Deck Hardware [1]

Description	Unit	Man-hr/unit
Bits	ea.	3
Bollards	ea.	4
Chocks	ea.	3
Cleats	ea.	2
Pad eyes	ea.	1

[1] Typical crew: 1 leader, 4 men.
Installation of deck hardware includes required drilling, handling, and fastening of bits, bollards, chocks, cleats, and pad eyes.

ABBREVIATIONS AND SYMBOLS
CONTENTS

			Page
1.	Abbreviations		1
2.	Symbols		3
	a.	Architectural	3
	b.	Plumbing	4
	c.	Electrical	4

ABBREVIATIONS AND SYMBOLS

1. Abbreviations

The following abbreviations in connection with lumber are used by the carpenter:

AD ---------- air-dried
al ---------- all length
av ---------- average
avw --------- average width
avl --------- average length
bd ---------- board
bd ft ------- board foot
bdl --------- bundle
bev --------- beveled
bm ---------- board (foot) measure
btr --------- better
clg --------- ceiling
clr --------- clear
CM ---------- center matched; that is, tongue-and-groove joints are made along the center of the edge of the piece
Com --------- common
Csg --------- casing
Ctg --------- crating
cu ft ------- cubic foot
D & CM ------ dressed (one or two sides) and center matched
D & M ------- dressed and matched; that is, dressed one or two sides and tongue and grooved on the edges. The match may be center or standard
DS ---------- drop siding
D & SM ------ dressed (one or two sides) and standard matched
D 2S & CM --- dressed two sides and center matched
D 2S & M ---- dressed two sides and (center of standard) matched
D 2S & SM --- dressed two sides and standard matched
Dim --------- dimension
E ----------- edge
FAS --------- firsts and seconds, a combined grade of the two upper grades of hardwoods
fbk --------- flat back
fcty -------- factory (lumber)
FG ---------- flat grain
Flg --------- flooring
fok --------- free of knots
Frm --------- framing
ft ---------- foot or feet
Hdl --------- handle (stock)
Hdwd -------- hardwood
Hrt --------- heart
Hrtwd ------- heartwood
in ---------- inch or inches

KD --------- kiln-dried
kd --------- knocked down
lbr --------- lumber
lgr --------- longer
lgth --------- length
linft --------- linear foot, that is, 12 inches
LR --------- log run
Lr MCO ------ log run, mill culls out
M --------- thousand
MFBM ------- thousand (feet) board measure
MCO -------- mill culls out
Merch ------- merchantable
MR --------- mill run
msm -------- thousand (feet) surface measure
mw --------- mixed width
No --------- number
1s & 2s ------ ones and twos, a combined grade of the hardwood grades of firsts and seconds
Ord --------- order
P ---------- planed
Pat --------- pattern
Pky --------- picky
Pln --------- plain, as in plain sawed
Pn --------- partition
Qtd --------- quartered (with reference to hardwoods)
rd ---------- round
rdm -------- random
res --------- resawed
rf g --------- roofing
Rfrs --------- roofers
rip --------- ripped
rl ---------- random length
rw --------- random width
S & E ------- surfaced one side and one edge
S2S & M ----- surfaced two sides and standard or center matched
S2S & SM ---- surfaced two sides and standard matched
Sap -------- sapwood
S1E -------- surfaced one edge
S1S1E ------ surfaced one side and one edge
S1S2E ------ surfaced one side and two edges
S2E -------- surfaced two edges
S4S -------- surfaced four sides
S & CM ----- surfaced one or two sides and center matched
S & M ------ surfaced and matched; that is, surfaced one or two sides and tongued and grooved on the edges. The match may be center or standard.
S & SM ----- surfaced one or two sides and standard matched
S2S & CM --- surfaced two sides and center matched
Sap -------- sapwood
SB --------- standard bead
Sd --------- seasoned

Sdg	siding
Sel	select
SESd	square-edge siding
sf	surface foot; that is, an area of 1 square foot
Stfwd	softwood
ShD	shipping dry
Ship	shiplap
Sm	standard matched
sm	surface measure
snd	sap no defect
snd	sound
sq	square
sq E	square edge
sq E & S	square edge and sound
sqrs	squares
Std	standard
stk	stock
SW	sound wormy
T & G	tongued and grooved
TB & S	top, bottom, and sides
tbrs	timbers
VG	vertical grain
wal	wider, all length
wdr	wider
wt	weight
wth	width

2. Symbols

Symbols commonly used in carpentry are given below. For additional information on the various symbols used in construction plans and blueprints, refer to TM 5-704.

a. *Architectural*

Tile	
Earth	
Plaster	
Sheet metal	
Built-in cabinet	
Outside door: Brick wall	
Frame wall	
Inside door: Frame wall	
Brick	
Firebrick	
Concrete	
Cast concrete block	
Insulation: Loose fill	
Board or quilts	
Cut stone	
Ashlar	
Shingles (siding)	
Wood, rough	
Wood, finished	
Cased or arched openings	
Single caseinent window	
Double hung windows	
Double casement window	

b. *Plumbing*

Bathtubs:
- Corner 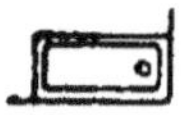
- Free standing

Floor drain

Shower drain

Hot-water tank

Grease trap

Hose bibb or sill cock

Lavatories:
- Pedestal
- Wall-hung
- Corner

Toilets:
- Tank 
- Flush valve

Urinals:
- Stall-type
- Wall-hung

Laundry trays

Built-in shower

Shower

Sinks:
- Single drain board 
- Double drain board

C. *Electrical*

Pull switch	Ceiling outlet
Single-pole switch — S_1	Wall bracket
Double-pole switch — S_2	Single convenience outlet
Triple-pole switch — S_3	Double convenience outlet
Buzzer	Ceiling outlet, gas & electric
Floor outlet	Motor
Bell	Light outlet with wiring and switches indicated
Drop cord	

GLOSSARY OF CARPENTRY AND BUILDING CONSTRUCTION TERMS

TABLE OF CONTENTS

	Page
Anchor … Ceiling	1
Center-hung sash … Gable	2
Gage … Ledgerboard	3
Level … Pitch board	4
Plan … Scotia	5
Scribing … Verge boards	6
Vestibule … Wooden brick	7

GLOSSARY OF CARPENTY AND BUILDING CONSTRUCTION TERMS

Anchor - Irons of special form used to fasten together timbers or masonry.

Anchor bolts - Bolt which fastens columns, girders, or other members to concrete or masonry.

Backing - The bevel on the top edge of a hip rafter that allows the roofing board to fit the top of the rafter without leaving a triangular space between it and the lower side of the roof covering.

Balloon frame - The lightest and most economical form of construction, in which the studding and corner posts are set up in continuous lengths from first-floor line or sill to the roof plate.

Baluster - A small pillar or column used to support a rail.

Balustrade - A series of balusters connected by a rail, generally used for porches, balconies, and the like.

Band - A low, flat molding.

Base - The bottom of a column; the finish of a room at the junction of the walls and floor.

Batten (cleat) - A narrow strip of board used to fasten several pieces together.

Batter board - A temporary framework used to assist in locating the corners when laying a foundation.

Batter pile - Pile driven at an angle to brace a structure against lateral thrust.

Beam - An inclusive term for joists, girders, rafters, and purlins.

Bedding - A filling of mortar, putty, or other substance in order to secure a firm bearing.

Belt course - A horizontal board across or around a building, usually made of a flat member and a molding.

Bent - A single vertical framework consisting of horizontal and vertical members supporting the deck of a bridge or pier.

Bevel board (pitch board) - A board used in framing a roof or stairway to lay out bevels.

Board - Lumber less than 2 inches thick.

Board foot - The equivalent of a board 1 foot square and 1 inch thick.

Boarding in - The process of nailing boards on the outside studding of a house.

Bollard - Steel or cast iron post to which large ships are tied.

Braces - Pieces fitted and firmly fastened to two others at any angle in order to strengthen the angle thus treated.

Bracket - A projecting support for a shelf or other structure.

Break joints - To arrange joints so that they do not come directly under or over the joints of adjoining pieces, as in shingling, siding, etc.

Bridging - Pieces fitted in pairs from the bottom of one floor joist to the top of adjacent joists, and crossed to distribute the floor load; sometimes pieces of width equal to the joists and fitted neatly between them.

Building paper - Cheap, thick paper, used to insulate a building before the siding or roofing is put on; sometimes placed between double floors.

Built-up member - A single structural component made from several pieces fastened together.

Built-up timber - A timber made of several pieces fastened together, and forming one of larger dimension.

Carriages - The supports or the steps and risers of a flight of stairs.

Casement - A window in which the sash opens upon hinges.

Casing - The trimming around a door or window opening, either outside or inside, or the finished lumber around a post or beam, etc.

Ceiling - Narrow, matched boards; sheathing of the surfaces that inclose the upper side of room.

Center-hung sash - A sash hung on its centers so that it swings on a horizontal axis.
Chamfer - A beveled surface cut upon the corner of a piece of wood.
Checks - Splits or cracks in a board, ordinarily caused by seasoning.
Chock - Heavy timber fitted between fender piles along wheel guard of a pier or wharf.
Chord - The principal member of a truss on either the top or bottom.
Clamp - A mechanical device used to hold two or more pieces together.
Clapboards - A special form of outside covering of a house; siding.
Cleats - Metal arms extending horizontally from a relatively low base used for securing small ships, tugs, and work boats.
Column - A square, rectangular, or cylindrical support for roofs, ceilings, and so forth, composed of base, shaft, and capital.
Combination frame - A combination of the principal features of the full and balloon frames.
Concrete - An artificial building material made by mixing cement and sand with gravel, broken stone, or other aggregate, and sufficient water to cause the cement to set and bind the entire mass.
Conductors - Pipes for conducting water from a roof to the ground or to a receptacle or drain; downspout.
Cornice - The molded projection which finishes the top of the wall of a building.
Counterflashings - Strips of metal used to prevent water from entering the top edge of the vertical side of a roof flashing; they also allow expansion and contraction without danger of breaking the flashing.
Cross brace - Bracing with two intersecting diagonals.
Deadening - Construction intended to prevent the passage of sound.
Decking - Heavy plank floor of a pier or bridge.
Diagonal - Inclined member of a truss or bracing system used for stiffening and wind bracing.
Drip - The projection of a window sill or water table to allow the water to drain clear of the side of the house below it.
Fascia - A flat member of a cornice or other finish, generally the board of the cornice to whic the gutter is fastened.
Fender pile - Outside row of piles that protects a pier or wharf from damage by ships.
Fitter - Piece used to fill space between two surfaces.
Flashing - The material used and the process of making watertight the roof intersections and other exposed places on the outside of the house.
Flue - The opening in a chimney through which smoke passes.
Flush - Adjacent surfaces even, or in same plane (with reference to two structural pieces).
Footing - An enlargement at the lower end of a wall, pier, or column, to distribute the load.
Footing form - A wooden or steel structure, placed around the footing that will hold the concrete to the desired shape and size.
Foundation - That part of a building or wall which supports the superstructure.
Frame - The surrounding or inclosing woodwork of windows, doors, etc., and the timber skeleton of building.
Framing - The rough timber structure of a building, including interior and exterior walls, floor, roof, and ceilings.
Full frame - The old fashioned mortised-and-tenoned frame, in which every joint was mortised and tenoned. Rarely used at the present time.
Furring - Narrow strips of board nailed upon the walls and ceilings to form a straight surface upon which to lay the laths or other finish.
Gable - The vertical triangular end of a building from the eaves to the apex of the roof.

Gage - A tool used by carpenters to strike a line parallel to the edge of a board.
Gambrel - A symmetrical roof with two different pitches or slopes on each side.
Girder - A timber used to support wall beams or joists.
Girt (ribband) - The horizontal member of the walls of a full or combination frame house which supports the floor joists or is flush with the top of the joists.
Grade - The horizontal ground level of a building or structure.
Groove - A long hollow channel cut by a tool, into which a piece fits or in which it works. Two special types of grooves are the *dado*, a rectangular groove cut across the full width of a piece, and the *housing*, a groove cut at any angle with the grain and part way across a piece. Dados are used in sliding doors, window frames, etc.; housings are used for framing stair risers and threads in a string.
Ground - A strip of wood assisting the plasterer in making a straight wall and in giving a place to which the finish of the room may be nailed.
Hanger - Vertical-tension member supporting a load.
Header - A short joist into which the common joists are framed around or over an opening.
Headroom - The clear space between floor line and ceiling, as in a stairway.
Heel of a rafter - The end or foot that rests on the wall plate.
Hip roof - A roof which slopes up toward the center from all sides, necessitating a hip rafter at each corner.
Jack rafter - A short rafter framing between the wall plate; a hip rafter.
Jamb - The side piece or post of an opening; sometimes applied to the door frame.
Joint-butt - Squared ends or ends and edges adjoining each other:
  Dovetail - Joint made by cutting pins the shape of dovetails which fit between dovetail upon another piece.
  Drawboard - A mortise-and-tenon joint with holes so bored that when a pin is driven through, the joint becomes tighter.
  Fished - An end butt splice strengthened by pieces nailed on the sides.
  Glue - A joint held together with glue.
  Halved - A joint made by cutting half the wood away from each piece so as to bring the sides flush.
  Housed - A joint in which a piece is grooved to receive the piece which is to form the other part of the joint.
  Lap - A joint of two pieces lapping over each other.
  Mortised - A joint made by cutting a hole or mortise, in one piece, and a tenon, or piece to fit the hole, upon the other.
  Rub - A flue joint made by carefully fitting the edges together, spreading glue between them, and rubbing the pieces back and forth until the pieces are well rubbed together.
  Scarfed - A timber spliced by cutting various shapes of shoulders, or jogs, which fit each other.
Joists - Timbers supporting the floorboards.
Kerf - The cut made by a saw.
Knee brace - A corner brace, fastened at an angle from wall stud to rafter, stiffening a wood or steel frame to prevent angular movement.
Laths - Narrow strips to support plastering.
Lattice - Crossed wood, iron plate, or bars.
Ledgerboard - The support for the second-floor joists of a balloon-frame house, or for similar uses; ribband.

Level - A term describing the position of a line or plane when parallel to the surface of still water; an instrument or tool used in testing for horizontal and vertical surfaces, and in determining differences of elevation.

Lintel (cap -) A horizontal structural member spanning an opening, and supporting a wall load.

Lookout - The end of a rafter, or the construction which projects beyond the sides of a house to support the eaves; also the projecting timbers at the gables which support the verge boards.

Louver - A kind of window, generally in peaks of gables and the tops of towers, provided with horizontal slots which exclude rain and snow and allow ventilation.

Lumber - Sawed parts of a log such as boards, planks, scantling, and timber.

Matching, or tonguing and grooving - The method used in cutting the edges of a board to make a tongue on one edge and a groove on the other.

Meeting rail - The bottom rail of the upper sash of a double-hung window. Sometimes called the check-rail.

Member - A single piece in a structure, complete in itself.

Miter - The joint formed by two abutting pieces meeting at an angle.

Molding Base - The molding on the top of a baseboard.

Bed – A molding used to cover the joint between the plancier and frieze (horizontal decorative band around the wall of a room); also used as a base molding upon heavy work, and sometimes as a member of a cornice.

Lip - A molding with a lip which overlaps the piece against which the back of the molding rests.

Picture - A molding shaped to form a support for picture hooks, often placed at some distance from the ceiling upon the wall to form the lower edge of the frieze.

Rake - The cornice upon the gable edge of a pitch roof, the members of which are made to fit those of the molding of the horizontal eaves.

Mortise - The hole which is to receive a tenon, or any hole cut into or through a piece by a chisel; generally of rectangular shape.

Mullion - The construction between the openings of a window frame to accommodate two or more windows.

Muntin - The vertical member between two panels of the same piece of panel work. The vertical sash-bars separating the different panels of glass.

Newel - The principal post of the foot of a staircase; also the central support of a winding flight of stairs.

Nosing - The part of a stair tread which projects over the riser, or any similar projection; a term applied to the rounded edge of a board.

Pad eyes - Metal rings mounted vertically on a plate for tying small vessels.

Partition - A permanent interior wall which serves to divide a building into rooms.

Pier-(a) Timber, concrete, or masonry supports for girders, posts, or arches. (b) Intermediate supports for adjacent ends of two bridge spans. (c) Structure extending outward from shore into water used as a dock for ships.

Piers-Masonry supports, set independently of the main foundation.

Pilaster - A portion of a square column, usually set within or against a wall.

Piles - Long posts driven into the soil in swampy locations or whenever it is difficult to secure a firm foundation, upon which the footing course of masonry or other timbers are laid.

Piling - Large timbers or poles driven into the ground or the bed of a stream to make a firm foundation.

Pitch - Inclination or slope, as for roofs or stairs, or the rise divided by the span.

Pitch board - A board sawed to the exact shape formed by the stair tread, riser, and slope of the stairs and used to lay out the carriage and stringers.

Plan - A horizontal geometrical section of a building, showing the walls, doors, windows, stairs, chimneys, columns, etc.

Plank - A wide piece of sawed timber, usually 1 1/2 to 4 1/2 inches thick and 6 inches or more wide.

Plaster - A mixture of lime, hair, and sand, or of lime, cement, and sand, used to cover outside and inside wall surfaces.

Plate - The top horizontal piece of the walls of a frame building upon which the roof rests.

Plate cut - The cut in a rafter which rests upon the plate; sometimes called the seat cut.

Plow - To cut a groove running in the same direction as the grain of the wood.

Plumb cut - Any cut made in a vertical plane; the vertical cut at the top end of a rafter.

Ply - A term used to denote a layer or thickness of building or roofing paper as two-ply, three-ply, etc.

Porch - An ornamental entrance way.

Post - A timber set on end to support a wall, girder, or other member of the structure.

Pulley stile - The member of a window frame which contains the pulleys and between which the edges of the sash slide.

Purlin - A timber supporting several rafters at one or more points, or the roof sheeting directly.

Rabbet or rebate - A corner cut out of an edge of a piece of wood.

Rafter - The beams that slope from the ridge of a roof to the eaves and make up the main body of the roof's framework.

Rafters, common - Those which run square with the plate and extend to the ridge.

   Cripple - Those which cut between valley and hip rafters.

   Hip - Those extending from the outside angle of the plates toward the apex of the roof.

   Jacks - Those square with the plate and intersecting the hip rafter.

   Valley - Those extending from an inside angle of the plates toward the ridge or center line of the house.

Rail - The horizontal members of a balustrade or panel work.

Rake - The trim of a building extending in an oblique line, as rake dado or molding.

Return - The continuation of a molding or finish of any kind in a different direction.

Ribband - (See Ledgerboard.)

Ridge - The top edge or corner formed by the intersection of two roof surfaces.

Ridge cut - (See Plumb cut.)

Rise - The vertical distance through which anything rises, as the rise of a roof or stair.

Riser - The vertical board between two treads of a flight of stairs.

Roofing - The material put on a roof to make it wind and waterproof.

Rubble - Roughly broken quarry stone.

Rubble masonry - Uncut stone, used for rough work, foundations, backing, and the like.

Run - The length of the horizontal projection of a piece such as a rafter when in position.

Saddle board - The finish of the ridge of a pitch-roof house. Sometimes called comb board.

Sash - The framework which holds the glass in a window.

Sawing, plain - Lumber sawed regardless of the grain, the log simply squared and sawed to the desired thickness; sometimes called slash or bastard sawed.

Scab - A short piece of lumber used to splice, or to prevent movement of two other pieces.

Scaffold or staging - A temporary structure or platform enabling workmen to reach high places.

Scale - A short measurement used as a proportionate part of a larger dimension. The scale of a drawing is expressed as 14 inch = 1 foot.

Scantling - Lumber with a cross-section ranging from 2 by 4 inches to 4 by 4 inches.

Scarfing - A joint between two pieces of wood which allows them to be spliced lengthwise.

Scotia - A hollow molding used as a part of a cornice, and often under the nosing of a stair tread.

Scribing - The marking of a piece of wood to provide for the fitting of one of its surfaces to the irregular surface of another.

Seat cut or plate cut - The cut at the bottom end of a rafter to allow it to fit upon the plate.

Seat of a rafter - The horizontal cut upon the bottom end of a rafter which rests upon the top of the plate.

Section - A drawing showing the kind, arrangement, and proportions of the various parts of a structure. It is assumed that the structure is cut by a plane, and the section is the view gained by looking in one direction.

Shakes - Imperfections in timber caused during the growth of the timber by high winds or imperfect conditions of growth.

Sheathing - Wall boards, roofing boards; generally applied to narrow boards laid with a space between them, according to the length of a shingle exposed to weather.

Sheathing paper - The paper used under siding or shingles to insulate in the house; building papers.

Siding - The outside finish between the casings.

Sills - The horizontal timbers of a house which either rest upon the masonry foundations or, in the absence of such, form the foundations.

Sizing - Working material to the desired size; a coating of glue, shellac, or other substance applied to a surface to prepare it for painting or other method of finish.

Sleeper - A timber laid on the ground to support a floor joist.

Span - The distance between the bearings of a timber or arch.

Specifications - The written or printed directions regarding the details of a building or other construction.

Splice - Joining of two similar members in a straight line.

Square - A tool used by mechanics to obtain accuracy; a term applied to a surface including 100 square feet.

Stairs, box - Those built between walls, and usually with no support except the wall.

Standing finish - Term applied to the finish of the openings and the base, and all other finish work necessary for the inside.

Stringer - A long horizontal timber in a structure supporting a floor.

Stucco - A fine plaster used for interior decoration and fine work; also for rough outside wall coverings.

Stud - An upright beam in the framework of a building.

Studding - The framework of a partition or the wall of a house; usually referred to as 2 by 4@s.

Sub floor - A wood floor which is laid over the floor joists and on which the finished floor is laid.

Threshold - The beveled piece over which the door swings; sometimes called a carpet strip.

Tie beam (collar beam) - A beam so situated that it ties the principal rafters of a roof together and prevents them from thrusting the plate out of line.

Timber - Lumber with cross-section over 4 by 6 inches, such as posts, sills, and girders.

Tin shingle - A small piece of tin used in flashing and repairing a shingle roof.

Top plate - Piece of lumber supporting ends of rafters.

To the iveather - A term applied to the projecting of shingles or siding beyond the course above.

Tread - The horizontal part of a step.

Trim - A term sometimes applied to outside or interior finished woodwork and the finish around openings.

Trimmer - The beam or floor joist into which a header is framed.

Trimming - Putting the inside and outside finish and hardware upon a building.

Truss - Structural framework of triangular units for supporting loads over long spans.

Valleys - The internal angle formed by the two slopes of a roof.

Verge boards - The boards which serve as the eaves finish on the gable end of a building.

Vestibule - An entrance to a house; usually inclosed.
Wainscoting - Matched boarding or panel work covering the lower portion of a wall.
Wale - A horizontal beam.
Wash - The slant upon a sill, capping, etc., to allow the water to run off easily.
Water table - The finish at the bottom of a house which carries water away from the foundation.
Wharf - A structure that provides berthing space for vessels, to facilitate loading and discharge of cargo.
Wind ("i" pronounced as in "kind") - A term used to describe the surface of a board when twisted (winding) or when resting upon two diagonally opposite corners, if laid upon a perfectly flat surface.
Wooden brick - Piece of seasoned wood, made the size of a brick, and laid where it is necessary to provide a nailing space in masonry walls.

www.ingramcontent.com/pod-product-compliance
Lightning Source LLC
Chambersburg PA
CBHW082035300426
44117CB00015B/2496